AF570679

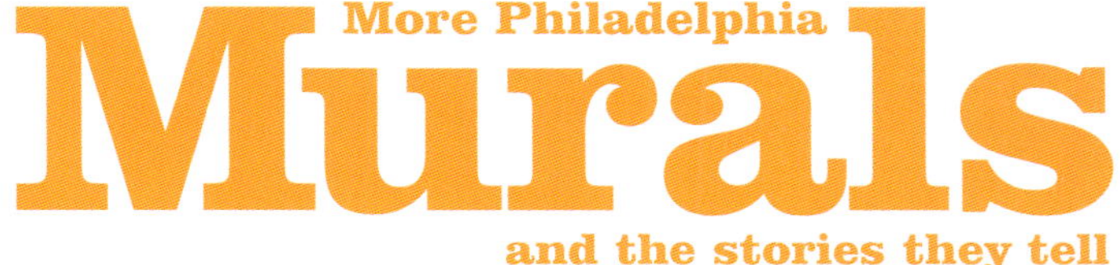
More Philadelphia
Murals
and the stories they tell

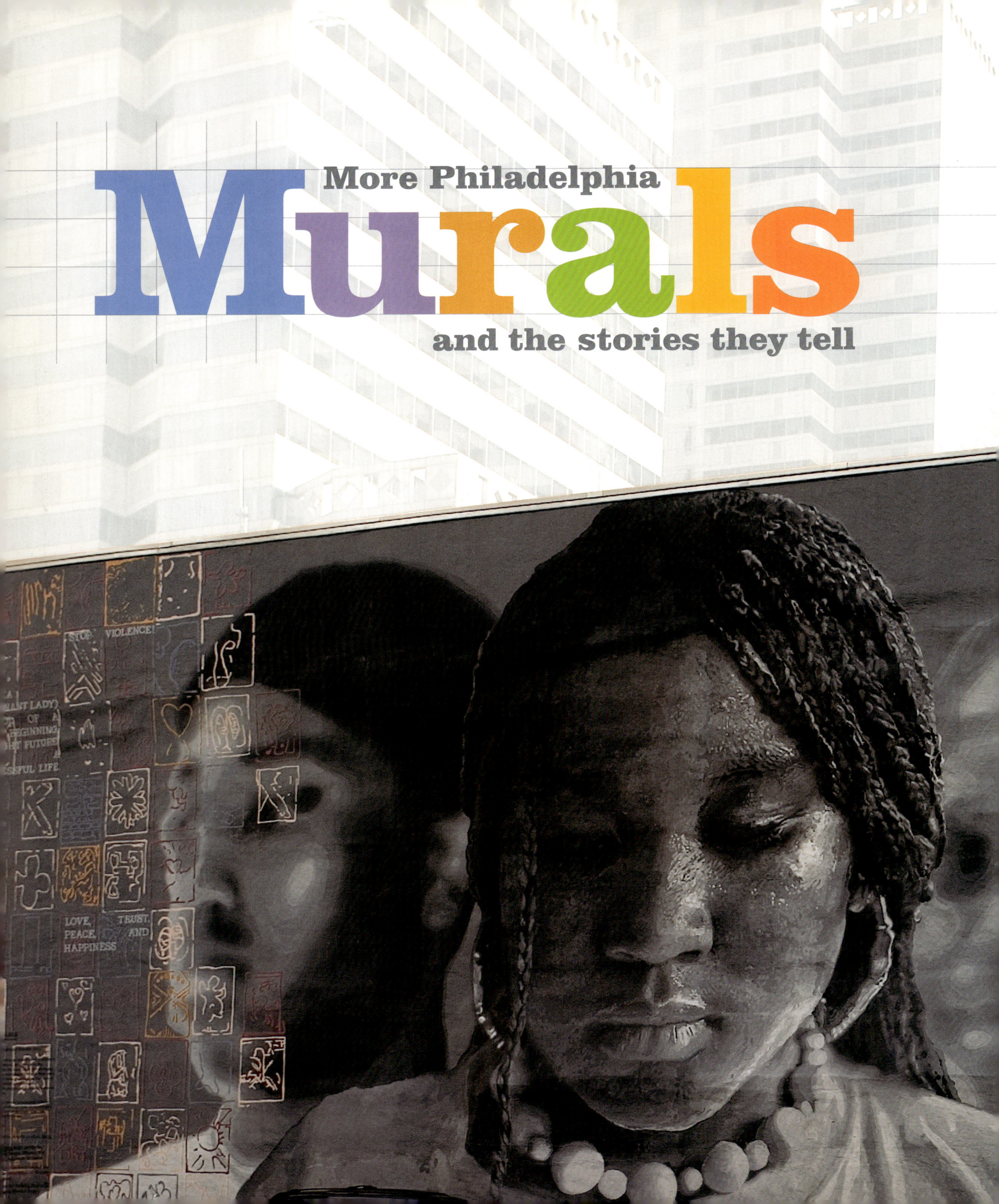
More Philadelphia
Murals
and the stories they tell
STOP VIOLENCE!
LOVE, TRUST,
PEACE, AND
HAPPINESS

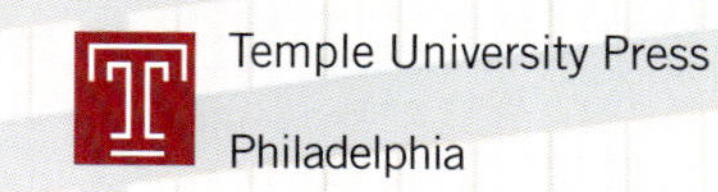

Jane Golden, Robin Rice & Natalie Pompilio

with photography by David Graham and Jack Ramsdale

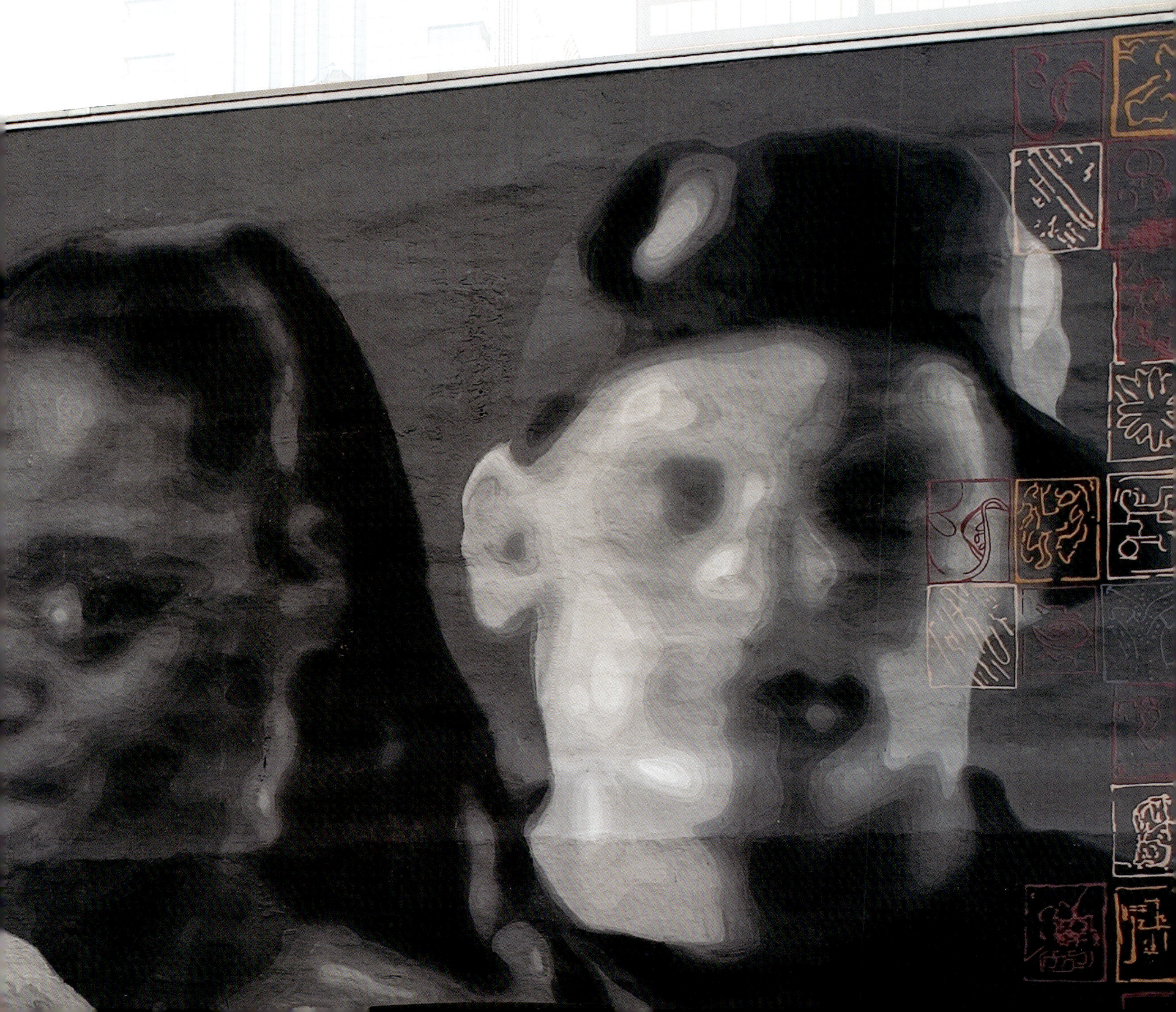

To the more than twenty thousand students who have gone through Mural Arts' programs—you inspire us with your resilience!

TEMPLE UNIVERSITY PRESS
1601 North Broad Street
Philadelphia PA 19122
www.temple.edu/tempress

Published 2006
Printed in Canada

This book is printed on acid-free paper for greater permanence and durability

Library of Congress Cataloging-in-Publication Data

Golden, Jane, 1953-
More Philadelphia murals and the stories they tell / Jane Golden, Robin Rice, and Natalie Pompilio ; with photography by David Graham and Jack Ramsdale.
p. cm.
Includes bibliographical references and index.
ISBN-13: 978-1-59213-527-1 (cloth : alk. paper)
ISBN-10: 1-59213-527-7 (cloth : alk. paper)
1. Street art—Pennsylvania—Philadelphia—History—21st century. 2. Mural Arts Program (Philadelphia, Pa.) 3. Community arts projects—Pennsylvania—Philadelphia. I. Rice, Robin, 1943- II. Pompilio, Natalie. III. Graham, David, 1952- IV. Ramsdale, Jack. V. Title.

ND2638.P48G648 2006
751.7'30974811—dc22
2006021755

2 4 6 8 9 7 5 3 1

In This City Called Philadelphia

In this City of universities and churches and museums. In this City of children's faces parading their fears and hopes and smiles. In this City where history stretches in aristocratic silence. In this City where hope continues to bloom like flowers in a procession of waves, there are the murals, celebrating neighborhoods and people. They say our names out loud. They say you can find us without maps, bursting out of alleys, secreted on minor streets, falling from the sky with a sound that has been handed down from generation to generation. A sound of immaculate voices. A sound of ancestral blood. A sound of eyes, uncrucified. Insistent with beauty.

These murals are everywhere. We know many by heart. Black. Brown. Yellow. White. Gay. Lesbian. Peaceful saints, pure as ivory. They wait for us to turn corners. They wait with open hearts. And if we listen, we will hear their gigantic laughter. Taste their purple smiles. See their elegant waists inscripted with love.

Lo profundo! (What is profound!)
These Murals!
Lo purisimo! (What is pure.)
These Murals!

Ten Haiku (for Phila murals)

1.
phila roots
lighting these walls
with fireflies.

2.
flowers stretched
in prayer on a
cornerstone wall.

3.
brownskinned
children dancing
with butterflies.

4.
these children's
faces humiliate
the stars.

5.
philadelphia
painted with
blue hallelujahs.

6.
winter,
a warrior's face.
I hear our bones singing.

7.
in the open
alley a galaxy
of dreams.

8.
common ground
is we, forever
tasting this earth.

9.
hands
in the green light
saluting peace.

10.
even in the
rain, these murals
pause with rainbows.

Sonia Sanchez

Publication of this book was made possible by the generous support of

Haas Charitable Trust

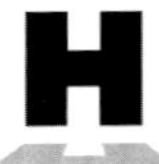

The Philadelphia Foundation
The Peter A. Wiley and Elizabeth Greene Wiley Fund
of the Philadelphia Foundation

Jane Golden and the Mural Arts Program gratefully acknowledge the sponsors of the programs and projects featured in this book:

Allegheny West Foundation
Anonymous
Asian Arts Initiative
Bank of America
Brandywine Realty Trust
Children's Investment Strategy
Christopher Ludwick Foundation
Citizens Bank
City of Philadelphia
Capital Program Office
Department of Human Services
Department of Recreation
Neighborhood Transformation Initiative/ Empowerment Zone
Office of the Managing Director
Prison System
Cuba Support Project
Delaware Valley Legacy Fund
The Dolfinger-McMahon Foundation
Eagles Youth Partnership
Eisenhower Fellowships
Fannie Mae Foundation
Ford Foundation
Forrest C. Lattner Foundation
Frank Guarrera Society
Girard Coalition, Inc.
Glenmede Trust Company
GMAC Mortgage
Lawrence Guzzardi / Chancellor Properties, Inc.
Independence Foundation
John C. and Chara C. Haas Charitable Trusts
Lincoln Financial Group Foundation
Lindback Foundation
Local Initiatives Support Corporation
Morris Animal Refuge
National Endowment for the Arts
Zach Oppenheimer
Pennsylvania Council on the Arts
Pennsylvania Department of Aging
Pennsylvania Horticultural Society
Philadelphia Green Program
Pew Charitable Trusts
Philadelphia Health Management Corporation
Philadelphia Housing Authority
Philadelphia Mural Arts Advocates
Philadelphia Safe and Sound
The Philadelphia Weekly
PNC Bank
Evelyn Richman
The Rockefeller Foundation
Angelo Rotchford in memory of John F. Staich
The Samuel S. Fels Fund
School District of Philadelphia
SEI Investments
Sheila Fortune Foundation
SmithKline Beecham
Sovereign Bank
Stockamp and Associates
Sunoco Welcome America
Support Center for Child Advocates
Surdna Foundation
Suzanne F. Roberts Cultural Development Fund
TLA Video
U.S. Department of Education
United Way of Southeastern Pennsylvania
Neighborhood Funding Stream
University City District
University of Pennsylvania
David Waxman
Westrum Development Company
Whole Foods Market
William Penn Foundation
WXPN and World Café Live!

Contents

Preface

A lot has happened since the first book about the Mural Arts Program (MAP) was published in 2002. Community mural art is now reaching more people than ever, in harder-to-reach places, and it is transforming lives. MAP now works with more than twenty-five hundred students around the city, engaging them in a rigorous curriculum that teaches not only artistic skills but also civic engagement and personal responsibility. We're working with students in Philadelphia public schools, those who are chronically truant, those who have been convicted of minor crimes, even those who are incarcerated. In part, this is a credit to the city of Philadelphia and the visionary and open-minded officials who recognize the benefits of public art. MAP has partnered with the criminal justice system, the Department of Human Services, the Philadelphia School District, and more opportunities abound. These partnerships mean that mural art has a greater role to play in transforming not only individual lives, but our civic life as well. I've been in government work long enough to know that when it comes to large bureaucracies and institutions, change is often incremental. That's why our progress feels so incredible to me.

Perhaps the best way to show what we've accomplished is to tell you about some of our kids.

Mural Corps, aimed at high school students, graduated its first group of teens last year. During a ceremony held in the backyard of our headquarters, the students talked about what they were planning to do next. One young man had won a full scholarship to Rhode Island School of Design, another was headed to the Tyler School of Art. A young woman, a gifted painter and musician, was going to college to study dental hygiene but promised she wouldn't let her artistic side slide. Several others said they were going to community college.

Why is this significant? Because these kids all came from rough neighborhoods. They faced challenges at a young age that some adults will never see. They weren't expected to succeed. But Mural Corps was their constant, their line to the outside. Through the program, they learned basic job skills, how to communicate with each other and adults, how to be a leader, and how to be led. Perhaps most important, they learned they could make a difference in their lives and in their community. Because of MAP's long-term commitment to these wonderful young people, they've been able to envision a future beyond their neighborhoods.

Our ArtWORKS! and ARTscape programs are aimed at truant and delinquent youth. Both programs started with several dozen young people a few years ago and now they each serve literally hundreds and hundreds of kids during the course of the school year and summer. Participants are sent to the program by the city's Department of Human Services and the court system. For the most part, these are young people who have been disengaged from both their schools and their communities. Some of them serve their time and move on. But every year, there are students so inspired by our teachers and so energized by the individualized attention that they keep coming back long afterward. Our teachers are professional artists and, to be completely honest, really wonderful people—caring, empathic, and accessible. The kids love their mentorship, their friendship, and their inspiration.

MAP also has brought hope to people and places many consider hopeless: a maximum security prison and three juvenile detention facilities. Life behind bars is mostly gray. We've brought in colors bright and bold. I've been astonished by how much talent we've found in the prison system, talent that was ignored until now. It makes me feel that everybody can be productive, everybody has strengths and gifts. Some of our artists have had art shows on the outside while remaining inside, receiving accolades from the public. For some of them, it's the first time in their lives they've had positive feedback. It's the first time they've been noticed for the good things they've done and not the bad.

One of our most unique ventures to date is the Healing Walls project. Against the odds, it brought together prisoners, community members, victims of crime, and victims' advocates. It was a project that required courage on all sides. The victims and their advocates had to overcome their fears and bias when they faced the inmates at the State Correctional Institution at Graterford. The same held true for the inmates: they feared they'd be stigmatized and some

Mural Arts Program Director Jane Golden standing in front of a classic Philadelphia mural work—Meg Saligman's *Philadelphia Muses* at 13th and Locust Streets.

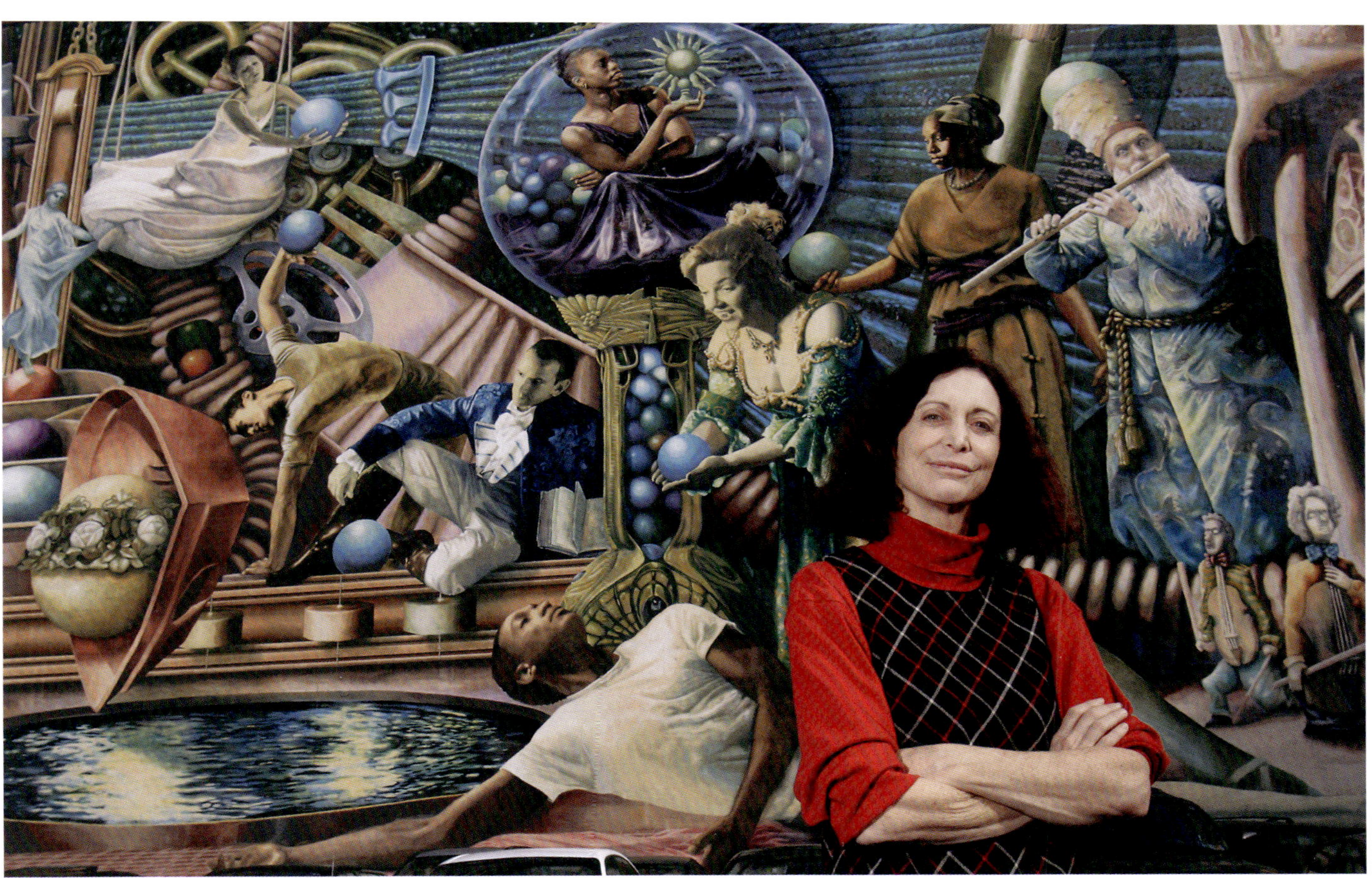

felt almost paralyzed by their feelings of guilt and remorse. But doing art together, meeting and talking about their feelings, these disparate groups found common ground. I remember watching the painting sessions and just stopping to listen to people connect. In the midst of talking about what color went where, they also would talk about their lives on a deeper level. In dealing with their collective pain, they learned there was a blurred line between victims and perpetrators. They saw that the impact and consequences of crime are more widespread than they thought.

...these kids all came from rough neighborhoods. They faced challenges at a young age that some adults will never see. They weren't expected to succeed. But Mural Corps was their constant, their line to the outside.

In so many ways, MAP has become more about changing lives than about art. Don't get me wrong: the art we're producing is still beautiful and inspiring and important to us. But the changes I see in the people we work with are also beautiful and inspiring and important. I've seen art provide comfort to troubled lives. I've seen art inspire people to change and do better. I've seen art become a way to rebuild community. And I've seen art serve as a tool of redemption.

The power of art helps us persevere despite all obstacles. In the end, the Mural Arts Program has been, for me, a journey of faith. And now, twenty-one years after I started working in Philadelphia, it is still about envisioning a dream and giving it form—it is about believing in things before they seem possible and inspiring people to sense, to believe, to feel what isn't quite there yet. This is the power of art—and it is why the arts so often inspire people to make changes. And this is exactly why my work has led me to believe that opportunity is everywhere and anything is possible in the future.

Acknowledgments

Jane Golden

I would like to thank my wonderful husband, Tony Heriza, for his love and support; my family for always encouraging me to follow my heart; my incredible staff and board for their dedication and hard work; and to all the city officials and funders who have the insight to know that art can play an important role in the life of a city, particularly the three mayors under whom I've worked: W. Wilson Goode, Edward G. Rendell, and John F. Street. And, finally, to my colleagues, who helped put together this book and to Temple University Press, thank you . . . for believing in the power of art to transform lives.

Robin Rice

I would like to express my gratitude for the support and generosity of my husband, David Utz, for the organizational skills of Kevin Gardner and the thoughtful feedback of Denis Snell. I also want to thank my favorite fellow authors, Jane Golden and Natalie Pompilio, and especially wish to acknowledge the achievements of the many hard-working and dedicated MAP muralists, teachers, and community leaders whose stories do not appear in this volume. I also gratefully acknowledge the scholarship of many historians of murals, wall-paintings, and other public art. I am especially indebted to the writing and insights of Penny Balkin Bach, Tim Drescher, Robin J. Dunitz, Mary Lackritz Gray, Tristan Manco, Jon Pounds, Jim Prigoff, and Bill Rolston.

Natalie Pompilio

I would like to thank my parents, Pat and Lou Pompilio, for their love and for always believing I'd get something published someday; T, for being a rip-roar; Walt, for his tireless search for my waterlogged notes; "Coach" Kristen, for her support and schedule-making; and Boudin and Schuster, for keeping my lap warm every time I sat down at the computer.

David Graham

We have great murals in our city, no doubt. There is so much brilliance, hidden around so many corners. I want to thank Jane and everyone else who helped put these pictures in the midst of my life. It makes me want to take pictures.

Jack Ramsdale

I would like to thank Jane Golden and the Mural Arts Program for creating the beautiful murals we see around the city and giving me the opportunity to work on this book. I would also like to thank Carl Toth for his vision and inspiration, Tish Ingersoll and my friends and family for all their support and understanding, and all the wonderful people of Philadelphia for accepting me and my camera into their neighborhoods.

The writers and the photographers would like to extend their deep gratitude to Brian Campbell, Kevin Gardner, and Amy Johnston, whose hard work and dedication helped bring this book to life.

A Key to the Mural Arts Program

The Mural Arts Program (MAP) began in 1984 as a component of Philadelphia's Anti-Graffiti Network. As part of this citywide initiative to eradicate graffiti and address neighborhood blight, the Anti-Graffiti Network hired mural artist Jane Golden to reach out to graffiti writers and redirect their energies from destructive graffiti to constructive mural painting. Mural painting provided a support structure for these young men and women to develop their artistic skills, empowering them to take an active role in beautifying their neighborhoods and communities. In 1996, the city of Philadelphia recognized MAP as a separate program, distinct from the Anti-Graffiti Network. At the same time, MAP established a nonprofit, the Philadelphia Mural Arts Advocates, with a broad mission of youth development and neighborhood revitalization through the arts.

MAP's current activities include:

Art Education

Programs targeting nearly three thousand underserved and at-risk youth at sixty neighborhood sites throughout Philadelphia, using mural-making as a dynamic means to engage youth and teach transferable life and job skills. With professional artists serving as role models and educators, MAP's art education programs engage youth in a rigorous artistic discipline, empowering them as artists, community organizers, and leaders. All programs are offered at no fee, ensuring accessibility for all participants.

The *Big Picture* Program – a year-round after-school program providing young people ages ten to eighteen with a structured environment and a high-quality visual arts education.
The *Mural Corps* Program -a year-round youth development and job readiness program engaging young people ages fourteen to twenty-one in advanced mural, mosaic, and mixed-media projects.
The *ARTscape* Program - offering youth offenders the opportunity to complete their community service requirements by participating in mural and community projects.
The *ArtWorks!* Program – providing mural painting courses to chronically truant youth as a complement to the comprehensive delinquency prevention services provided by the Philadelphia Department of Human Services.
The *Educational Outreach* Program – providing workshops for adjudicated youth at schools, long- and short-term residential placement facilities, and youth detention centers.
The *School District of Philadelphia Partnership* – a five-year partnership to create one hundred murals in Philadelphia schools, involving students of all ages in the mural-making process.

Community Mural-Making

MAP works with over one hundred communities each year to co-create over 130 murals serving the needs of the neighborhood, stabilizing abandoned lots, revitalizing open spaces, and inspiring civic pride. Since 1984, MAP has facilitated the creation of over twenty-five hundred murals throughout the city of Philadelphia that incorporate a variety of art forms and materials, including mosaic, metalworking, photography, and stained glass. The organization's street-level approach to mural-making involves block captains, neighborhood associations, public schools, community development organizations, and several city agencies in the struggle against blight and economic underdevelopment.

Prevention and Rehabilitation

MAP uses mural creation for two powerful purposes: the reparation and prevention of crime. Its work with men at local prisons, including the State Correctional Institute at Graterford, brings together prisoners, victims, victims' advocates, and community members to create healing, meaningful dialogue and powerful art. MAP's collaborations with alternative sentencing programs, detention centers, schools, and the Philadelphia prison system provide powerful crime deterrents for juvenile offenders and chronically truant youth, and provide solid community reentry experiences for youth recently released from detention centers and prisons.

Public Engagement

Philadelphia is nationally and internationally recognized as America's City of Murals. Every year, MAP brings more than six thousand tourists and residents on community mural tours throughout various neighborhoods of the city. Additionally, every October is Mural Arts Month, featuring popular special events such as community mural dedications, community paint days, lectures, and gallery exhibitions at MAP's headquarters in the historic Thomas Eakins House.

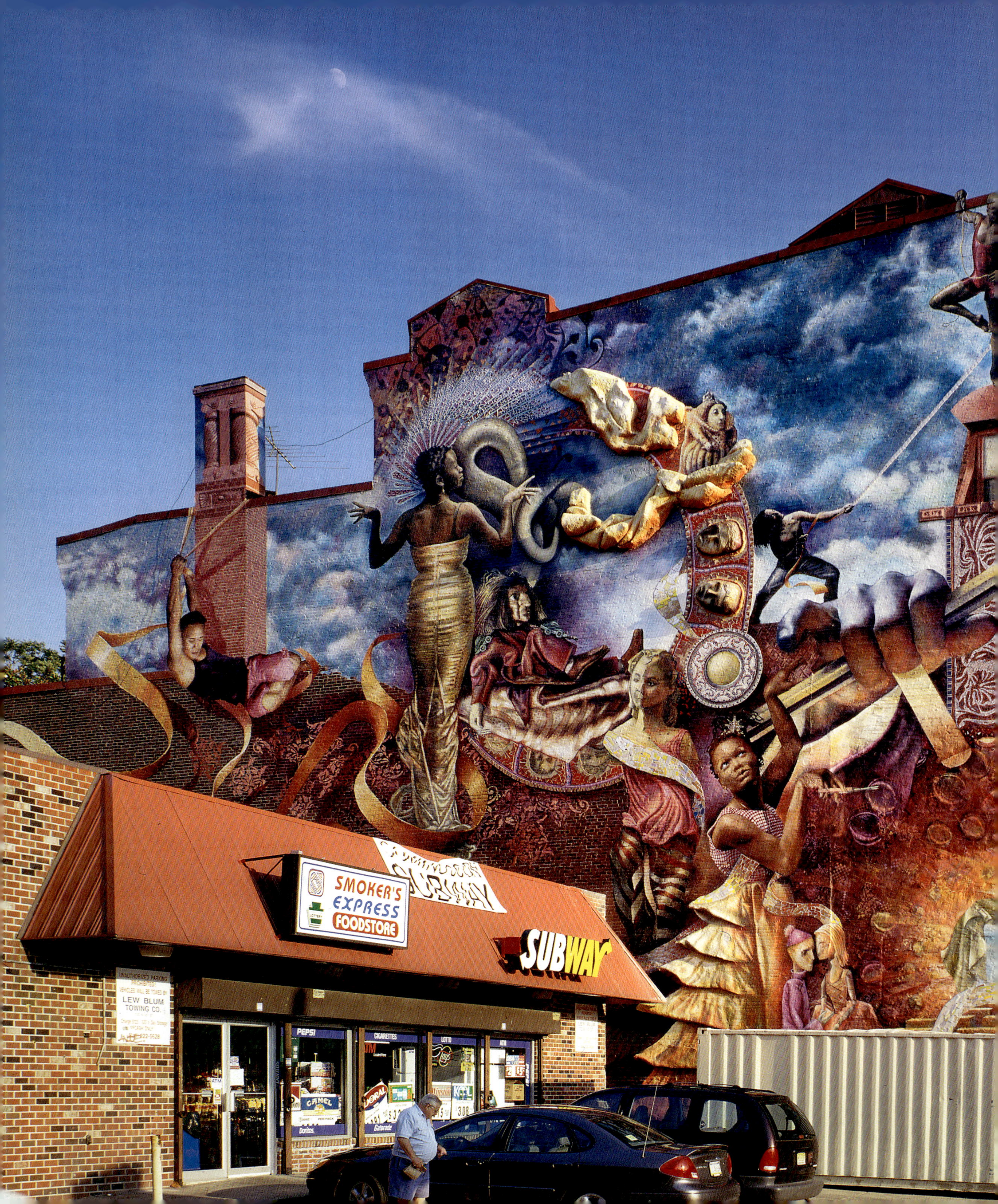
SMOKER'S
EXPRESS
FOODSTORE
SUBWAY
LEW BLUM
TOWING CO.

Chapter 1

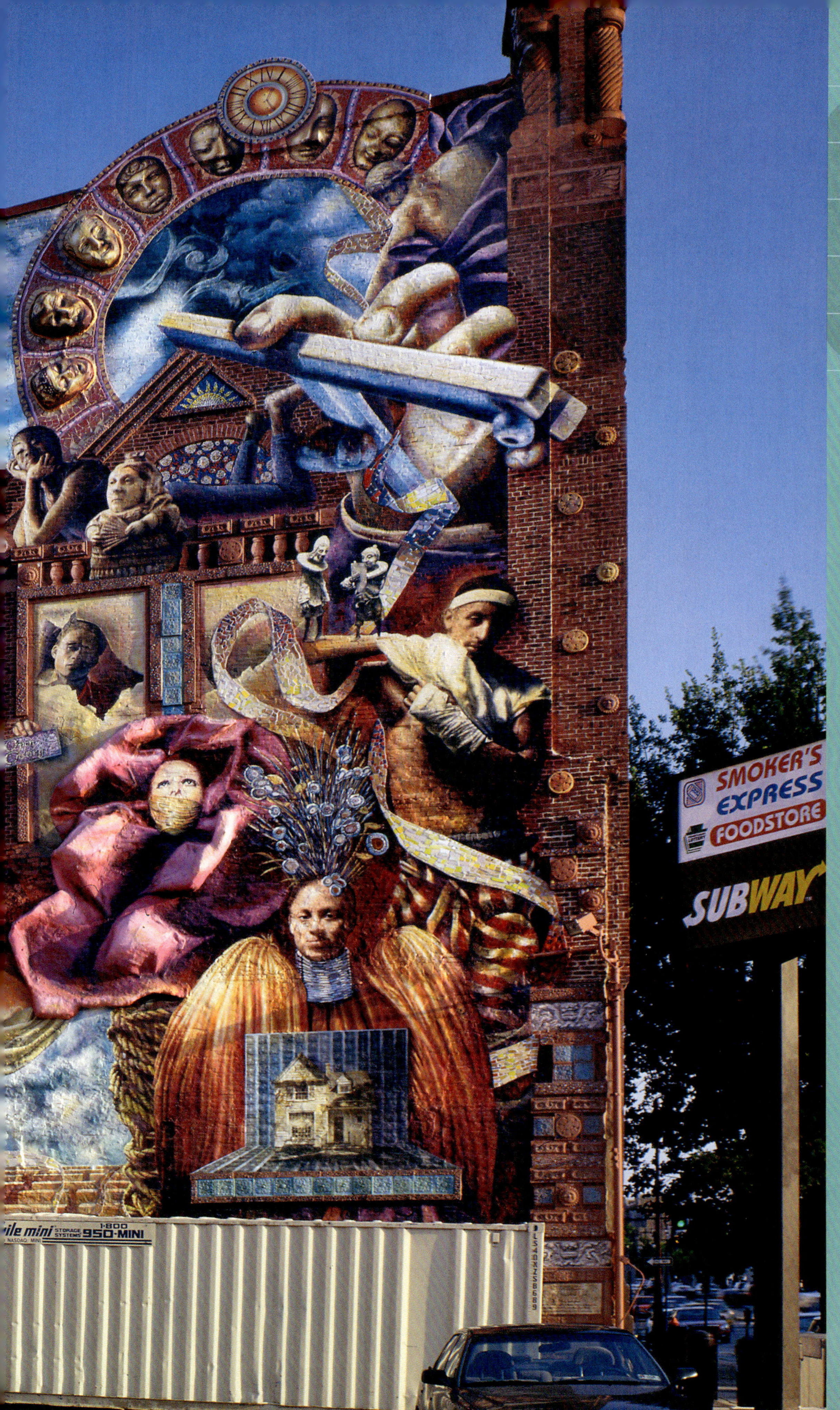

Meg Seligman's Avenue of the Arts masterpiece of sculpture, glass, tile, and paint, *Theatre of Life,* at Broad and Lombard Streets. Made possible by the Independence Foundation.

Chapter 1

Aspects of American Muralism

The name doesn't say it all. The Philadelphia Mural Arts Program, despite its name, is not just about artwork, larger than life, filling this rapidly rejuvenating city's walls—it's about people. *Muralism,* a term coming out of the Mexican mural movement, has resurfaced as a way of talking about contemporary mural-making. As practiced today by MAP, muralism is more about process and communication than about decoration. It is about exchanging ideas, hopes, and visions over time, not individual expression. Long-time Philadelphia muralist Peter Pagast acknowledges this emphasis on process when he says, "There's more good from this program, but it's not necessarily about murals."

MAP makes many kinds of artwork, including mosaics, fences, sculptures, and three-dimensional structures. The stakeholders in this vigorous process include educators and students, municipal employees, elected officials and taxpayers, community service workers and funding organizations, even incarcerated offenders and victims of crime: folks of all ages and all walks of life. Muralism does not claim to be a social cure-all, but today's community muralists do strive to orchestrate activities of communication and sharing into a singular and satisfying whole, a visual emblem of community. Often they accomplish a great deal.

Public Art, Process, and Kitsch

There is a risk in attempting to please too many: the triumph of the lowest common denominator expressed with greeting-card simplicity. As we will see in the discussion of MAP's diverse projects and its individual artists, muralism has become something both commemorative and transformative. Effective murals have a life beyond the wall. Murals may have pleasing and accessible surfaces, but if the artist and the process succeed, the work rewards repeated viewing with subtle new resonances. It is conceptually layered. It offers different answers for different people and occasions.

In contrast to MAP's belief in the human and humanizing value of muralism, almost everyone who expresses negative thoughts about murals utters one damning word: *kitsch*. Associated with pretentiousness, imitation, and sentimentality, kitsch entered the English language through the German *kitsch* and the related Yiddish *verkitschen,* pejorative terms for "cheap" or "garbage." This catch-all condemnation became part of the vocabularies of art-conscious Americans in the 1930s, when several writers sought to oppose it to the idea of high quality and significant art.

In 1939, Clement Greenberg made an enduring mark with his essay "Avant-Garde and Kitsch," published in the *New Partisan Review*. Greenberg tried to draw a clear distinction between high-quality, serious art and worthless entertainment. The year of Greenberg's essay is a convenient point to begin a survey of the arts and the course of muralism in the United States. In many ways, 1939 was a pivotal year in the development of Modernism and its ultimate evolution into Postmodernism.

Greenberg himself later disavowed some of his polemics in "Avant-Garde and Kitsch." He was only twenty-nine when he wrote it and had not yet discovered Jackson Pollock and other Abstract Expressionists with whom he will forever be identified. The paintings he saw as cutting-edge in 1939 were twenty or more years old; however, Greenberg's passionate denunciation of "ersatz culture . . . destined for those who, insensible to the values of genuine culture, are hungry nevertheless for the diversion that only culture . . . can provide," made a striking contribution to the critical dialogue on Modern painting. It prefigured the insights of later movements like Pop Art, which responded to American commercial culture with irony and sometimes unacknowledged nostalgia.

When Greenberg describes kitsch as "the debased and academicized simulacra of genuine culture," he is thinking not just of painting but of culture in its larger sense. He sees the United States as a disseminator of this ersatz popular and profitable culture to the rest of the world. Writing in the year Nazi Germany occupied Czechoslovakia and invaded Poland, which it invaded on September 1, the date generally accepted as the beginning of World War II, Greenberg no doubt realized that the United States would soon be at war. But, in spite of his insights into the American genius for confecting and selling cheap visual culture, he could hardly have imagined the global power of postwar U.S. entertainment and marketing.

In 1939, Greenberg also critiqued Soviet socialist culture and politics, in particular the communist attempt to level the social classes. Having seriously flirted with and rejected Marxism, Greenberg believed that only the elite classes have the leisure to study and understand intellectual art, music, and literature. Ordinary people, he says, can't be expected to appreciate the best art.

If we look at modern murals—or, indeed, most well-loved public art from the Statue of Liberty to Claes Oldenburg's and Coosje Van Bruggen's *Clothespin* in the center of

Philadelphia to Chicago's fifty-foot steel Picasso to Ann Hamilton's installations heaping up thousands of similar objects—in the light of Greenberg's discussion, several congruent aspects emerge:

1. Kitsch and murals are popular; that is they appeal to the populace or ordinary people, as distinct from the intellectual elite.
2. Kitsch and murals tend to be composed of represented or recognizable elements. They are only rarely completely abstract or nonobjective.
3. Kitsch and murals usually support basic, conventional values.
4. Kitsch and murals have to do with identity.

The history of murals is entwined with our core national, cultural, and human selves and also with innovative political ideas.

Kitsch, according to Greenberg, is "ersatz," fake, a superficial gesture. Like any other aesthetic judgment, the ultimate identification of kitsch will always be in the eye of the beholder; but, in theory, the best public art gets at deeper cultural truths. The history of murals is entwined with our core national, cultural, and human selves and also with innovative political ideas.

The Great Depression and Regionalism

MAP has created more than twenty-five hundred murals in one city. These are descended from a similar number of Depression-era murals commissioned throughout the United States by the Federal Arts Project, part of the Works Project Administration (WPA, 1935–1943). This big arts initiative was part of President Franklin Delano Roosevelt's New Deal, which aimed to rescue a struggling economy. American history, the American landscape, and American workers were typical subjects for muralists like Thomas Hart Benton, Sid Larson, Reginald Marsh, Ben Shahn, Charles White, and others who were making murals in post offices, hospitals, libraries, prisons, and schools.

The Depression-era painters' interest in native subject matter signaled an important shift of direction in American art away from European Modernists such as Cézanne, Picasso, and Braque. As a young man, Thomas Hart Benton, a key figure in the revival of mural painting in the United States, was attracted to Modernist abstraction. Benton even went to Paris to study, but he returned to America and to American subject matter even before the stock market crash of 1929. In the face of the grim economic crisis of the Great Depression, the intellectual disengagement of abstraction or the personalized angst of European Expressionism seemed empty to Benton and to many others. A style of painting about local lives, struggles, myths, and landscape—sometimes called Regionalism or American Scene Painting—came to the fore. This focus on America, although more socially oriented, echoed the nationalism of Thomas Cole, Robert Scott Duncanson, Thomas Moran, and other Hudson River style landscape painters of the previous century. Artists like Benton saw the sweep of murals as a good way of recording this American society, sometimes democratic, often colorful, and always in flux.

Mexican Muralism—1920s

Mexico provided a model for the WPA's mural program during the Great Depression and prototypes for the murals themselves. In 1920, the Mexican government initiated an ambitious mural program as a way of rallying and educating citizens about the 1910 revolution. Mexican muralists had stylistic and thematic freedom. *Los Tres Grandes* (The Big Three)—Diego Rivera, José Clemente Orozco, and David Alfaro Siqueiros—inspired North American painters and the world. Rivera and Siqueiros executed influential murals in the United States. In particular, Siquerios, who was exiled from Mexico in the 1930s, painted in New York and Los Angeles. He used a spray gun–like graffiti-related muralists of today, experimented with acrylic paint, and developed compositions that wrap around a building.

The Black WPA muralist Hale Woodruff, like some other Depression-era muralists, studied with Rivera. He painted many murals, including the Amistad Murals (1938 and 1939) at Alabama's Talladega College. His later work reflects the influence of Thomas Hart Benton.[1]

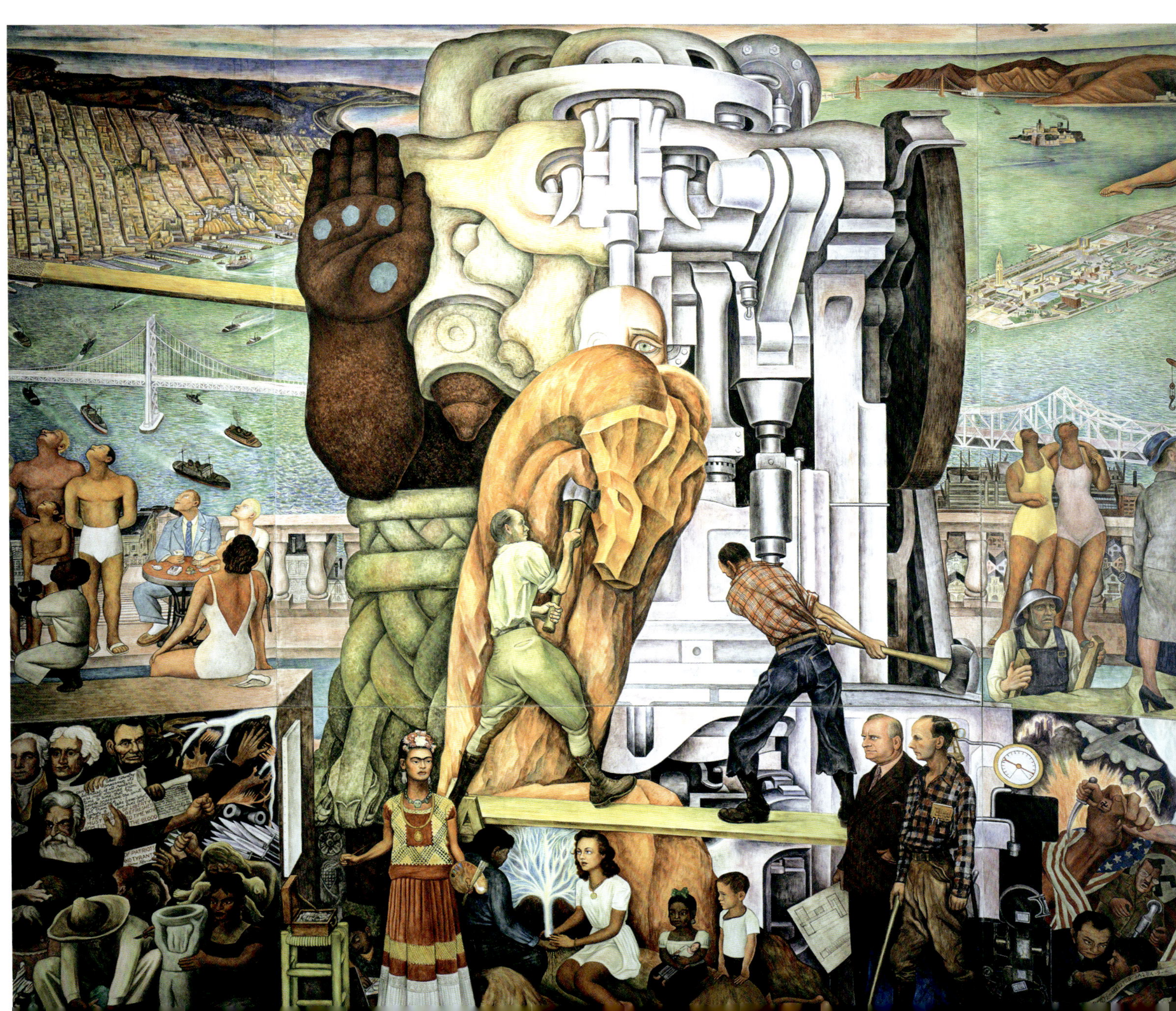

The Pan American Unity Mural painted by Diego Rivera in 1940 and located in the Diego Rivera Theater at the City College of San Francisco, 50 Phelan Avenue, San Francisco, California.

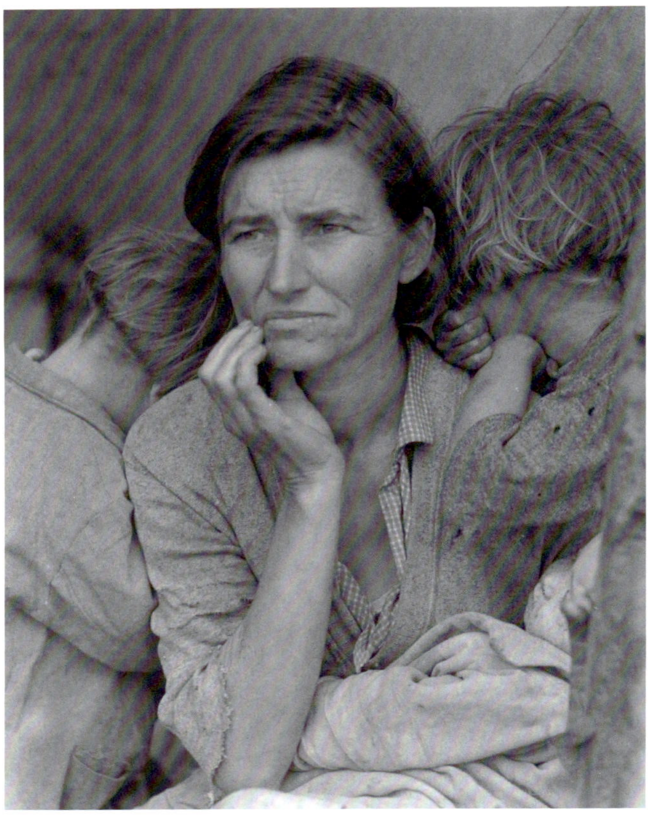

Dorothea Lange's photograph, *Destitute pea pickers in California. Mother of seven children. Age thirty-two,* 1936, from the Migrant Mother series.

Social Realism versus Socialist Realism—1930s and 1940s

The Cubist-related style of representation and proletarian subject matter of Mexican murals and of leftist painting in general is often called "social realism." This term is easily confused with *Socialist Realism,* the officially sanctioned pedagogical or propagandistic approach of socialist governments to all art, especially murals and posters. The governments of China, Nazi Germany, the former East Germany, and the former Soviet Union preferred or still prefer Socialist Realism.

The two categories overlap to some degree, but social realism tends to critique society, illustrating difficulties people face, whereas Socialist Realism tends to present a didactic, idealized picture, such as scenes of well-fed, smiling children saluting a leader. The real point of Socialist Realism is ideological. It is heroic and optimistic. In Socialist Realism, the word "realism" simply means that the viewer can recognize what is represented; the style of painting *looks realistic.* Advertising uses this same tool to make the represented ideal appear to be a reality. Thus, the appealing photograph of food on a pretty china plate on the box containing a frozen dinner is a "serving suggestion," not what you will find inside the box.

Didactic art tends to resemble Socialist Realism. *The Saturday Evening Post* magazine covers by Norman Rockwell were not socialist but, like much religious, narrative art, they illustrated simplistic cultural values. Maoist or Soviet posters represented the ideal in similar terms. Different societies—identical strategies. These tactics often surface in murals.

In contrast, *social realism,* prominent during the Depression, tries to be objective and descriptive. Although it clearly has an agenda of improvement, its artists typically aim to record simple human lives. The word "realism" here does not describe the appearance of the work (although it may be photographic or illusionistic) but, rather, the subject matter. It means that the artist is trying to represent *real life,* not a fiction, fantasy, or ideal. This more politically neutral but compassionate stance informs the work of many WPA muralists, as well as photographers like Dorothea Lange. Social realists do not flinch from poverty, injustice, and suffering, and sometimes seek them out. When they depict people enjoying kitsch entertainment in dance halls, brothels, bar rooms, and movie theatres, they are showing us something that happens. Today's murals are also directly related to social realism.

Violet Oakley: The First Philadelphia Muralist of International Stature

An important muralist working throughout the first half of the twentieth century and residing primarily in Philadelphia, Violet Oakley (1874–1961) was neither a regionalist nor social realist but, rather, a political activist, successfully supporting herself with art that advocated peace and women's rights. She painted a series of murals in the Pennsylvania State Capitol complex in Harrisburg in the 1920s before moving to Geneva, Switzerland, to serve as the official muralist for the League of Nations. Later, she painted murals depicting the delegates to the United Nations. She painted an altarpiece for the sanctuary of the Samuel Fleisher Art Memorial in Philadelphia and in 1949, at the age of seventy-five, she completed a cycle of ten murals, *Great Women of the Bible,* at the First Presbyterian Church in Germantown.

Postwar Influences on Murals

Advertising on billboards and in print inspired twentieth-century graffiti; it began as a form of visual vandalism with roots in prehistory. Tagging and even piecing (large multicolored grafitti "masterpieces") are home-grown branding, protests against personal meaninglessness and marginalization. A few middle-class graffitists such as Jean-Michel Basquiat, Futura 2000, and Philadelphian Steve Powers (ESPO) moved on to commercial careers, but grafitti has been more an influence than a presence in contemporary art. It continues to impact murals, typography, and other art forms.

At mid-century, the paranoia of the McCarthy Era stifled dissent; however, conformity soon was challenged by strident political protest, a context in which art challenged all sorts of rules. Improvisational performance art and political activism relating to civil rights and the Vietnam War developed almost simultaneously, and the spirit of both contributed significantly to the way muralism is practiced today.

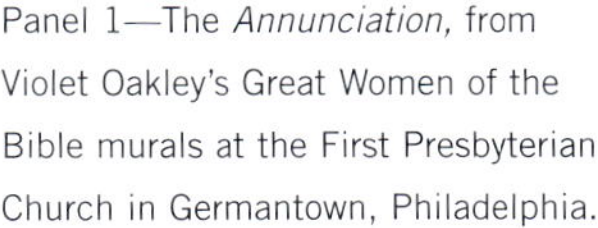

Panel 1—The *Annunciation,* from Violet Oakley's Great Women of the Bible murals at the First Presbyterian Church in Germantown, Philadelphia.

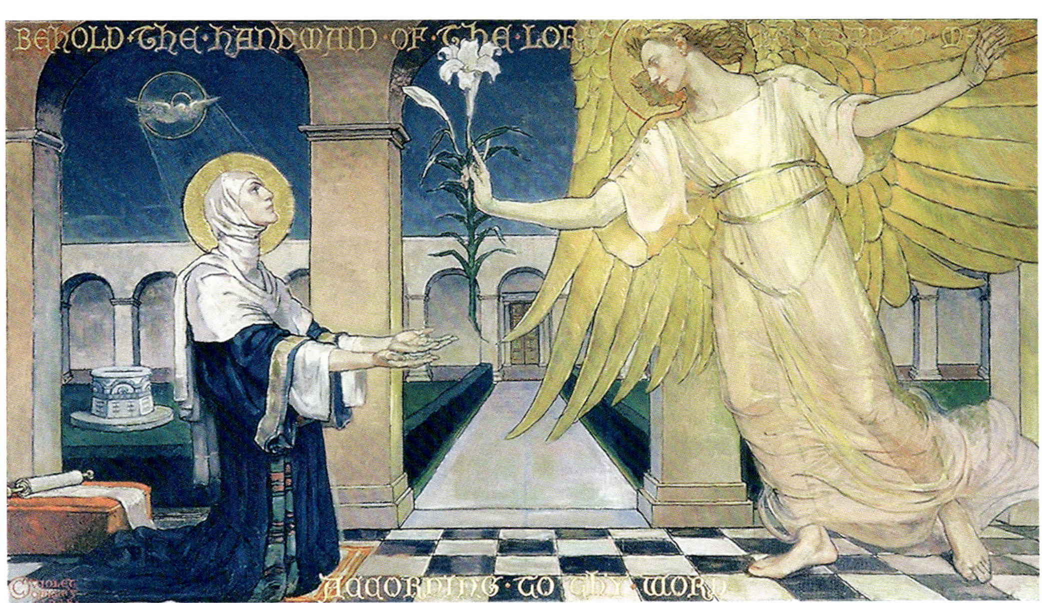

To quote Greenberg one last time, "Kitsch pretends to demand nothing of its customers except their money—not even their time." He cynically observes that "the Russian masses" prefer Hollywood movies to more arty films. Two 1939 Hollywood classics of fantasy and escape, *Gone with the Wind* and *The Wizard of Oz,* defined much that remains quintessentially American. Both films depict the triumph of dreams over adversity and both stories originate in family and farmland, emblems of America that would be more hallowed and paradoxically threatened by big business and urbanism following World War II.

Along with the movies, Greenberg lists popular music, tap dancing, and "pulp fiction" as leading examples of kitsch. He had already identified affordable consumer goods, made possible by the Industrial Revolution, and universal literacy, made possible by democratic political revolutions, as key events in the growing market for kitsch.

From Advertising to Action—1950s and 1960s

Following World War II, mid-twentieth-century America entered an unprecedented period of affluence. American families in cars and on couches passively absorbed visual and auditory stimulation. Advertising—notably billboard advertising and, later, television advertising—became pervasive elements of the everyday context.

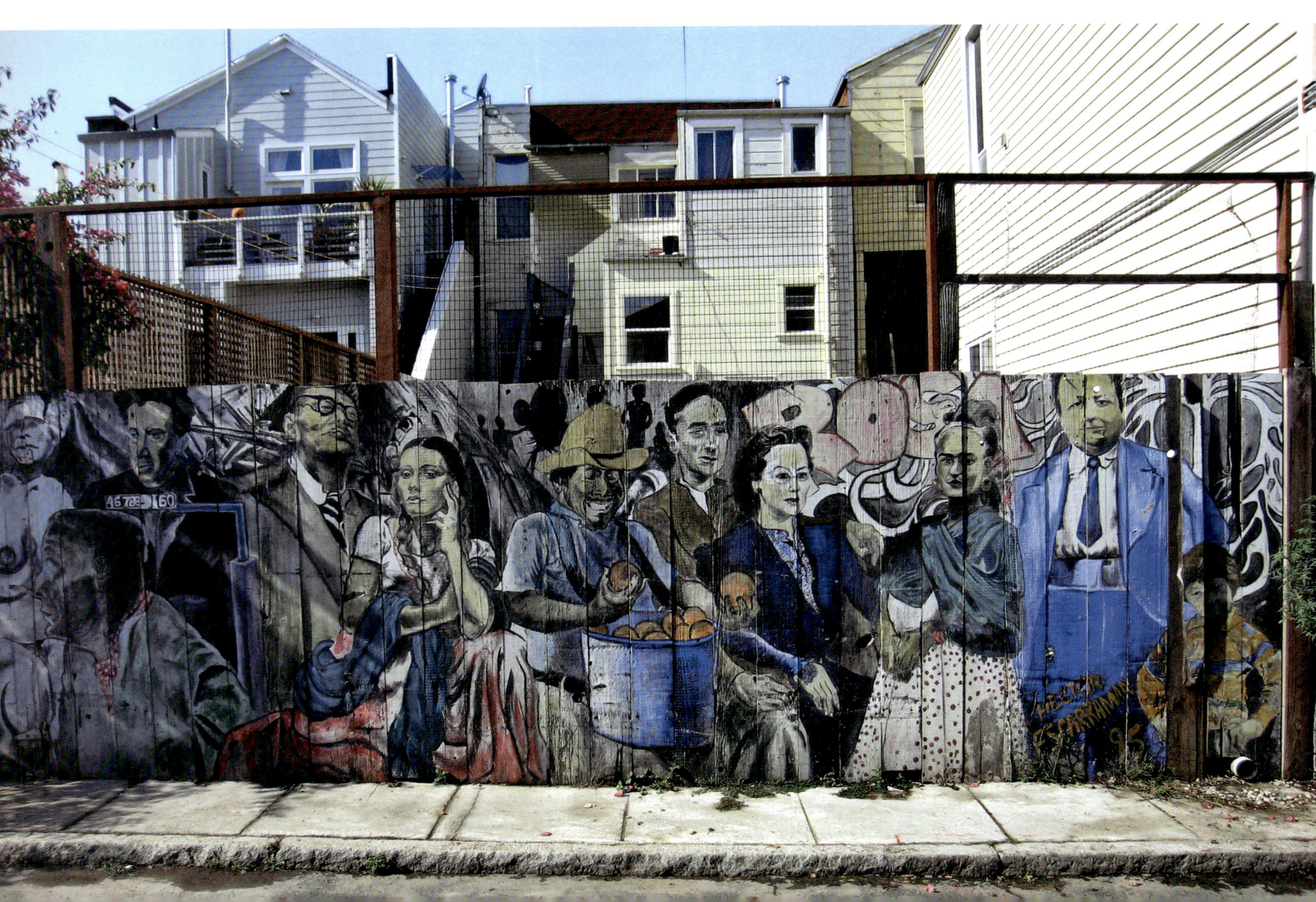

Hector Escarraman's tribute to Diego Rivera and Frida Kahlo, one of the many murals found on Balmy Alley—a narrow street in San Francisco's Mission District active with mural work since 1971.

It is no coincidence that Pop Art—an intellectual response to consumerism—and graffiti took off independently in the 1960s. Each draws inspiration from the shallow passions of consumer society and the advertising that drives it. Both art forms emphasize words and distinctive letter forms as pictorial elements. Pop artists such as Robert Indiana and Andy Warhol, who began his career as a commercial artist, acknowledged commodification and the print media as sources for art-making. Graffiti writers, ingenuously or not, typically cite "branding" and billboard advertising in poor urban neighborhoods as primary sources.

Provocatively, Philadelphia was a seminal city for the development of twentieth-century graffiti or graf. Graffiti was and often still is an expression of gang identity; however, the early independent Philly wall writer known as "Cornbread" gave it a more benign aspect. He is said to have placed his peace sign tag on a jet plane in the Philadelphia International Airport—some say it was a plane that carried the Beatles—and on an elephant in the zoo.

In addition to self-promoting graffiti, gangs pioneered the painting of memorial walls, usually text-based murals listing the names of gang members who had been murdered or died in some untimely way. Occasionally, mural groups have used this technique to remember innocent victims of violence, but some mural programs feel that the link to gang activity is too blatant.

Grassroots public art sprang up in the idealistic 1960s. Local political groups and individuals with a message chose walls as a vehicle for communication. Their messages, often statements of cultural identity, borrowed strategies from billboards and posters to reclaim the visual field in the urban environment. Ethnic pride was the subject of the collaborative *Wall of Respect.* Begun in Chicago (43rd and Langley Streets) in 1967, it is usually identified as the first important example of contemporary American muralism. Until it was destroyed in 1971, the wall was an evolving statement, which was well documented photographically.

The overarching subject of the *Wall* chosen by artists of the Organization of Black American Culture (OBAC), a group sympathetic to the Black Power Movement, was *black heroes.* William Walker is often identified as initiating the project, in which twenty-three African-American artists drew up a list of heroes who might be included. Community members were invited to comment. Local businesses provided paint. This wall became a collage of images, including photographs, and various sections were modified over time in response to political events.

On the West Coast, in San Francisco's Mission District, community muralists decorated Balmy Alley in 1971. The narrow street has been home to layers of murals ever since, including work by the *Mujeres Muralistas* (Women Muralists) and the *PLACA* (to mark or speak out) group of about forty artists who made many political murals. Recent Balmy Alley murals are technically adventurous and some protest the war in Iraq.

Artist Profile

Cavin Jones

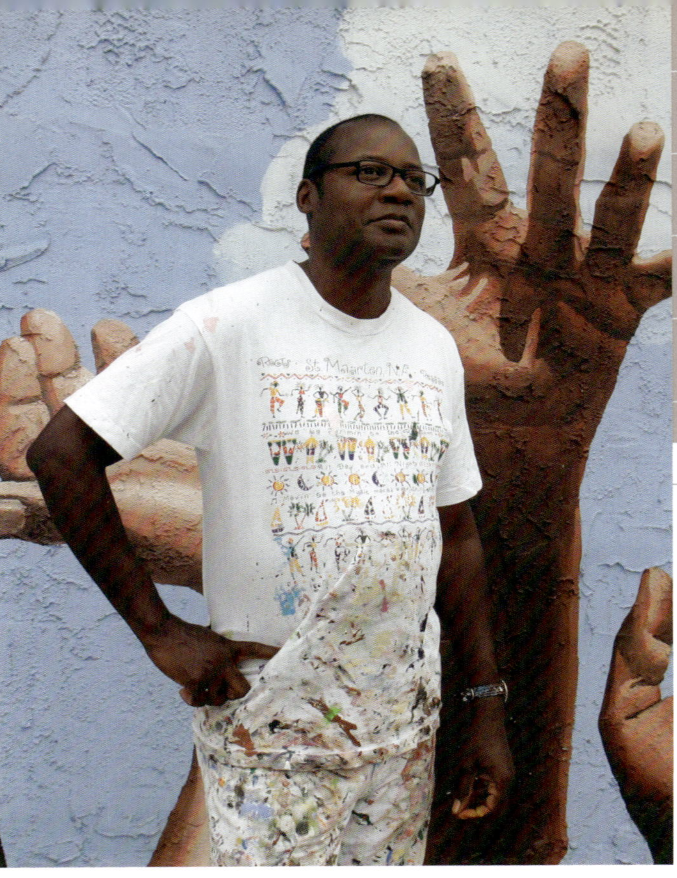

In over a decade of painting regularly for MAP, Cavin Jones has come to rely on the power of illusionism to attract viewers and convey a message. "I think that my paintings are easy to look at even though they are dealing with some pretty difficult subject matter. The human touch of painting has a calming effect," he says. He shows his surreal politically-charged studio paintings at Philadelphia's prestigious Seraphin Gallery, but Jones has "always believed that art should be in people's lives—not that it should be exclusively in museums and galleries. Murals give me an opportunity to do this."

Jones earned a BFA in Philadelphia at Tyler School of Art at Temple University and, after a stint in the U.S. Air Force, completed his MFA at Washington University in St. Louis. As a student, he did a series of paintings on paper with themes of political protest, but he didn't dream his future work would have such public exposure. "I would never have thought that I would be doing what I'm doing now, especially working outside the studio and being watched while working."

When Jones returned to Philadelphia, a married man with a baby daughter, he happened to revisit Smith Memorial Playground, a fondly remembered favorite from his own childhood. He sadly noted that it no longer matched his "dream-like memories of bright colors from childhood." After learning that the playground was privately owned, Jones contacted the director with a proposal to spruce it up. He was hired to repaint the equipment in his chosen color scheme. There, in a basement play area called "Smithtown," Jones painted his first public mural. (He'd previously done one in his sister's home.) Through the "Smithtown" project, Jones met parents who commissioned more indoor murals. He did jungles in kids' rooms and a desert landscape in an office in Glenside. One patron asked him to represent his house exterior on an inside wall of the same building. These jobs eventually led Jones to Jane Golden and then to the Philadelphia Anti-Graffiti Network.

Today, Jones is frequently asked to do murals with very specific themes and he is "as straightforward as possible" in addressing them. Usually communities prefer uplifting, cheerful, or sublime imagery no matter what the subject of the mural is; however, for an early antidrug wall, Jones was asked to paint "some dark elements," including somebody in a coffin, somebody being arrested, and a woman smoking a crack pipe. He did, but by using monochromatic tones and strategies suggestive of Picasso's Blue Period—in which the Spanish artist painted emaciated, grieving peasants—Jones was able to infuse the mural with beauty.

"I'm willing to compromise and I accept that as a reality of doing community murals. I actually embrace it. If they want a flower, I can choose a flower that I really want to do. When I do a mural design, I do images that I really want to draw." He particularly enjoyed researching American history for a series of murals for the Society of Friends.

In planning the *I Too Have a Dream* mural (2203 W Somerset St., 2004), Jones worked with a group of elementary school children who read and discussed Dr. Martin Luther King's "I Have a Dream" speech. The students made mobiles of cloud shapes on which they wrote down their dreams. The dreams varied from personal (future careers) to social (a world without guns) to silly (corn chips falling from the sky). Jones interpreted it all in a single mural and even found the shape of curved chips fun to paint. A little girl's head in the foreground seems to generate the cacophony of hopes and fantasies bubbling around an image of Dr. King.

Jones crisply conceptualized future careers and young people in the *Careers: Heads to the Sky* mural (22nd St. and Lehigh Ave., 2005). The group of students from Dobbins Area Vocational Technical High School that worked with him had no art experience. They did not attempt to present ideas in visual terms; however, Jones turned that possible defect into a virtue by using language in the mural. On the long horizontal wall, job titles ("ELECTRICIAN ACTOR PSYCHIATRIST HAIRSTYLIST NURSE") move across the blue sky in three blocky, horizontal graphic tracks suggesting an almost endless series of possibilities above a row of oversize por-

Opposite
Cavin Jones, muralist and creator of *Heads to the Sky*, 22nd St. and Lehigh Ave.
Below
Inspiring text and expressive portraits in Cavin Jones's *Heads to the Sky*, 22nd St. and Lehigh Ave.

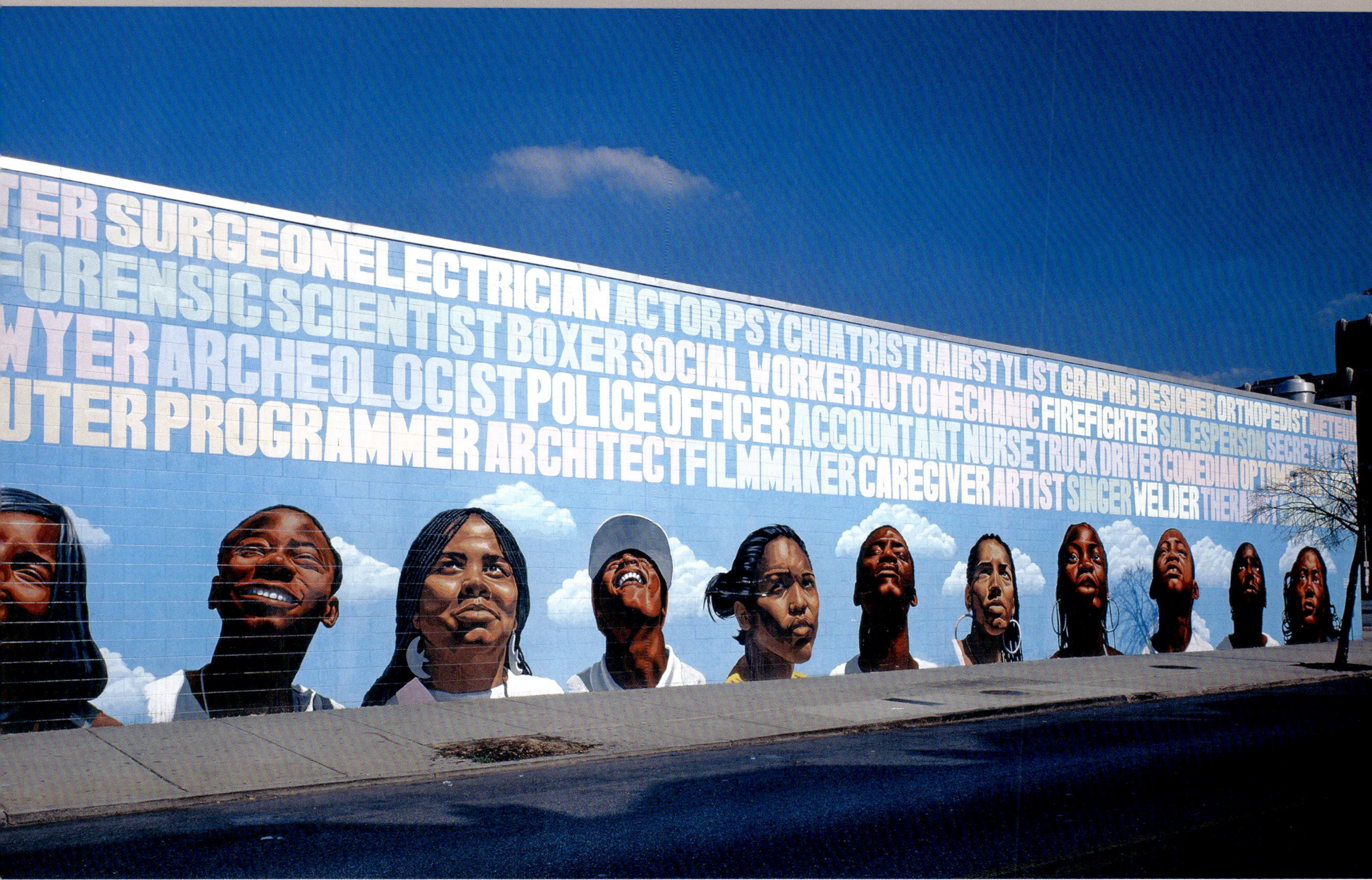

trait heads. The candylike colors of the letters, pastel but intense, provide a fantasy contrast to the naturalistic skin tones of the youthful faces below.

With his part of the design complete, Jones gave the students an opportunity to paint the mural. He drew the expressive heads directly on the wall and broke them down into simplified color areas. He mixed paint so that the students could simply fill in areas. They learned that making a mural is real work, but it is rewarding work.

Even though Jones had simplified the job, he says, "It was still a difficult thing for them to do. They had a problem with neatness. They enjoyed the first and second days. By the third day, some began getting frustrated. But once they filled in more and more of the faces, they really got excited about it."

New ways of understanding the role of process and authorship characterized much fine art in the second half of the twentieth century. Movement of the artist's body and of paint itself was the dominant characteristic of Abstract Expressionism, a style Greenberg and others once viewed as the ultimate development of the history of Western painting. Also called "action painting," Abstract Expressionism is a record of gestures, drips, and pours in which chance plays a role. Improvisation in jazz deeply influenced many artists of this time.

But the nature of art history is dialogue. Soon, Pop artists reintroduced imagery with a twist, reveling in the accidents of off-register printing. Young graffiti artists were more deeply immersed in physical action, addicted to the rush of doing something dangerous and secret. These sources feed directly into the development of contemporary muralism.

In retrospect, it's not surprising that process as an end in itself came to be so important in art. The escapist and spiritual side of the psychedelic drug culture and Asian philosophies that emphasize the value of living in the moment attracted a generation of idealistic baby boomers. They sought alternatives to the hypocrisy and conformity they found in mainstream religions, institutional racism, and a futile war in Vietnam (1957–1975).

Similarly, during World War I, artists who felt politically impotent and unable to derail a conflict they saw as pointless invented Dada, a deliberate descent into nonsense, a form of protest that laughs at its own futility. In the 1960s, the absurdist ghost of Dada happily met the Zen Zeitgeist of the composer John Cage in Allan Kaprow's *Happenings,* art events that

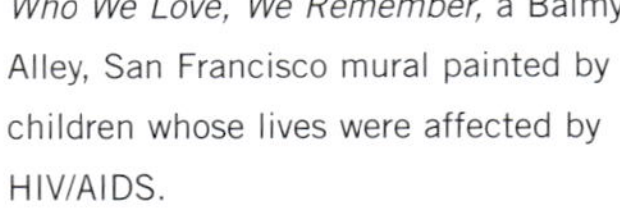

Who We Love, We Remember, a Balmy Alley, San Francisco mural painted by children whose lives were affected by HIV/AIDS.

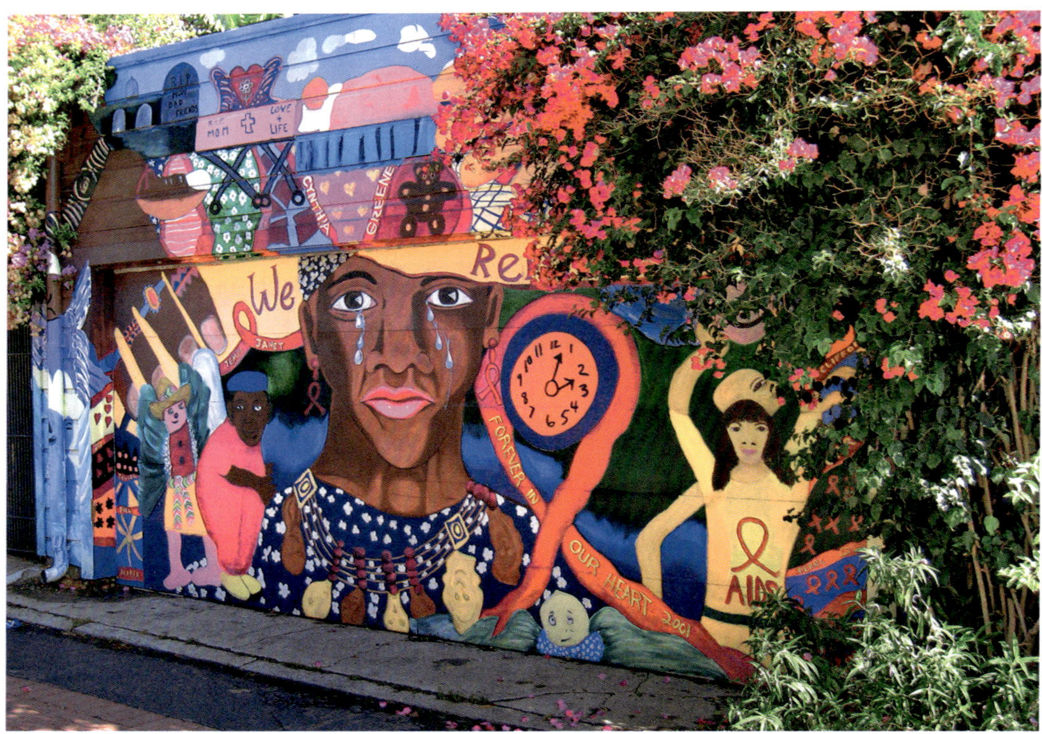

unfold as collective experiences. Although often documented on film, Happenings do not result in permanent works of art. Kaprow, who is now regarded as an authority on public art, staged the first Philadelphia Happening at the Gershman Y in 1960. The importance of Happenings and similar art events to muralism partly lies in the participation of nonartists as both makers and consumers. Their *experience* is the center of the work.

Kaprow writes:

When art as a practice is intentionally blurred with the multitude of other identities and activities we like to call life, it becomes subject to all the problems, conditions, and limitations of those activities, as well as their unique freedoms . . . the means by which we measure success and failure in such fleeting art must obviously shift from the aesthetics of the self-contained painting or sculpture, regardless of its symbolic reference to the world outside of it, to the ethics and practicalities of those social domains it crosses into. And that ethics, representing a diversity of special interests as well as the deep ones of a culture, cannot easily be disentangled from the nature of the artwork. Success and failure become provisional judgments, instantly subject (like the weather) to change.[2]

One consequence of this emphasis on process and interaction was demystification. Untrained people can and do make meaningful contributions to art works, especially in the realm of ideas, language, and subject matter. Mural artists have developed several techniques for organizing the participation of nonartists in order to maximize their contributions while maintaining a sense of visual structure.

Muralism Revives—1970s and 1980s

After a dry period in Philadelphia, the newly founded Department of Urban Outreach/ Department of Community Programs of the Philadelphia Museum of Art, led by Penny Balkin Bach, painted approximately 130 murals during the early 1970s. Working for the museum, the artists Don Kaiser and Clarence Wood were committed to allowing neighborhood people to choose the subjects and the specific imagery of murals. They took the position that they as artists simply facilitated the community's mural-making, claiming no pride of authorship. The subjects of these murals tended toward primordial waterfalls, but some neighborhoods chose to celebrate heroes such as Malcolm X, the educator Mary McLeod Bethune, and the entertainer Aretha Franklin.

Political murals were springing up all over the country. Some of the most exciting work was done on the West Coast in places like Balmy Alley (see page 22). These ephemeral and ever-evolving walls were often painted by unpaid, uncommissioned, sometimes untrained artists familiar with the Mexican mural tradition and mural painting in churches. Sometimes they combined religious imagery with a political agenda. It has often been documented that artists who paint over previous murals will visually frame and retain an earlier representation of the Virgin of Guadalupe, leaving the sacred image intact. If the image of the Virgin has weathered, chipped, or faded, it will be refreshed with new colors.

Judith Francisca Baca, the "Mother of American Muralism," is the preeminent figure in the history of California murals. Her first mural, a portrait of her grandmother (*Mi Abuelita*), combined two themes that continue to engage her: feminism and cultural heritage. By 1970, Baca was the Resident Fine Artist for the Cultural Affairs Division in Los Angeles. She recognized the importance of locating murals in neighborhoods and the necessity of involving local residents in the richness of the mural process.

Her most famous achievement, *The Great Wall of Los Angeles*—painted over seven summers beginning in 1976—is a series of murals covering the sides of a flood control channel in the San Fernando Valley. *The Great Wall* tells the story of the people of California, a story partly constructed through oral histories, a secondary component of the mural project. At a half-mile long, the mural is sometimes described as the largest single artwork in the world. By 1983, more than four hundred young people, including rival gang members, and one hundred professional artists had contributed to the work-in-progress. It is an ongoing project, as sections continually require repainting and conservation. Baca still maintains connections with some of the kids, now grown, who participated in the original painting.

Baca founded S.P.A.R.C. (Social and Public Art Resource Center) in Venice, California, in 1976 to promote "art with a social voice, art reflecting . . . the lives and concerns of America's diverse ethnic populations, women, working people, youth, and the elderly." MAP Director Jane Golden, who was living in Los Angeles at that time, received her first mural commission, *The Ocean Park Pier*, from S.P.A.R.C.

A scattering of whimsical or surreal murals also popped up in commercial and industrial areas during the 1970s and 1980s. People do not feel comfortable with large, uninflected building surfaces. As William H. Whyte wrote in his important 1988 analysis of urban spaces, *City: Rediscovering the Center:*

Blank walls proclaim the power of the institution and the inconsequence of the individual, whom they are clearly meant to intimidate. . . . The walls fairly cry for something to set them off—some inspired graffiti, for example, a touch of the vulgar. . . . The best thing to do with blank walls is to do away with them, or, at the very least, . . . to fill the vacuum or replace nothing with something . . . (p. 226)

Although Whyte did not envision the effectiveness of murals as an antidote, wall paintings today inject a sense of warmth and fun in to otherwise stark settings.

Until 1985, developers in Philadelphia adhered to a gentleman's agreement to ban buildings higher than the hat on the statue of "Billy Penn" atop City Hall, thus avoiding the canyon of skyscrapers that characterizes other major U.S. cities. Through most of the twentieth century, this wisdom preserved a unique skyline with relatively few empty, dehumanizing walls.

Like Simon Rodia's brilliantly eccentric *Watts Towers* (1921–1954) in Los Angeles, Isaiah Zagar's Philadelphia mosaics reflect the maverick sensibility of a single individual. Unlike Rodia, Zagar is a trained artist with a long exhibition history. However, working almost entirely alone, Zagar has made a significant visual impact on the city with improvisational mosaics incorporating bits of broken ceramic, found objects, and countless glittering splinters of mirror. Zagar's emphasis on direct visual experience rather than a representational image is unusual in Philadelphia wall arts. Among the city's many murals and mosaics, playful, abstract, or decorative ones are a delightful and noteworthy minority.

In 1986, Philadelphia artist Lily Yeh embarked on a single project to beautify an abandoned lot in North Philadelphia. Her effort and interest grew into the multifaceted Village of Arts and Humanities, which has absorbed several blocks of its Germantown Avenue neighborhood while making murals, mosaics, and sculptures, renovating buildings, and planting gardens. The Village of Arts and Humanities offers classes in many subjects. Yeh directed an organization that has transformed the neighborhood and continues to provide an outstanding example of effective neighborhood reclamation and growth.

Muralism Is Institutionalized—1990s

Golden was forced to break off her career as a muralist in California when she returned to the Philadelphia area in 1983 to seek treatment for lupus. The following year, she began teaching young people in Mayor Wilson Goode's newly founded Philadelphia Anti-Graffiti Network (PAGN). PAGN's mission was to offer kids positive alternatives to graffiti. Under Golden's guidance, murals, originally only one among many activities, became a key component in the program, one that effectively attracted the eager participation of teens. For many years, antigraffiti activists felt they had to forbid the use of spray paint, the medium of graffiti, in murals. Nevertheless, PAGN hired a number of former wall writers and commissioned graffiti-inspired muralists. Since PAGN became the Mural Arts Program, muralists also have begun to incorporate spray paint.

Taking Los Angeles and Philadelphia as models, communities around the country began using mural painting as a way of combating graffiti while providing positive activities for youth at risk.

Taking Los Angeles and Philadelphia as models, communities around the country began using mural painting as a way of combating graffiti while providing positive activities for youth at risk. Mural paint is a cost-effective alternative to marble or bronze. Even the fact that murals have a comparatively short life span has an up side: if the mural does not remain popular, it need not be restored.

The 1980s taught the Philadelphia muralists that people value the act of contributing ideas and their own labor almost as much as they appreciate the finished wall; however, the program was almost abandoned by the city that had so brilliantly demonstrated its effectiveness. In 1996, Mayor Ed Rendell restructured PAGN. Golden became head of the newly created Mural Arts Program, a specialized mural-painting project in the Department of Recreation. PAGN's teaching components were dissolved or shifted to other programs. MAP optimized this mostly mural period by emphasizing high quality art. It nurtured a diverse group of mural painters that was more skillful and more stylistically varied than those associated with any other organized mural program in the world. This collection of skilled and committed muralists remains central to the achievements of MAP today.

But Golden always dreamed of introducing more young people to Philadelphia's growing pool of talent. She believes that mural painting offers unique opportunities for kids to build the discipline, confidence, sense of identity, and the social and creative skills that are the basis of effective adulthood. Golden formed the Mural Arts Advocates, a small nonprofit organization, in 1996. "After watching then Department of Recreation Commissioner Mike DiBerardinis raise money to open up swimming pools," she says, "I decided to take the lead in forming a separate nonprofit that could assist us in raising private money to help stabilize MAP. I had just gone through the program Leadership Inc., so I asked the executive director, Liz Dow, to help me form the board. The Mural Arts Advocates were charged with providing MAP with both programmatic and fiscal support. The Advocates have a strong interest in youth development through the arts." Among the original board members were Dow, Andy Toy, and Bob Yermish.

Opposite
Ann Northrup's unique skill in making a mural painting not unlike an easel painting in her *Growing Up in Germantown,* Germantown Avenue and Rittenhouse Street.

Another key moment for MAP was when John F. Street was elected mayor of Philadelphia in 2000. The mayor appointed Estelle Richman to be his director of social services. She became a key figure in the development of MAP as an independent organization that interacts with numerous city programs and departments. Richman had been a successful health commissioner and was a supporter of MAP before assuming her new position. Golden was inspired by Richman's ideas about city government. She always spoke of needing an "integrated model of city government." "Estelle says that all too often city departments have a silo mentality which ultimately leads to a lack of partnership and collaboration," Golden recalls. Richman actively promoted working relationships between departments within the Division of Social Services. Not only did she increase MAP's funding, she also made sure that, even though MAP was still part of the Department of Recreation, it became an independent entity within the Division of Social Services. This meant that Golden was at the table with commissioners of major departments. Golden says, "I credit Estelle, who is now Secretary of the Department of Public Welfare for the State of Pennsylvania, with a major transformation of our program."

For a couple of years in the late 1990s, MAP offered no classes, but gradually it reintroduced mural-related activities for kids of middle-school age as well as teens, before moving to its current headquarters in Thomas Eakins House. With a new home came expanded programming. The beautiful four-story row house was once the residence of Thomas Eakins (1844–1916). Often described as Philadelphia's most illustrious realistic painter, Eakins was an influential and sometimes controversial teacher at the Pennsylvania Academy of the Fine Arts. Eakins House is located in the old township of Spring Garden (for a short time in the mid-nineteenth century, it was one of the ten largest cities in America; now it is solidly part of Philadelphia). Today, Eakins's narrow dwelling is home to classrooms, computers, and

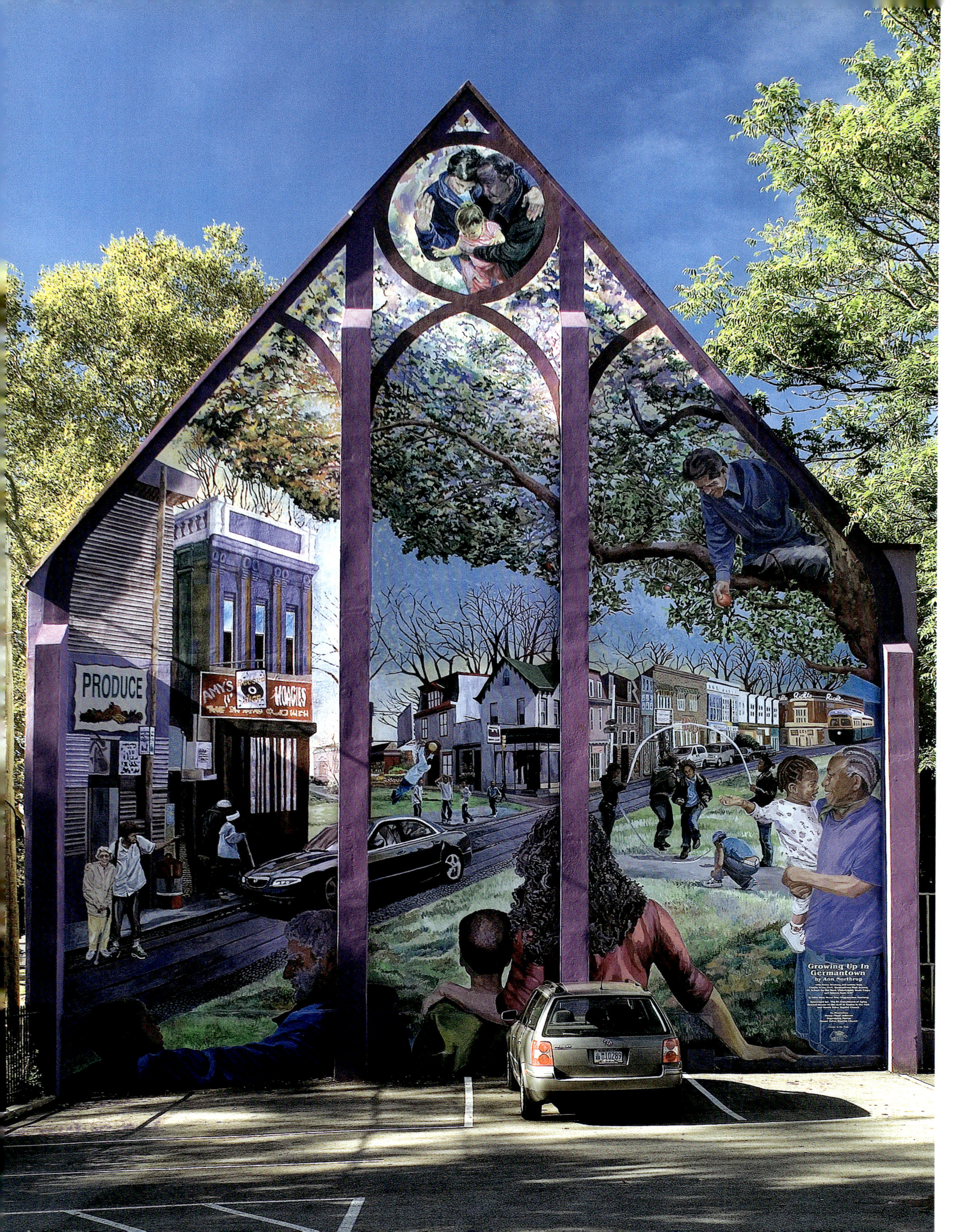
PRODUCE
HOAGIES
Growing Up In
Germantown
by Ann Northrup

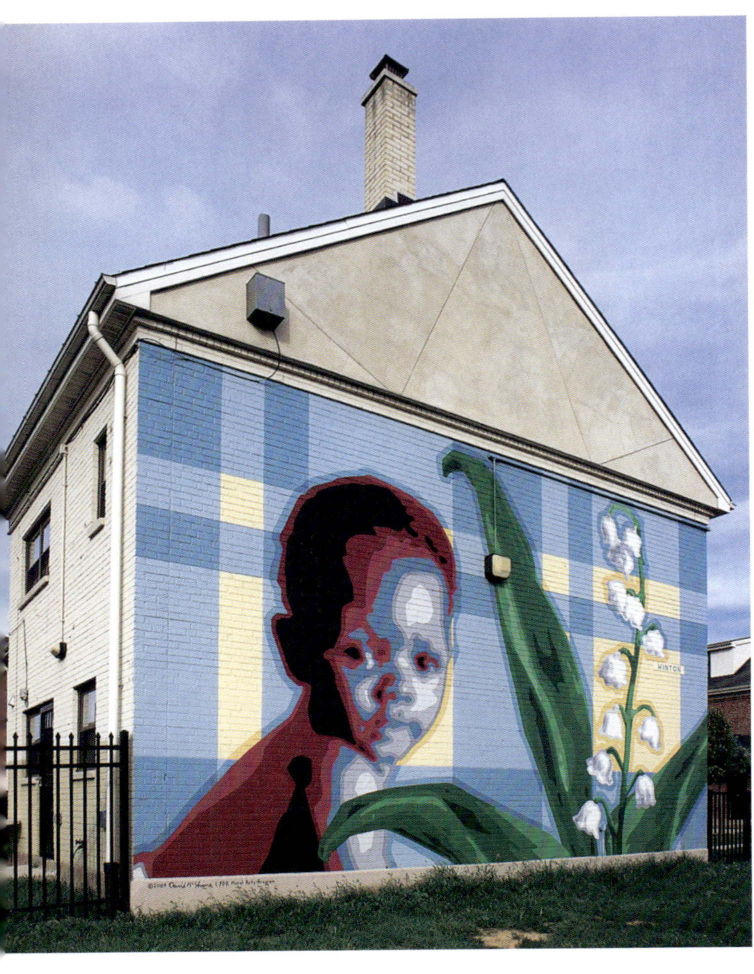

other art equipment, which support after-school and summer classes for kids.

With the unprecedented support from Mayor Street's administration, MAP blossomed. His commitment to education and MAP has encouraged the development of ArtWORKS!, Mural Corps, MuralARTscape, and other initiatives that involve kids of different ages and locations, including public schools, recreation centers, detention centers, and residential facilities. The Big Picture Program works throughout the year in thirteen different locations in the city with kids from ten to eighteen who are paid for their work. The Mural Academy works with sixty tenth and eleventh graders in the Philadelphia School District. The Rivera Institute teaches in-depth art history to twenty selected graduates of the Mural Academy. Experienced muralists and instructors, many of them with advanced degrees, work with incarcerated or adjudicated youth.

Students can go as far as they want. There are opportunities to study art continuously from grade school classes through high school. Most students have fun, make friends, and bring home some nifty artworks. Sometimes they even sell a few pieces. Eric Okdeh proudly says that his classes always sell everything they show. Students who are more serious and persistent can put their experience into practice, even developing portfolios that prepare them for art school. Guided by professionals, including Okdeh or Jennie Shanker, the most skilled and dedicated students work with community organizations to plan and paint murals on their own.

David McShane combines design and representation in this portrait of a baby for his mural *Life Span*, at Wilson Park, 25th and Jackson Streets, a unique partnership with the Philadelphia Housing Authority.

In America, murals like Aaron Douglas's 1934 *Aspects of Negro Life*, painted for the New York Public Library, traditionally have had a redemptive quality, affirming the identity and values of communities within the larger American whole. This mission recently has been expanded and personalized with MAP's Prison Program. The innovative movement for restorative justice suggested the potential for murals to serve as a liaison between incarcerated men and the victims of crime and their families (although not involving individuals connected to one another). Muralist César Viveros-Herrera, assisted by Parris Stancell, led work on two *Healing Walls* murals. Utilizing a method of painting on sections of nonwoven fabric, which are later mounted on an exterior wall, inmates who participate in the program in the maximum-security Pennsylvania State Correctional Institution at Graterford have been able to collaborate with outside groups in planning and making murals. Children in the Youth Study Center, the House of Corrections, and St. Gabriel's Hall, a residence for juvenile offenders, have worked with the adult prisoners of Graterford and neighborhood residents—but not necessarily side by side—to make murals.

The first pair of restorative justice murals and Viveros-Herrera's third mural in the series (East Lehigh Avenue between Tulip and Trenton Streets) were particularly challenging projects because they responded to the needs of unrelated though intertwined stakeholders: children, teens, and adults; victims, transgressors, and ordinary citizens; and, like every mural, people with social agendas, people who yearn for something beautiful in the neighborhood, and those who daily experience the finished mural even if they don't participate in planning or painting. Every Philadelphia community mural necessarily embraces some of this complexity and, even, contradiction, although perhaps not in such clear-cut terms.

Finding a mutual language is easier when the message is a simple one. The shared feelings and commitment that enable murals to speak to a diverse public inevitably render them vulnerable to accusations of kitsch. From its beginnings in the late 1960s, the new mural movement was purposeful. It reflected the need, hope, and self-defining idealism of the Depression era. Drawing on popular culture for its imagery and subject matter, undoubtedly it was sometimes simplistic, perhaps kitsch; but it was also experiential, challenging, and even revolutionary. Much of the power of contemporary community murals grows from the blending of many voices in considering thematic material and aesthetic presentation.

When we make art for public spaces, we define ourselves: *this* is what we think is worth remembering, *this* is what we believe. The driving forces of Philadelphia muralism are human concerns and our murals commemorate human history, understanding, and interaction. An effective mural reminds us of what we share. It reminds us on several levels: beautifully, eloquently, and in a way that makes the city a more harmonious and welcoming place.

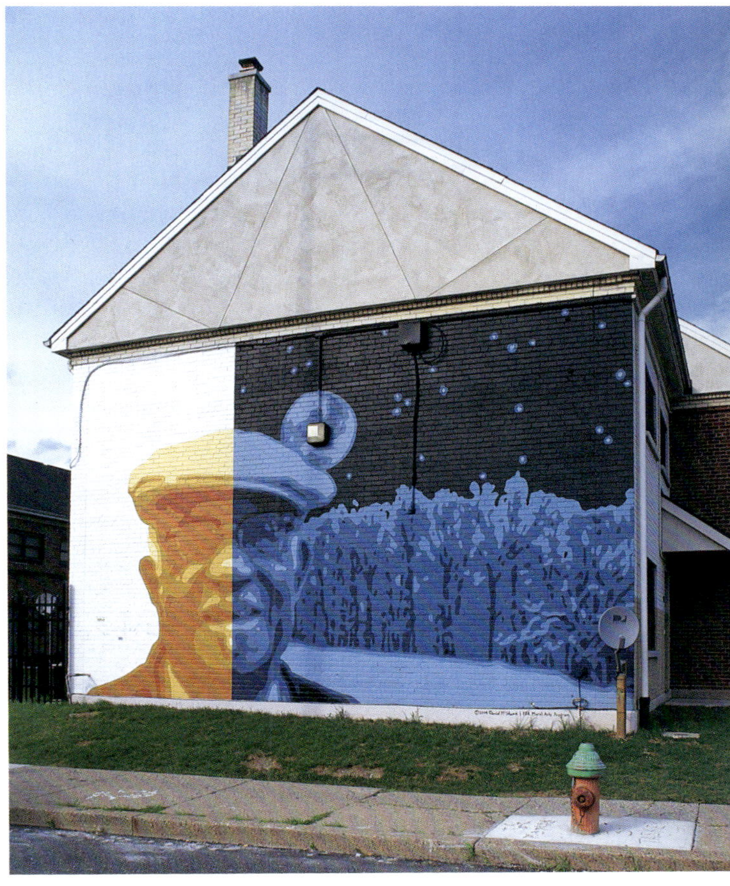

Right
From morning to dusk, David McShane captures the generations of life in *Life Span,* at Wilson Park, 25th and Jackson Streets.

NOTES

1. James Prigoff and Robin J. Dunitz, *Walls of Heritage/Walls of Pride: African American Murals* (Rhonert Park, CA, 2000), 15, 16.

2. Allan Kaprow, "Success and Failure When Art Changes," in *Mapping the Terrain: New Genre Public Art*, ed. Suzanne Lacy (Seattle, WA, 1995), 157.

Artist Profile
Peter Pagast

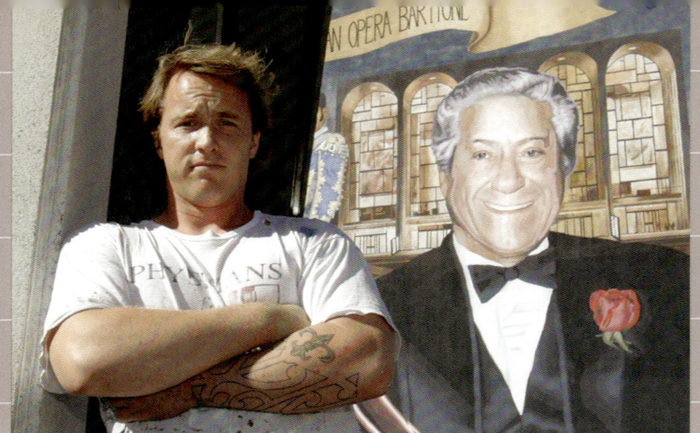

"Peter is a master at making things look right from a distance. It's a special skill: if you're looking at a face from several hundred feet, it's different from painting a studio portrait and he knows that. He's amazing!" That's how Michael Webb, one of Philadelphia's most highly regarded and experienced muralists, speaks of colleague and occasional collaborator Peter Pagast. (For more on Webb, see the profile on page 146.)

Quietly and consistently, Pagast has built a reputation as one of the city's premier portrait painters. He receives a steady stream of studio commissions and paints other somewhat surreal figure compositions, but he especially enjoys the sweep of murals and working outdoors in the city. His larger-than-life subjects include Patti LaBelle, the late Congressman and long-time City Councilman Lucien Blackwell (1931–2003), the first elected African-American Pennsylvania State Senator Roxanne H. Jones (c. 1928–1996), and the nationally recognized community leader Peaches Ramos. The Mural Arts Program commissioned Pagast to paint a portrait of Paul Robeson (1898–1976) at a time when the U.S. Postal Service had refused to issue a postage stamp of the Philadelphia resident, a mistake that has since been rectified. Pagast's simple, formal portrait (4502 Chestnut Street) is one of his most popular works. Robeson's image is framed subty by the words, "Citizen of the World / Scholar / Actor / Attorney / Author / Humanitarian / Athlete / Singer / Bibliophile / Activist."

An outstanding high school athlete, Pagast perhaps became a painter because a knee injury ended his dreams of a football scholarship. His fallback career, pilot, was grounded due to boredom and Pagast's realization that he was not "hanging out with the pilots. My friends were all studying English and art." At a community college in Kankakee, Illinois, he became intrigued by an art course, and went on to earn an Associate's degree from the American Academy in Chicago. He worked with a successful but "smarmy" portraitist there, he says, roughing in heads and learning the business. Soon, he was driven to further hone his skills in traditional anatomy classes.

A scholarship to the Pennsylvania Academy of the Fine Arts, a premier institution for traditional painting techniques, brought Pagast to Philadelphia, "an older city with a more European feeling. Everything fits together really tightly. I was living in an old house in West Philly and there were trolleys."

After seeing MAP Director Jane Golden painting a mural, Pagast showed her his portfolio and soon was working for the Philadelphia Anti-Graffiti Network. "I've seen so much of the city because of the Mural Arts project. I've learned a lot about people and communities. There are so many unique buildings, like the tiny factories in North Philly. Plus, I like the fact that I'm an hour away from the shore. It's near New York and I can bike to most (mural) sites." Not all of Pagast's Philadelphia experiences have been pleasant. On one occasion, he and another muralist had to hide behind a building to keep clear of a shootout.

He still possesses an athlete's discipline and relentless drive for improvement. As a full-time member of the MAP staff, he builds scaffolding between mural projects or assists other muralists.

He habitually studies the work of other artists. "If you look at something daily, it is a learning experience. I get as close as I can and try to figure out how the painting is done." For him, few can match the skills of turn-of-the-twentieth-century American portrait painter John Singer Sargent. Sargent was revered for his ability to capture a likeness in which psychological insight is matched by elegance and bravura. "I've heard that Sargent would finish the face and then add on brush strokes at the end to make it look like it was effortless," Pagast muses.

Pagast may finish portraits that way, but he begins a mural using the traditional grid method to enlarge a drawing. "I like to paint directly on the wall because I can see it all. I break it into three tones: dark, middle, light. I just keep breaking it up and seeing the subtleties."

His *Tribute to Frank Guarrera* (2003, 1532 S. Broad Street), represents the legendary baritone in five signature roles, including that of Escamillo from Bizet's *Carmen,* in which he debuted at the Metropolitan Opera in 1948. The cape of the toreador drapes dramatically out of the frame of the picture and over a curb running along the bottom of the wall.

The lighted arches of Lincoln Center can be seen behind the largest smiling image of the handsome star wearing a rosebud in his buttonhole. Pagast rose to the challenge, juxtaposing a half-dozen likenesses of the same face at different ages and in different guises—while still conveying the idea of a singular personality.

In Philadelphia, most portrait murals are posthumous. But Frank Guarrera lived to see this tribute, which was facilitated by the Frank Guarrera Society and friend Angela G. DeVita who "rallied the support and appreciation for the mural. Guarrera loves that mural," Pagast reports with satisfaction.

Opposite

"When you paint a tribute mural, you become a part of that person's life," says muralist Peter Pagast.

Below

Tribute to Frank Guarrera, Broad and Tasker Streets, by Peter Pagast.

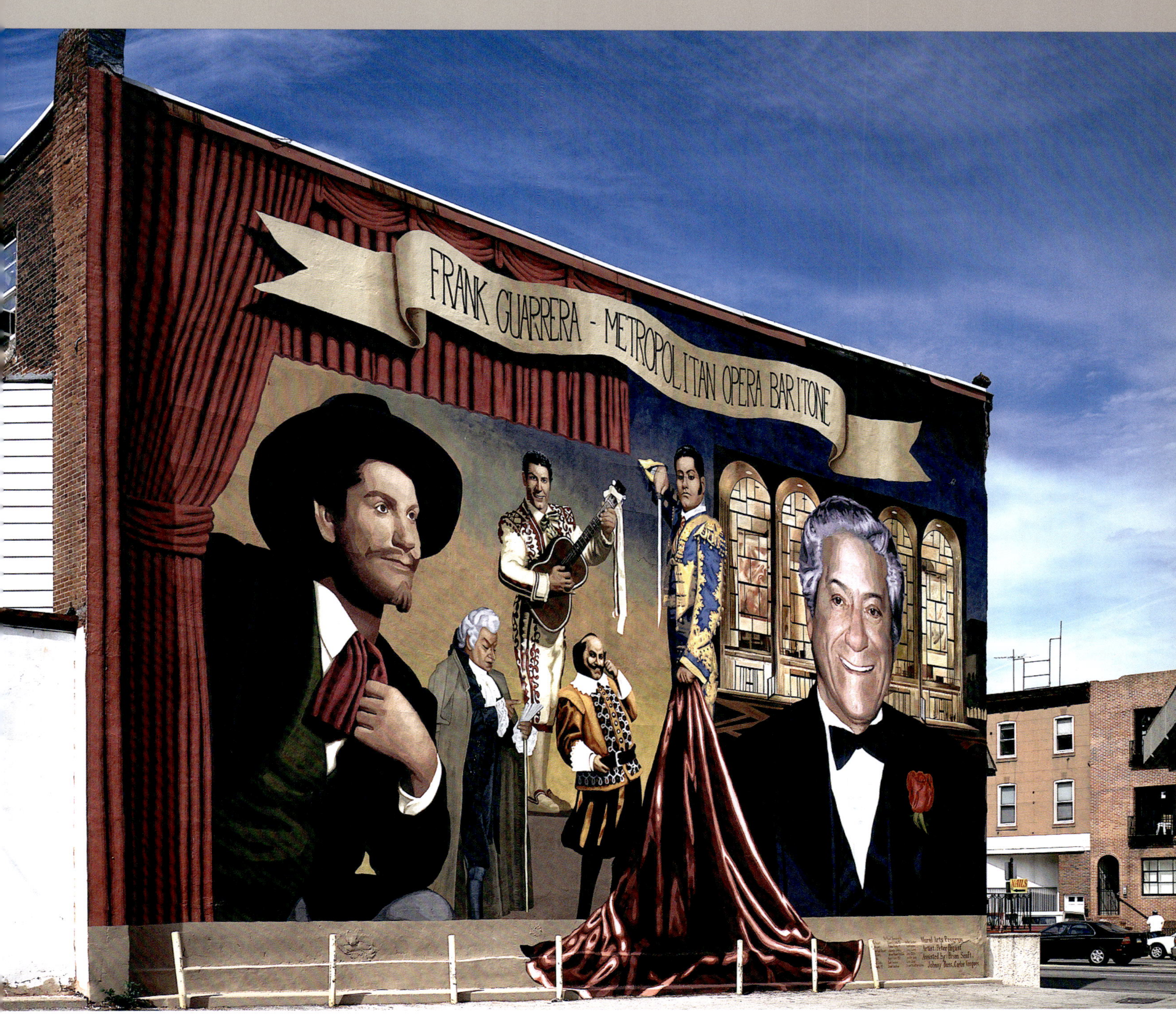

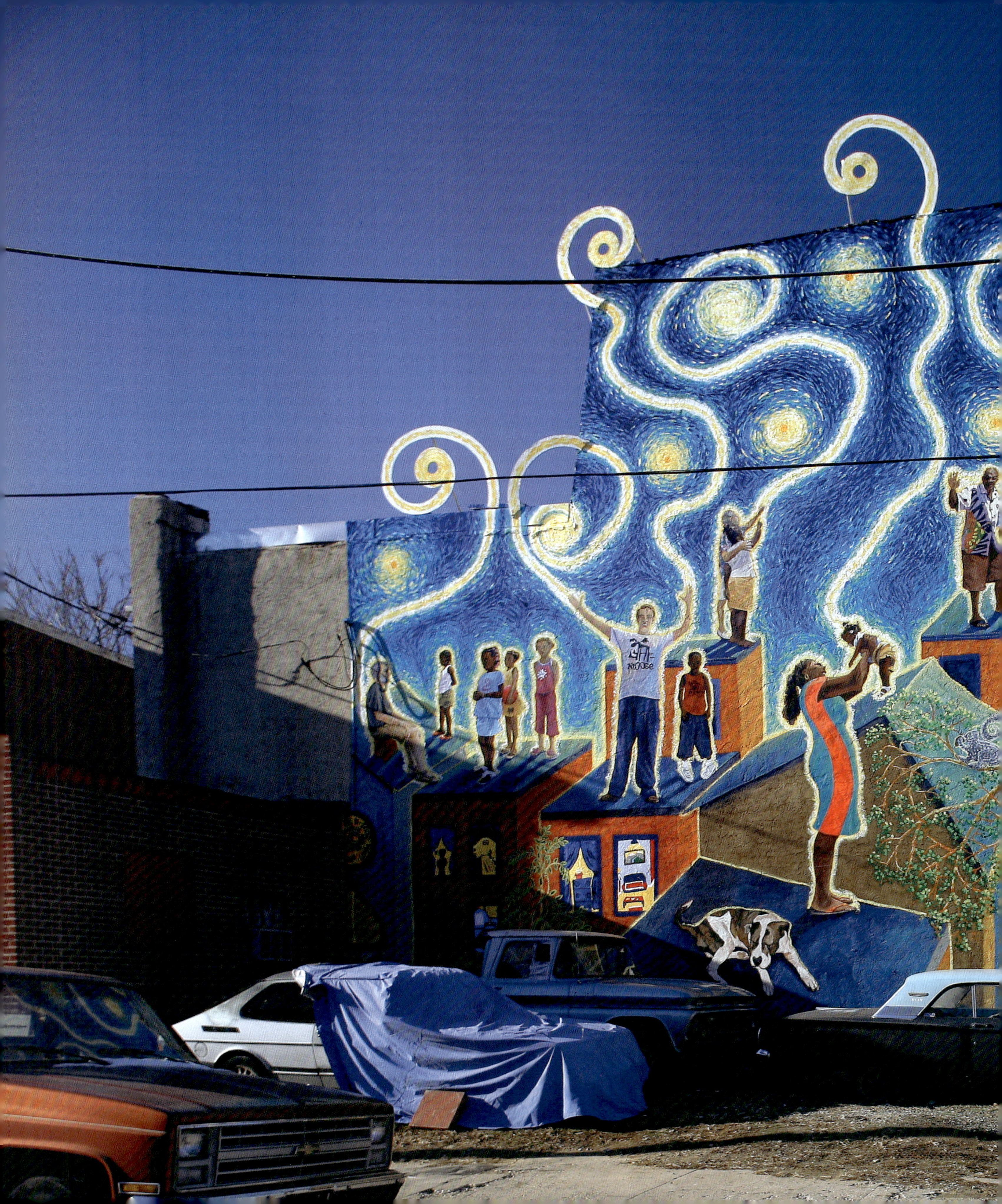

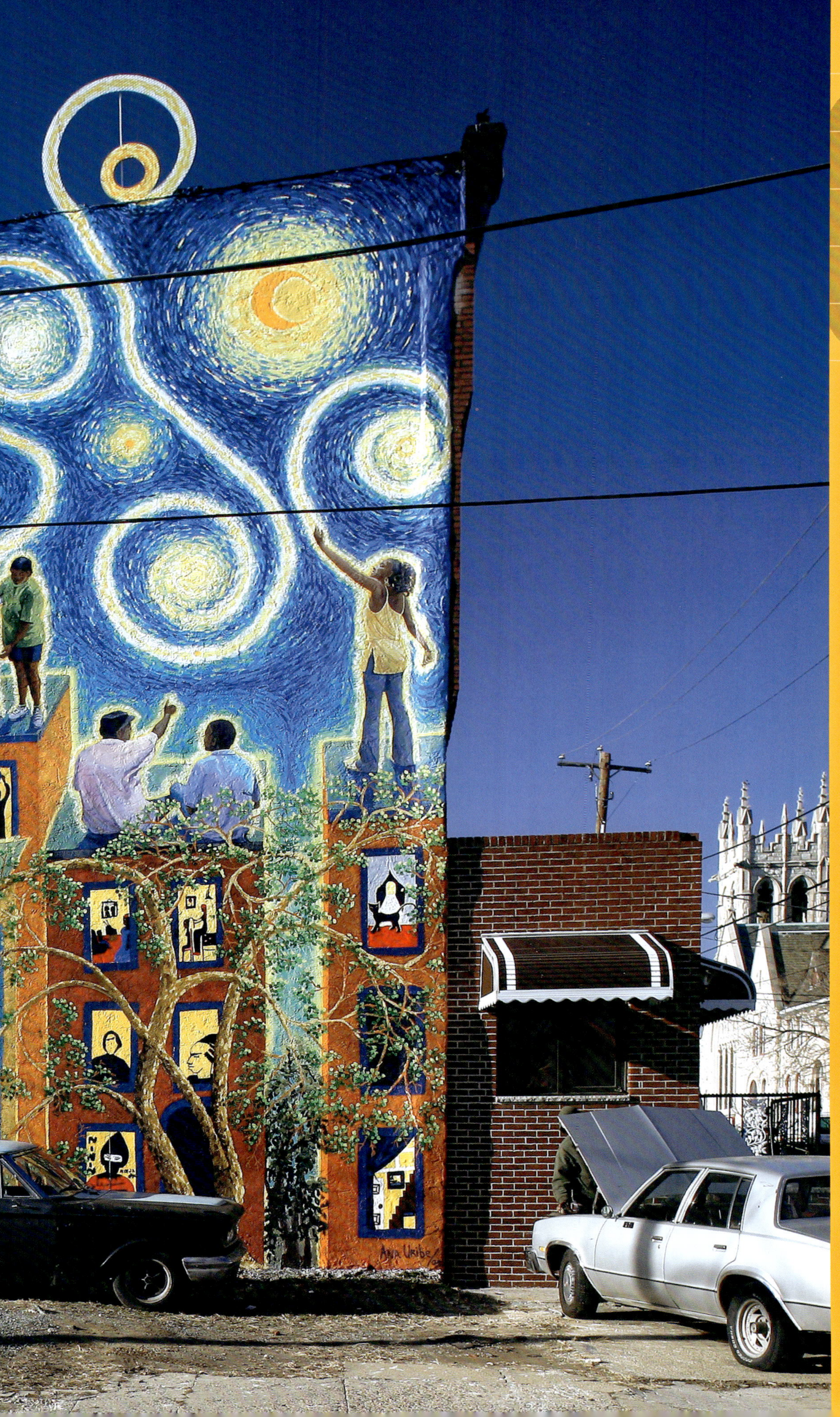

Chapter 2

Ana Uribe's *The Magic Wall* at 1230 S. 47th Street, painted with participants from the Big Picture Program's site at the 48th and Woodland Recreation Center.

Chapter 2

An Ounce of Prevention

The Big Picture classroom at the HERO Center in North Philadelphia was a small section of a much larger room, a corner separated from the rest by curtains and cardboard. From the other side of the makeshift walls, the art students could hear preschoolers running and playing and chanting things like, "Good morning to you, good morning to you . . . " The air was thick from the July heat and buzzing flies fluttered around the students' damp faces.

It was hard for these kids, roughly ages ten to fifteen, to stay focused. They didn't have to be here. They weren't getting extra credit for school or serving time as punishment. They could have been playing with friends in the streets or watching television in air-conditioned rooms.

Yet they chose to be here.

When lead instructor P. T. Schwab and assistant Retina Wearing gave the class an assignment on diversity—If you could create your own race of people, what would they look like? What would they be interested in? Would they be like you? Different from you?—they dug in. With heads bent low, they drew their new races: people with big ears because they're good listeners; people whose lives revolve around shopping; people who are half human, half animal. It tested their imaginations, got them thinking and talking.

Opposite
Instructor Michelle Ortiz mapping out a new mural project with Mural Corps participant Nathan Garrett at the Market Place Design Center.

And although no one is saying anyone here will grow up to be an artist or even a true appreciator of art, this class is crucial: It's keeping them safe, letting them speak, giving them options. Art may not be the solution, but it certainly has a powerful impact.

"I see us reaching a group of kids who really need us—really need us," says Schwab. "Without the Mural Arts Program, these kids might never realize the artist in them or what they're capable of. It opens their eyes to art, shows them it can be fun and a good way to express themselves. We engage them in something positive in a world where there are a lot of drugs,

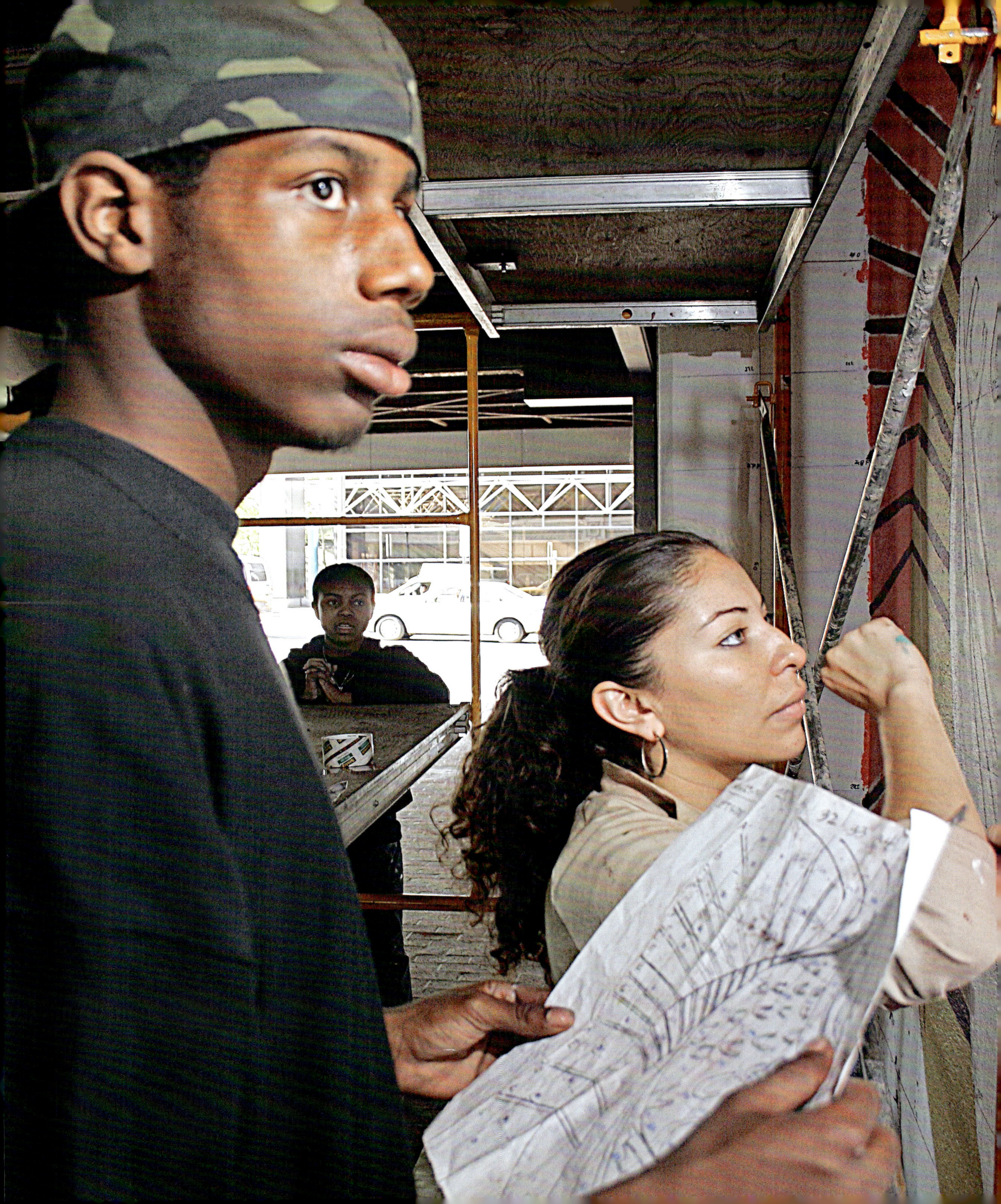

a lot of opportunities to do the wrong things and go down the wrong paths. We connect with them and plug them into something positive and channel their energy in positive ways."

Youth have been the backbone of MAP since it started as the Philadelphia Anti-Graffiti Network in 1984. Director Jane Golden sought out those defacing the city—mostly a crew of angry young men—and offered them something new: creative work, art classes, even a steady paying job. No questions were asked about their pasts. All that mattered was their futures.

By 1990, more than five hundred former graffiti taggers were on a waiting list for Golden's class. By 1996, Philadelphia officials recognized that MAP was more than just a citywide cleanup effort. It was changing lives—not just those of the repentant artists but also those of residents who were happy to see the graffiti go and who welcomed the new murals. Still, says Golden, "We didn't want to become merely a public art program. I think what we're good at is working with kids who could fall through the cracks. It's really about art education and rehabilitation and, at some level, it's about redemption."

A Message to the Child . . . The Hero Can Be Found mural located at 17th and Ontario Streets painted by John Lewis along with the Big Picture Program, an after-school and summer art program for Philadelphia youth.

Since Mural Arts began offering educational programming in 1984, more than twenty-five thousand youth have gone through its programs and taken part in the creation of almost one thousand murals, small and large—indoor and outdoor. One current youth program, Big Picture, for those ages ten to eighteen, has been a success since its earliest days in 1999. Big

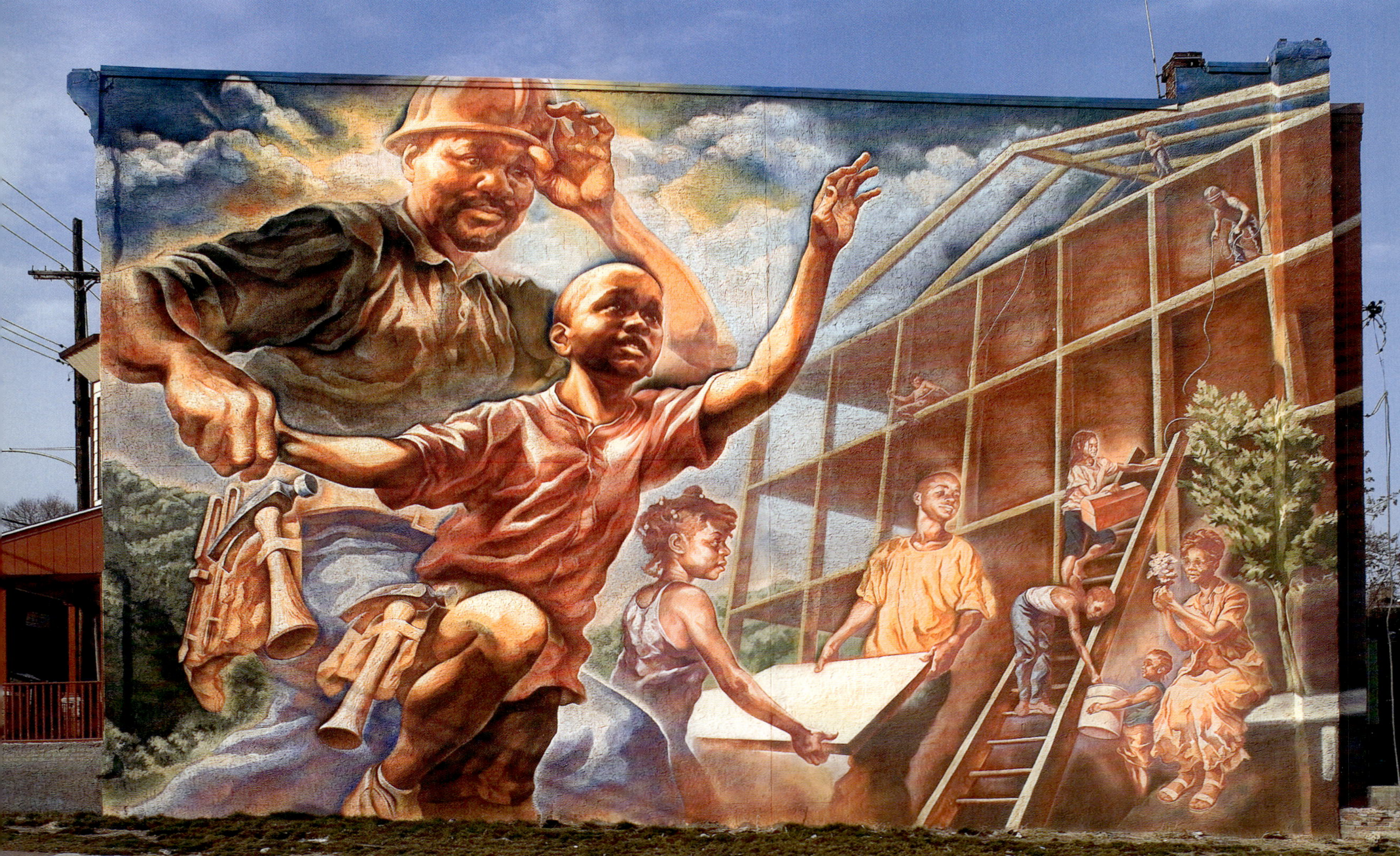

Instructor James Burns demonstrates for two Mural Corps participants. The mural, painted on pieces of transportable parachute cloth, can later be adhered to a permanent outdoor site. Photo by Jack Ramsdale.

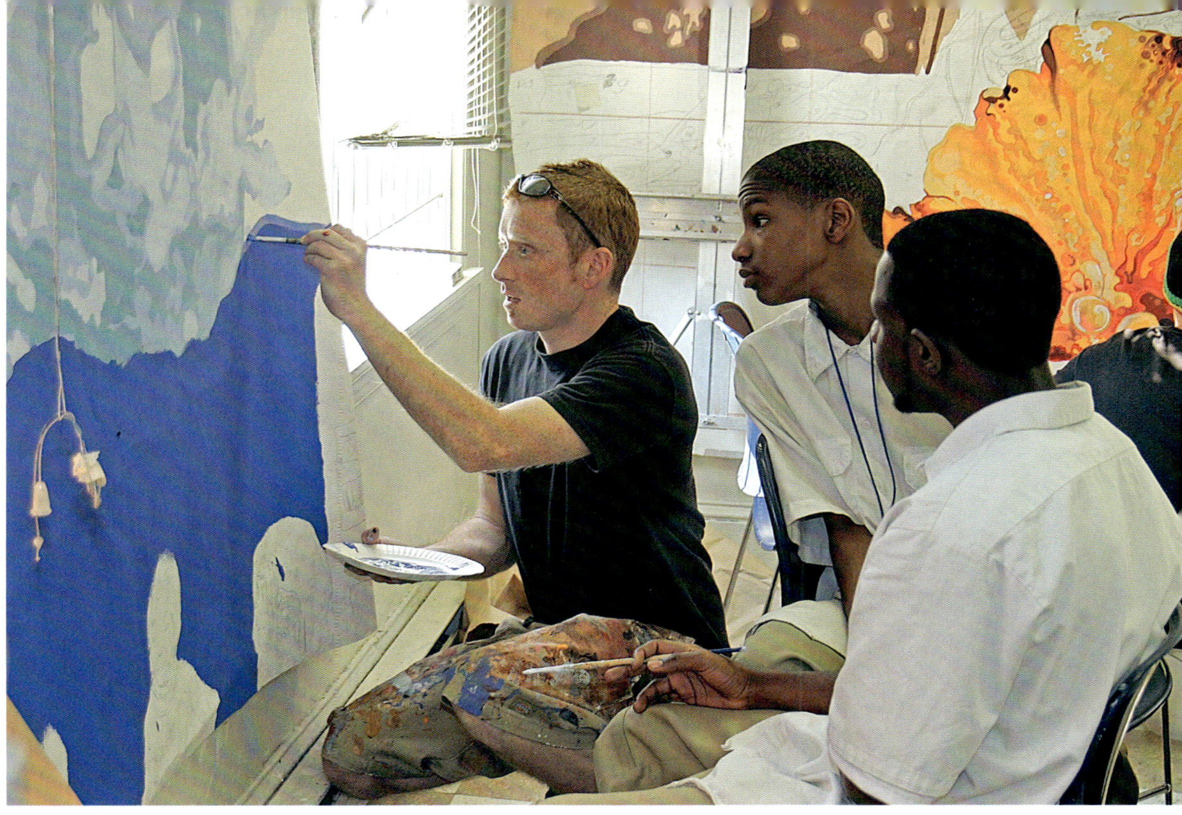

Picture started with five sites and then tripled that in one year. It now has thirteen. Available year-round, the classes teach mural history and techniques and aim to inspire the participants to think creatively. The students learn to work together, to solve problems, to contribute to something bigger than themselves. Art Education Director Kathleen Ogilvie notes that although the public knows MAP for the murals, "It's what is behind the murals that's really impressive to me. That's where the real work is and where the real story is. That's where the magic happens."

After Big Picture, students can move on to Mural Corps, which serves youth ages fourteen to twenty-two; "a Peace Corps of young muralists," as Golden says. In 2005, with the help of funding from Philadelphia's Department of Human Services, Mural Corps jumped from three locations to six. These students are considered "at-risk": their challenges include exposure to violence and substance abuse, an absence of positive role models, neighborhoods without essential services, and homes where they don't get enough heat in the winter or food any time, tough streets that beckon and cajole. They have to win their spots with applications and artwork, proving they have the talent and—more important—the commitment. "We're looking for something that shows they're really interested, not the best technically, but the most devoted," says Shari Hersh, the program's coordinator. "Mural Corps is about the development of pride in what they do. Some of them are good artists. Some are not. But there's something they're all getting out of the program."

MAP supporter Estelle Richman, Pennsylvania Secretary of Public Welfare and the former City of Philadelphia Managing Director, puts it bluntly: "Fewer kids dying." The after-school programs keep this vulnerable group occupied from 3 P.M. to 6 P.M., the deadliest time of day for them, statistics show. The summer programs keep them off the streets during the hottest, angriest hours. "Anything that cuts down on youth violence is a plus," Richman says. "All of this is designed to give kids something to do because they get in trouble when there's nothing to do."

And it builds self-esteem, Richman says. When she worked in Philadelphia, she never missed the dedication of a new mural because it was wonderful to see kids so excited. "They love to see their work up. The fact that their names aren't on it doesn't matter. They don't have that adult vanity yet. They take pride in being able to say, 'This is me and I did that,'" Richman says.

Briana Dawkins, fifteen, says she loves "to walk around with paint on my clothes and look like an artist because people stop me on the street and talk." This is her second year in Mural Corps, and she says she's learned so much about drawing and painting. And she's learned a lot about herself—how to handle herself in public, how to overcome obstacles. She's inspired, she says, by her past instructor, artist Michelle Ortiz. "She's a woman artist who's successful. In class, she would talk about racial issues and she has her own outlook that everybody's related and everyone's equal. Which, in society's eyes, we're not, but we're going to work our way up to it."

Jesse Mitchell (left) and Sean Hewitt working on a mosaic tile project at the Big Picture Program's EOM Community Center site. Their work helped create an inspiring mosaic mural on the side of the Lutheran Settlement House.

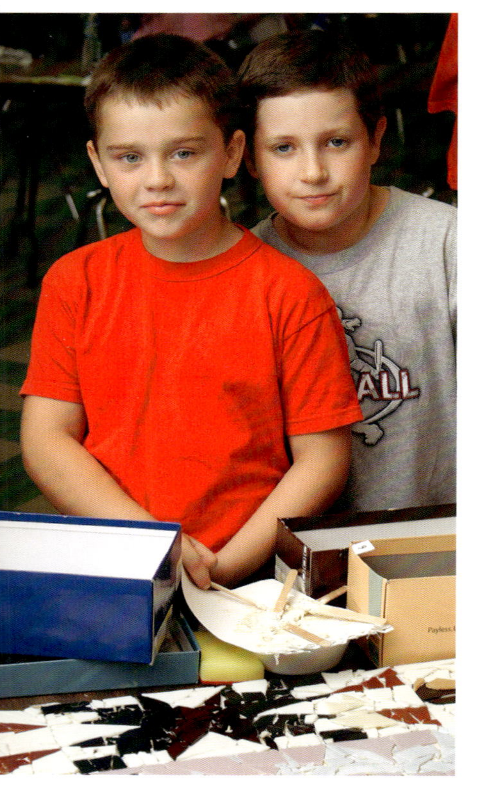

Joining forces with professional artists is an ego boost for the kids. One muralist likes to remind surly students how much he charges for private commissions—hundreds, thousands of dollars—while they're getting his services for free. When muralist Don Gensler, a former Mural Corps instructor, was working on a wall in Grays Ferry, a group of his students stopped by almost every day. Sometimes they just said "hi" and watched him work. Other times they had questions, like how he'd mixed certain shades or why he'd chosen a color. "They'd done some stuff in class, but to really see an artist working, doing all these things they'd learned a little bit about, was actually impressive," Gensler says. "Kids need to see real artists to look up to, to be impressed by."

One of the most difficult aspects of leading these classes is keeping problems from the students' lives outside of the classroom. It's not just a case of adolescents and hormones, although those are factors, too. It's the problems children face when they grow up in an urban area: violence, vices, pockets of poverty, and inferior services. Some do not come from stable homes. Some have been kicked onto the streets. "The biggest problem is hunger, I'd say. A lot of these guys are super skinny and they don't eat much, quite frankly. There's not a lot of money coming in," says Mural Corps instructor Eric Okdeh. "I know for a fact some of them operate on an empty stomach and that's a pretty big hurdle. An empty stomach and your head's not there."

When Gensler was teaching, one of his students had a tooth knocked out during a fight and was so embarrassed that he missed some classes. In another instance, a mother asked Gensler to speak to her son, who had stopped going to school but kept showing up for Corps classes. The boy's father was absent, she said, and he seemed to look up to Gensler. "I told him, 'It might be a day here or there, but it's going to get easier,'" Gensler says. "I don't know if everything changed right then, [but] he's still in school now."

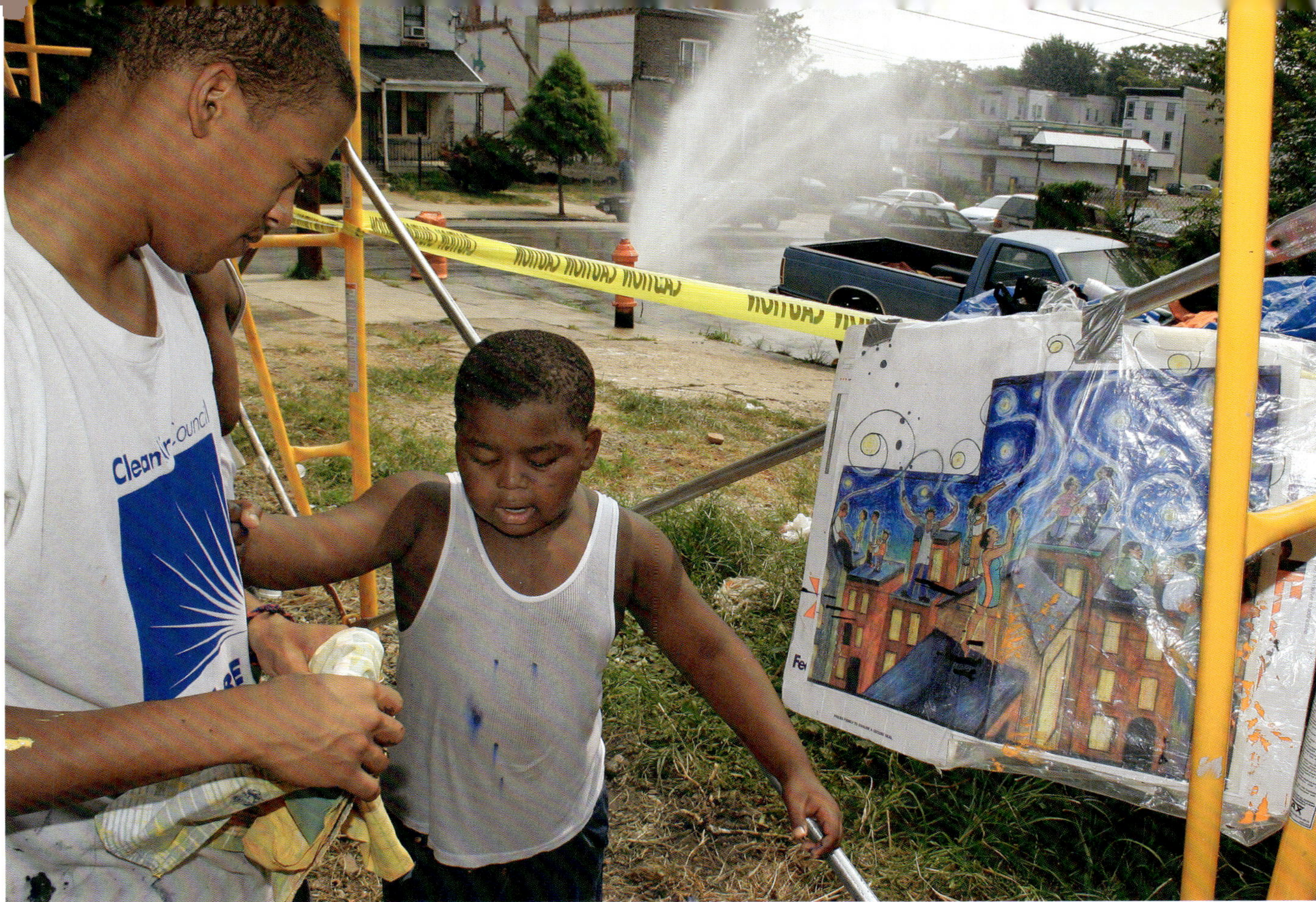

Art Instructor Jared Wood and Big Picture participant Naim Palmer spend a hot summer afternoon working on Ana Uribe's mural project at 1230 S. 47th Street, made possible by the Bank of America.

Tyree Carter dropped out of high school—but kept coming to Mural Corps, as he's done for the last four years. Tyree, eighteen, says he's not like the other boys in his tough South Philadelphia neighborhood—he doesn't like "standing on the corners and doing things like that. Their object is fun." Those boys question him, he says, but it doesn't bother him. "Every time I come around, they ask, 'Where was you?' and I say, 'I was at my art program' and they kind of look down on you a little bit. But I live for me," he says. "I'm different. I always knew it. It just took a matter of time for me to be comfortable with myself and not worry what everyone else thinks of me."

After Tyree dropped out of school, Hersh directed him to a GED program. Now he's almost completed it and thinking about a two-year college. He would like to be an animator, perhaps study at one of the art schools in Philadelphia. "The thing that's really important about these kids is, in a way, they're kind of brilliant," Hersh says. "Many of them grow up in extraordinarily difficult situations. They live in neighborhoods that are violent and have no resources and no phones in their homes and no food on the tables and they're very underserved but they are kind of geniuses because they don't define themselves based on the neighborhoods where they grew up. How many people do you know who aren't defined by their upbringing? They are astonishing. They never fail to amaze me."

Okdeh says one of his goals is expanding his students' horizons. "There's life beyond the five blocks they're used to. I want them to realize there's a much bigger world out there," Okdeh says.

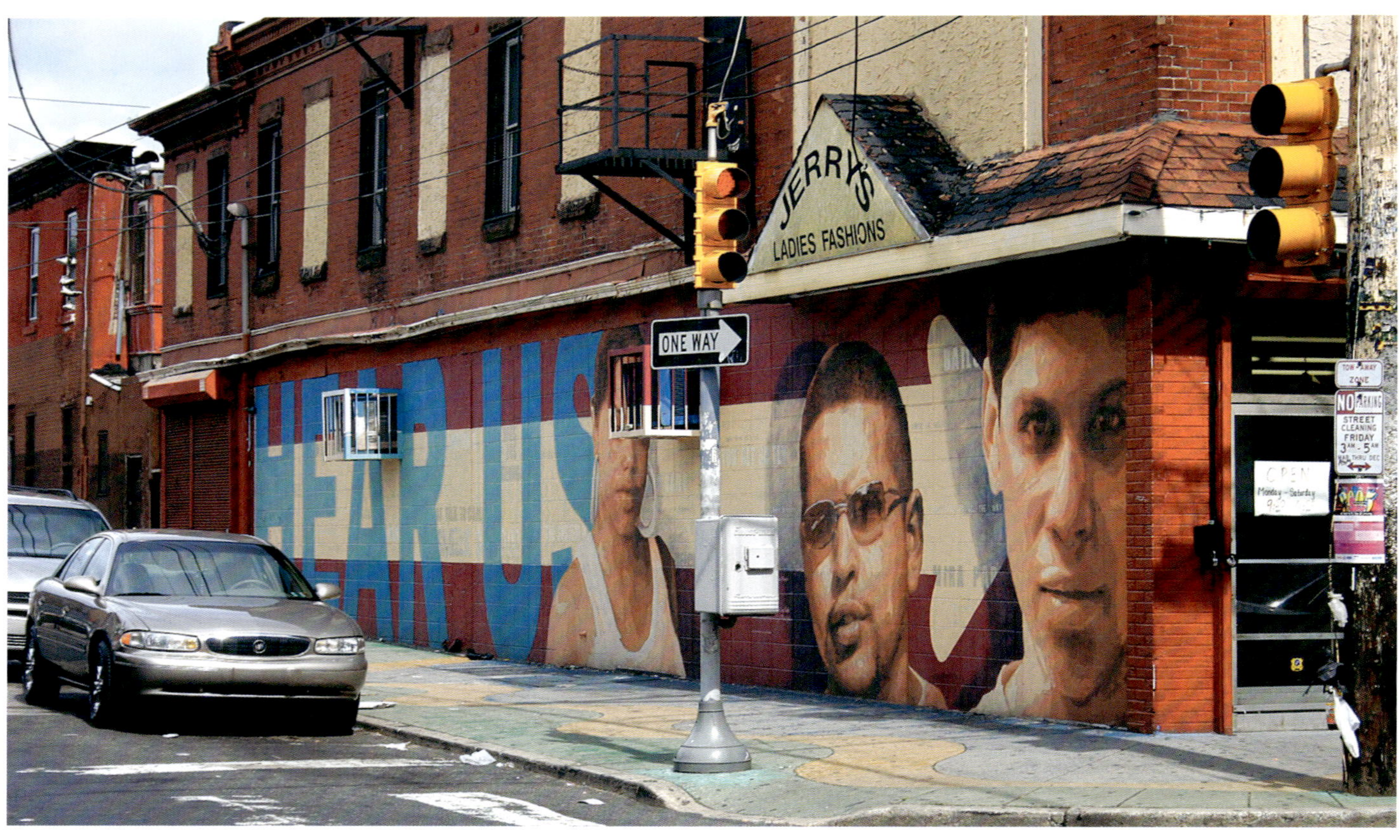

Look/Listen, painted by James Burns and participants in the Mural Corps Program. This engaging project at 5th and Cambria Streets was part of Meg Saligman's *Passing Through* series.

With his Big Picture students, Schwab's goal was to teach them techniques but also to build such a bond that "they can come to me for anything, from help with art, to help with homework, to help with any problem they're having in their lives. Anything." Watching him in his classroom, it was clear he'd accomplished that. A girl who was upset after an argument with her sister clung to Schwab like glue. He engaged her by making her his "assistant," giving her personal attention and making her feel special. After a workshop about domestic violence, one boy stopped Schwab in the hallway and started talking about his stepfather—how the man's behavior toward his mother bordered on violent, and how he and his brothers had to "step up" before their mother was hurt. Then he told Schwab about his older brother, who was shot more than a dozen times and killed while the two of them were walking together. He rolled up his pants and showed Schwab the scars on his legs from where the stray bullets had struck him.

"The big thing that happened that day was he opened up to me. He really had been a quiet guy all through class and that day, he really opened up," Schwab says. "A lot of my students grew up with a lack of a positive male role model in their lives and I found that as we built a strong student-teacher relationship, they started to mimic or imitate my behaviors. They just started to take each others' feelings into account more."

But Schwab's proudest teaching moment that summer involved a fifteen-year-old girl named Trashana. For weeks, she'd been uninterested in classes, saying she preferred poetry and fashion design to drawing and painting. "I had a really hard time getting her motivated," Schwab says. "I had an equally hard time getting her to finish a piece of art."

Then, after the domestic violence presentation, the students had the chance to enter a piece of their own antidomestic violence art in a contest. After a sit-down and idea session, Trashana was gripped by an idea: a collage showing two sides of a woman's face. The left side represented a healthy relationship, with bright colors and sunshine. The right side showed an abusive one, with tears, raindrops, and cool colors. "I've never seen a student transform like that," Schwab says. "Prior to this project, she was kind of sitting in her desk and not working and talking a lot, and in the two-week period we had to work on the contest, I did not hear a single word out of Trashana's mouth and she was just jamming on her art project. She even sat there until the last possible second. She put her heart into that piece."

Her efforts paid off: Trashana was one of the contest's grand prize winners.

"It opened her eyes to the process of coming in, day after day, working really hard, and then being rewarded," he says. "I just saw a real sense of accomplishment in her eyes. It was a really nice way to end the session."

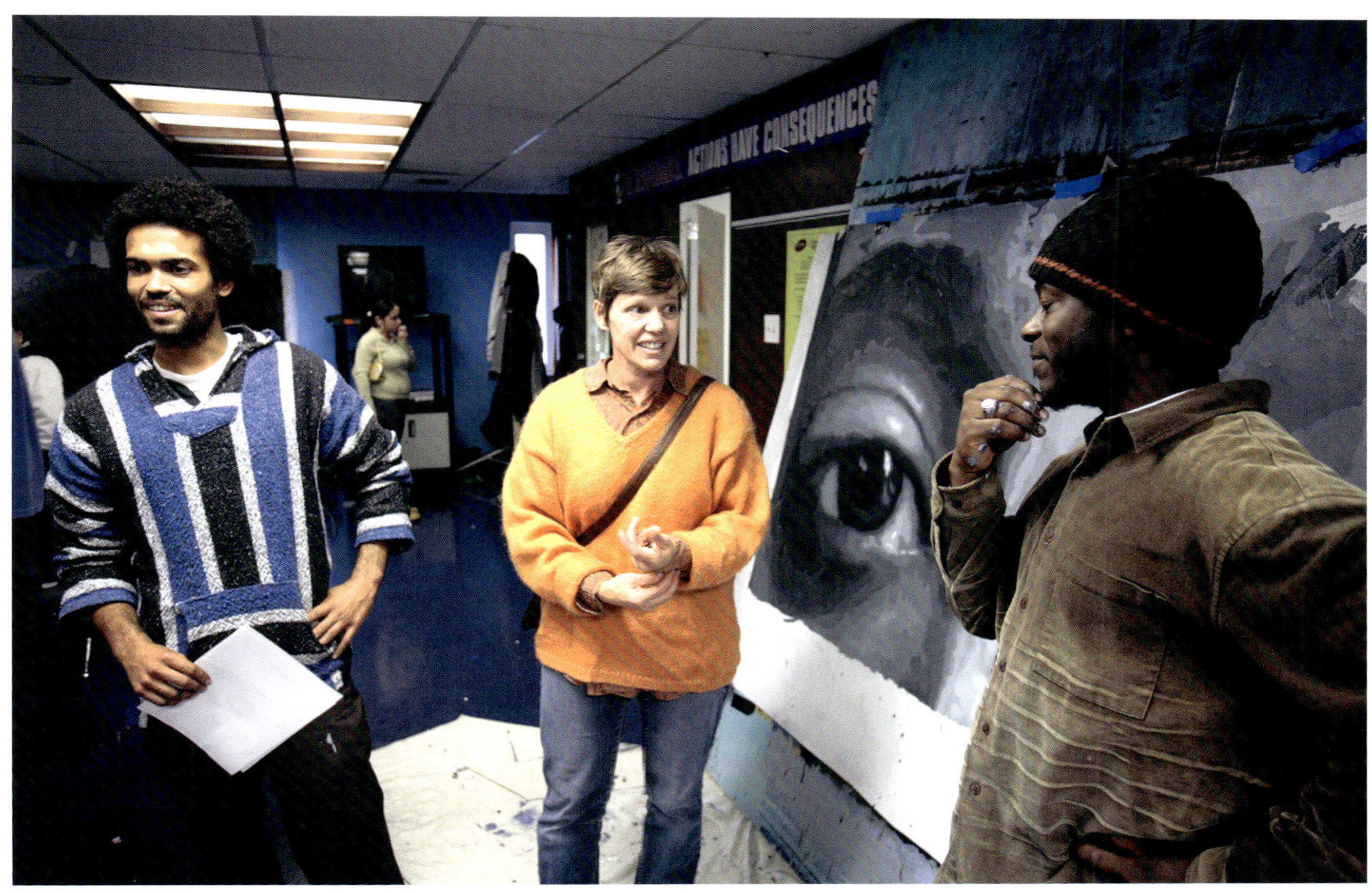

Mural Corps Coordinator Shari Hersh (center) with Corps instructors Keir Johnston (left) and Ernel Martinez (right) at an antiviolence workshop at a Corps E3 site. These workshops play an important part in the citywide antiviolence project called *All Join Hands—Visions of Peace.*

Artist Profile

Eric Okdeh

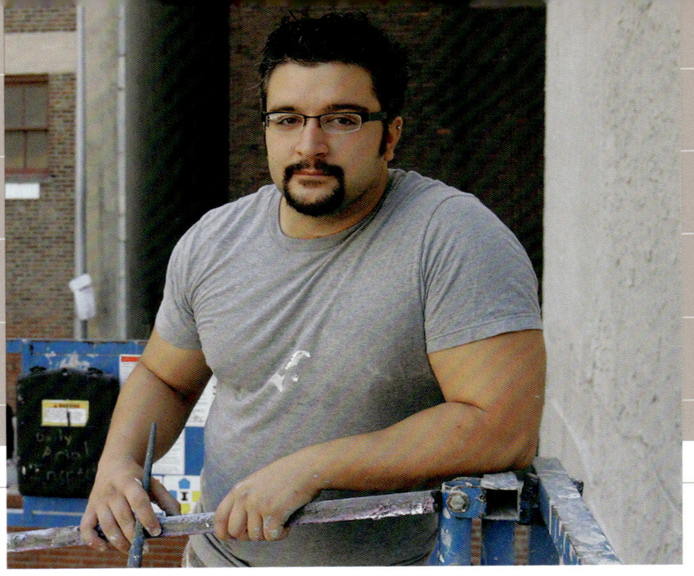

One reason that Eric Okdeh is so in synch with the Mural Art Program's ideals is that he practically grew up in the program. He began with preteen activities and progressed to assisting other muralists while an undergrad at Temple University's Tyler School of Art. Now Okdeh, a full-time staff member, works with young artists, as well as residents in Our Brother's Place, a shelter for homeless men, and lifers at Graterford prison.

All told, Okdeh estimates he's been involved in sixty or seventy MAP murals. Then, there are private commissions and his easel paintings. Okdeh and fellow muralist Jason Slowik are famous in the mural community for executing the two-story *Flag Day,* depicting the evolution of the American flag (1021 S. 8th Street near Washington Avenue, 1999) in two weeks, half the rush deadline they'd been given.

Not surprisingly, Okdeh identifies with his students. "They're fortunate to be in this program. They are from bad neighborhoods, just like I was, and their circumstances are pretty dire." He attended Philadelphia's Creative and Performing Arts High School and went on to college. He continues to exhibit and sell studio paintings, but he says, "There's so much more to art than the Whitney Biennial. I think art in a gallery is limiting. Something about it was not for me. So much hobnobbing, it seemed kind of false. I like the idea that in Philadelphia, you can see art right around the corner. Community-based work is much more inviting."

Young people who have attended satellite programs in recreation centers all over the city come to MAP headquarters at the Thomas Eakins House for a crash course in Photoshop on the well-equipped computers donated by Comcast. One technique Okdeh teaches utilizes a mapping or "posterizing" approach that enables even the most unskilled beginner to transform a Polaroid snapshot into a recognizable likeness.

Most of his advanced high school students in Mural Corps have completed seven years of study with MAP. In the summer of 2005, Okdeh's Mural Corps team, "the cream of the crop," made a Stuart Davis-style indoor mural for the nonprofit Neighborhood Bike Works. They handled all stages of the process from community meetings to design to a completed wall which honors two cyclists: Lance Armstrong, contemporary champion and cancer survivor, and Marshall "Major" Taylor, who in 1899 was the first African American to win a world cycling championship.

Okdeh distinguishes between his own work and that of his students, but notes, "At the same time, I don't hold back in showing them what I know." Under his supervision, each advanced student builds an individual portfolio and resume for college art programs. Already, one of them, Antoine Johnson, has been hired as an assistant muralist, joining MAP's third generation of artists.

Stylistically, Okdeh's been influenced by the computer-manipulated fashion photographs of David LaChapelle. Extensive underpainting and traditional figurative representation characterize both his easel paintings and murals. He brings the completed work to a high finish with coatings of glossy polyurethane.

One of Okdeh's favorite murals is *Ridge on the Rise* (2125 Ridge Avenue, 2004), designed with some input from senior muralist Josh Sarantitis. Okdeh interviewed people in the community and studied its history when planning this "story-telling" mural.

He learned that older residents remembered the area as home to the glamorous Pearl Theatre, where jazz greats like John Coltrane performed. In the mural, the art deco façade of the long-gone theatre contrasts with the forbidding ten-foot stone wall that still encloses the grounds of Girard College, the location of a landmark Civil Rights struggle.

For over a hundred years, that cold gray wall was a palpable symbol of segregation. Stephen Girard, who died the richest man in America, left a bequest founding the high school for "poor white orphan boys." Because it was private, Girard refused to desegregate with public schools, but, beginning in May 1965, Philadelphia attorney and NAACP leader Cecil B. Moore led daily demonstrations outside the school. As months passed, dozens of protestors swelled to thousands. Finally, the Commonwealth of Pennsylvania, the City of Philadelphia and the NAACP filed suit against Girard. Moore declared victory and concluded the protest, but it was not until 1968 that the U.S. Supreme Court upheld a lower court decision admitting boys of color. The enrollment at Girard College today is predominantly African American.

Moore (also honored in a 2002 mural painted by Cavin Jones at 1704 Cecil B. Moore Ave.) was a prickly, confrontational individual who once picketed the NAACP,

Opposite
"Through involving people in the work we do comes a sense of ownership in what is created," says muralist Eric Okdeh.

Below
Ridge on the Rise, 2125 Ridge Avenue, by Eric Okdeh.

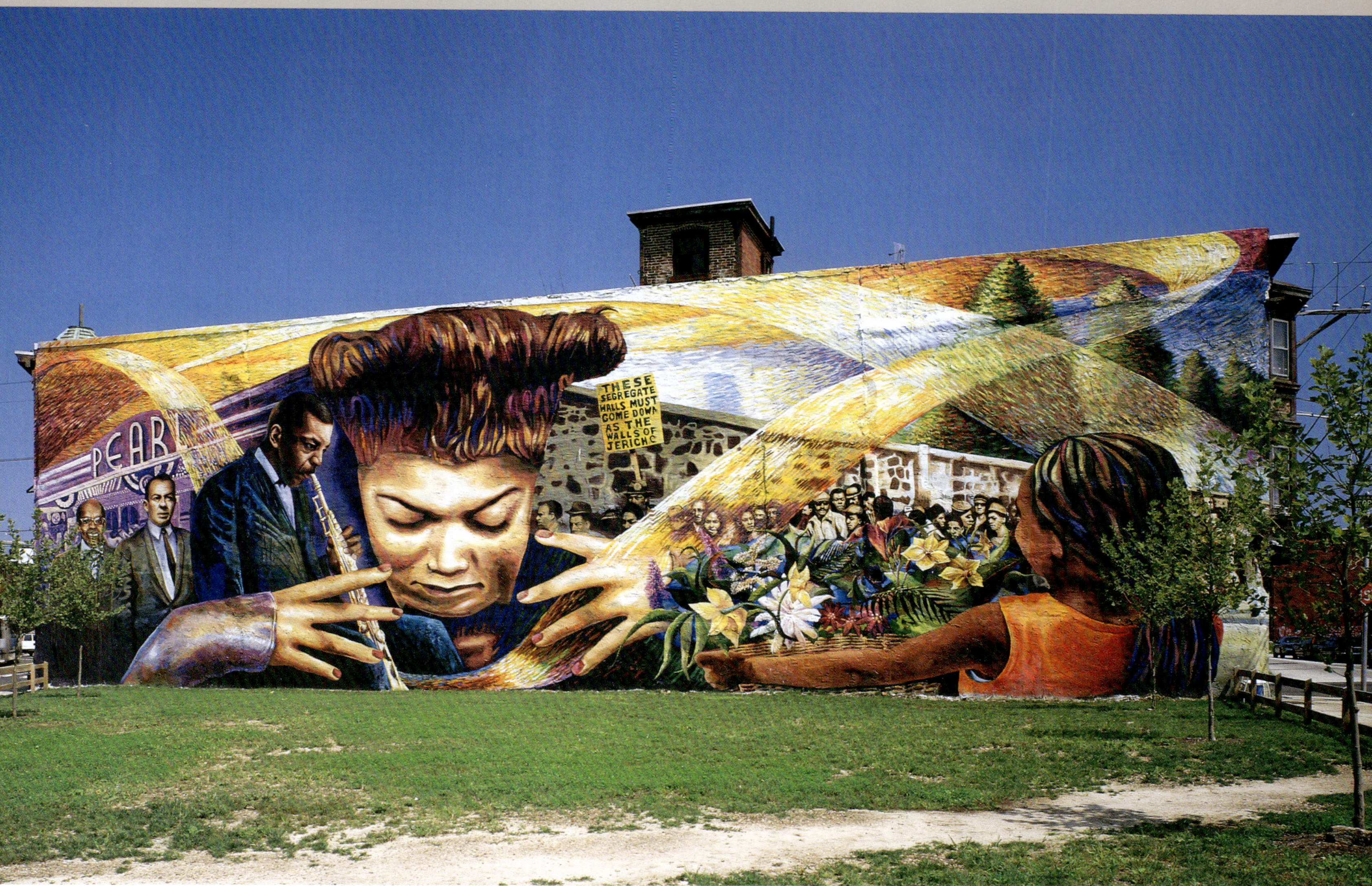

although he was a past president of the Philadelphia chapter. In his career, Moore represented hundreds of African Americans for little or no money. He remains a Philadelphia legend. "People would talk about those times. You could really see the effect that he had," says Okdeh.

Okdeh says he's pleased with the mixture of "teaching and community in my work. Through involving people in the work we do comes a sense of ownership in what is created." Through his association with MAP, he's witnessed the destruction of some murals for building projects and the loss of others for lack of care. Okdeh was entrusted with the 2004 restoration of Philadelphia's treasured Keith Haring mural (2147 Ellsworth Street). He hopes the community's sense of ownership of his murals will "help them have a long life."

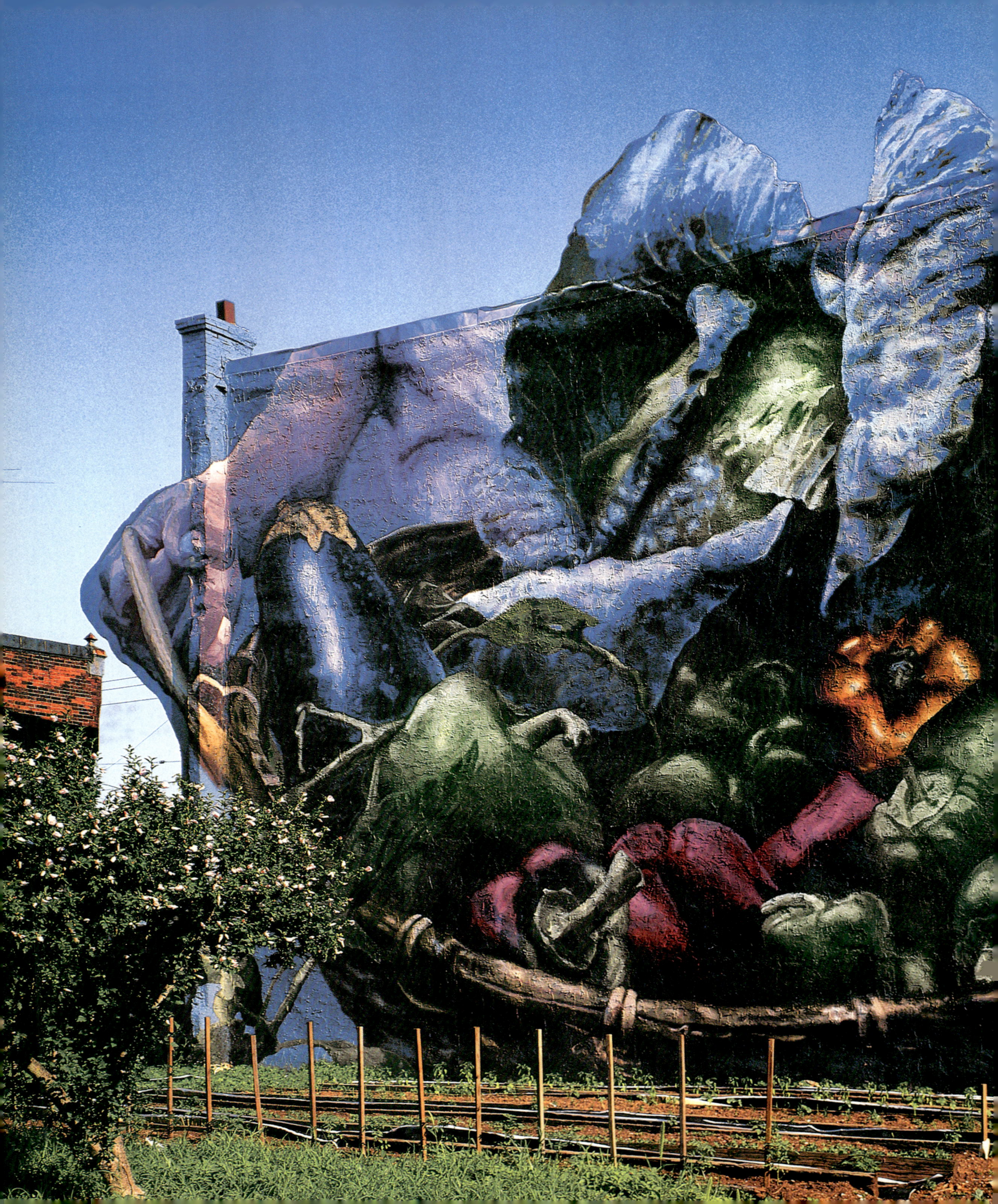

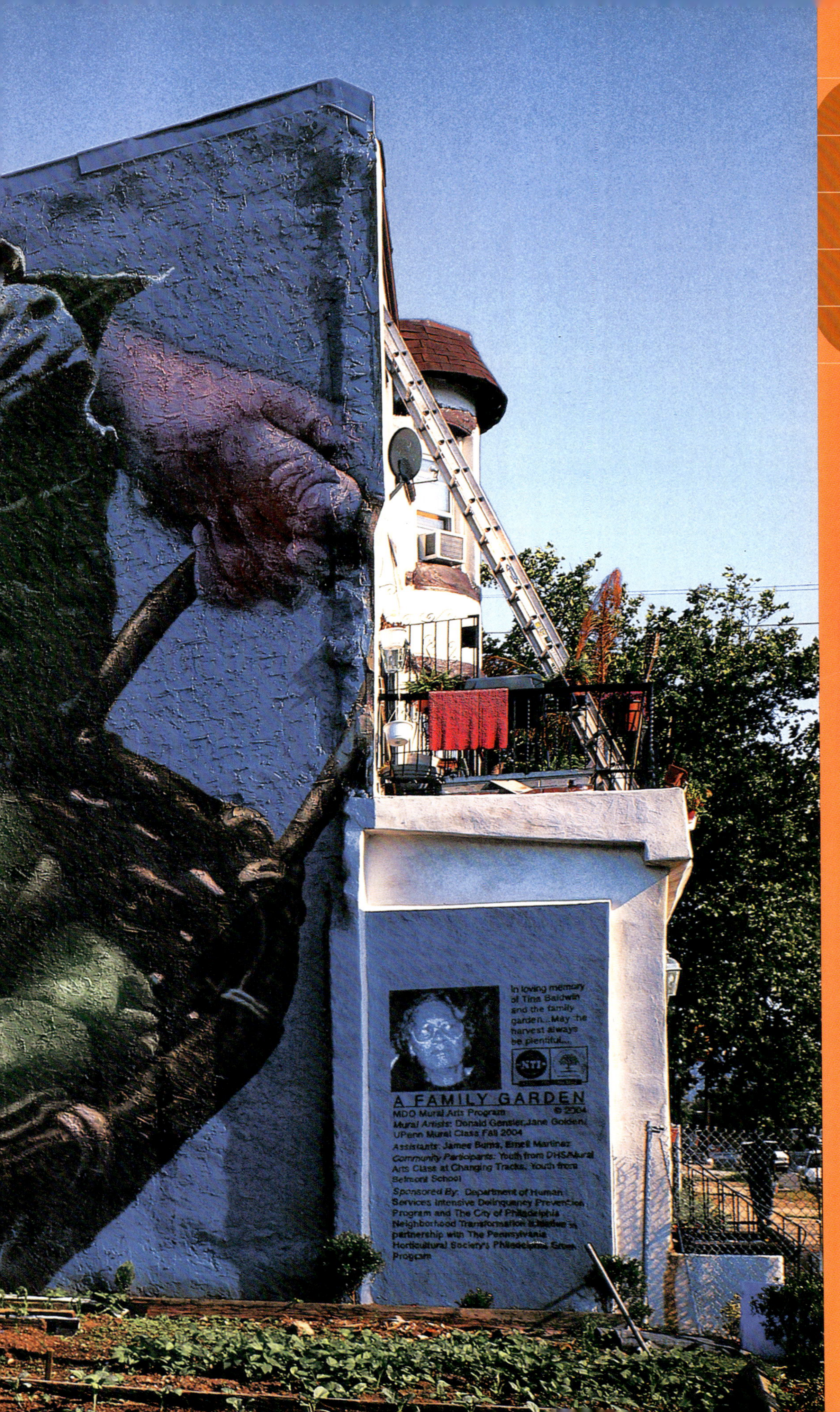

03

Chapter 3

Assisted by participants in the ArtWORKS! Program, a delinquency prevention program, *A Family Garden* by Don Gensler, 40th and Brown Streets.

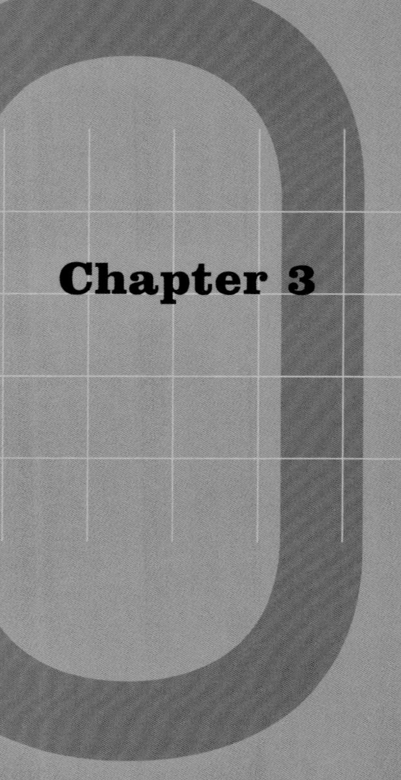

Chapter 3 A Pound of Cure

None of Aaron Traister's students at Philadelphia's House of Correction are over seventeen. But when he asked one class of seven boys if they'd ever been shot, three of them raised their hands. A fourth boy said he'd been grazed by a bullet.

"That was a wakeup call," Traister says. But he dealt with it, like he dealt with the student who had been shot seven times and loved showing off his pus-filled, bloated belly. Like he regularly dealt with yards of bureaucratic red tape, missing artwork, lesson plans that had to be discarded because guards decided certain equipment, such as safety scissors, were permitted one day but banned the next.

But one incident finally made him realize he needed a break from teaching art to these troubled boys. That week, he had learned his wife was pregnant with their first child. That day, he went to work and saw a boy who had had half of his ear bitten off during a fight.

"The look on his face, it wasn't anger. He wasn't screaming in pain. It was just this look of dead complacency, that he's in jail and he got his ear bit off," Traister says.

Kids slip through the cracks, even when you try your best. Even with all the art programs in the world, some still end up in trouble for little things like skipping school and big things like robbery and assault. The folks at the Mural Arts Program know that. They also know some of these kids are still savable.

"All my kids think they can rap because they speak every day. None of them think they can draw because they don't use pencils every day," Traister says. "The first time you put a pencil in their hands, they say, 'I can't do this.' But once they realize they can do it, they have a new language to work with. They have a positive outlet. And the most important thing, for me, is it gives them a sense of individual accomplishment."

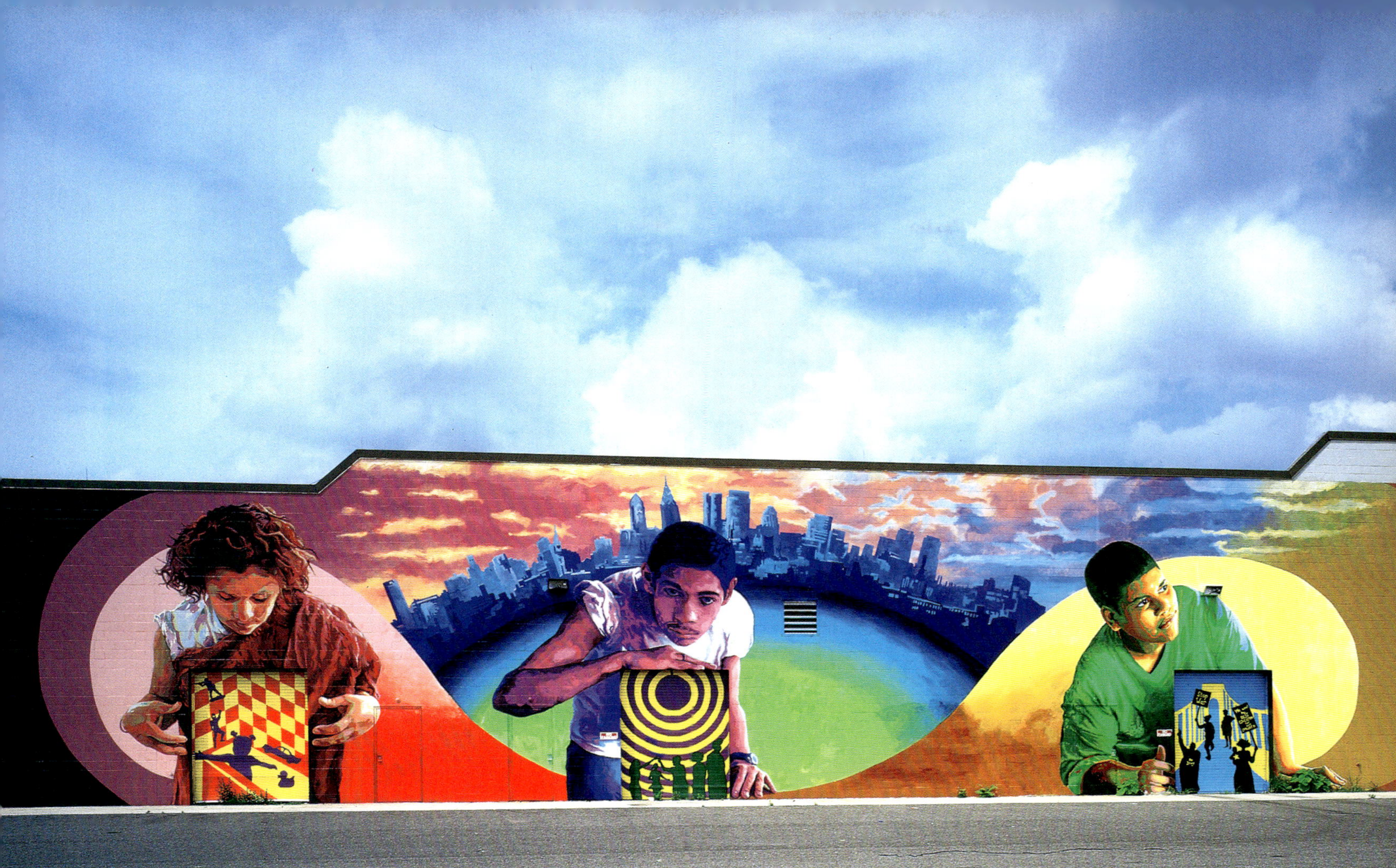

Painted by ArtWORKS! participants and Michelle Ortiz, *The Doors of Destiny Are in Your Hands,* American and Somerset Streets, a beautiful integration of a building's architecture with a mural's design.

MAP has offered art programs for young offenders and those on the cusp of serious trouble for more than five years. For chronically truant youth, there's ArtWORKS!, an afterschool program operated in cooperation with the Intensive Delinquency Prevention Program of the city's Department of Human Services. For those who have been arrested or are awaiting trial or sentencing, there are the outreach programs at the Youth Study Center. ARTscape, which has multiple sites, is for adjudicated youth fulfilling community service requirements. And for the most serious offenders, there's Traister's class at the House of Correction, a minimum-security facility that houses a significant number of minors who have been tried as adults.

"For many of these kids, there's not much forgiveness in their lives for what they've done and I see them as kids who are vulnerable and in need of love and support," says MAP Director Jane Golden. "Contact with Mural Arts isn't necessarily life-changing for everyone, but for those kids in particular, they gain a connection with a caring adult, have a program that's consistent and those things take on a great deal of meaning."

Traister compared the incarcerated boys to "bullets in a box." Stacked on top of one other, each is ready to explode and no one is doing anything to stop that.

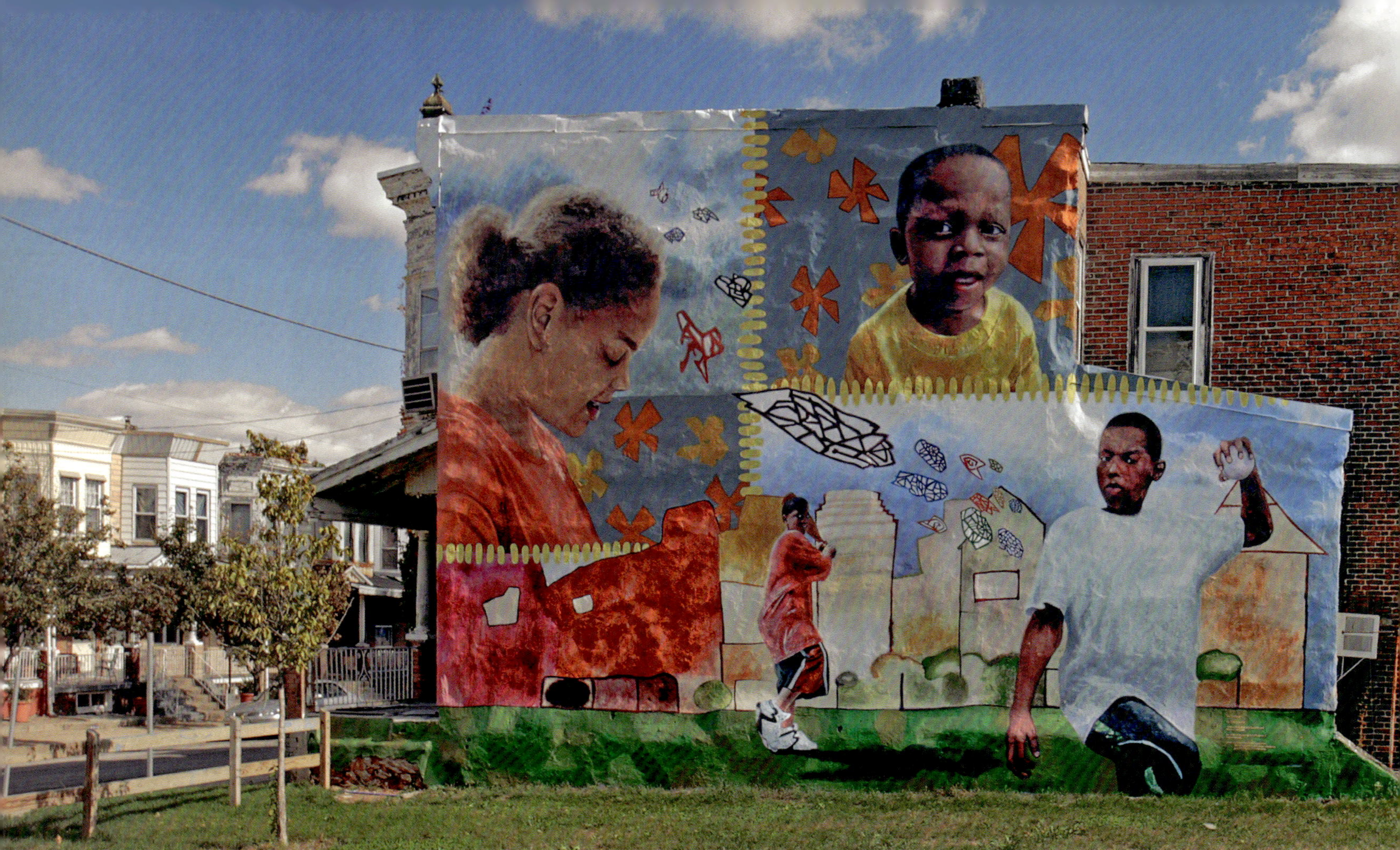

Created with participants in the ArtWORKS! program, *On the Block,* by James Burns at 40th and Pennsgrove Streets.

Philadelphia Prisons Commissioner Leon King says he supports the art programs precisely because they do offer alternatives and he aims to expand them. Already, MAP is starting to work at the Riverside Correctional Facility, the city's womens' prison, and is employing some of the male facilities' former inmates.

"It's good for the inmates, generally speaking, to have something to do because idle minds lead people to do things they shouldn't do. It's a way to keep things orderly and safe," King says. "But it also gives inspiration by showing the kids that if they channel their energies and emotions, they can accomplish something. It sort of turns on that light bulb in their heads and maybe they'll go on to do things that will help them not end up in jail."

MAP instructors are trying to reach the kids before that deadness Traister saw settles behind their eyes. Reformed graffiti artist Pose II, who works with students at the Youth Studies Center and in ArtWORKS!, says he's most surprised at how scared the youths really are. They're afraid to make a mistake. They're afraid to fail. They're afraid to dream. One student asked Pose II if she could work for him some day. When he asked her what she wanted to do, she shrugged and said she could clean his studio. He was stunned: "I said, 'That's how you see yourself? You want to sweep my floor?'" he recalls. "If you can't dream, man, forget about it. You're lost."

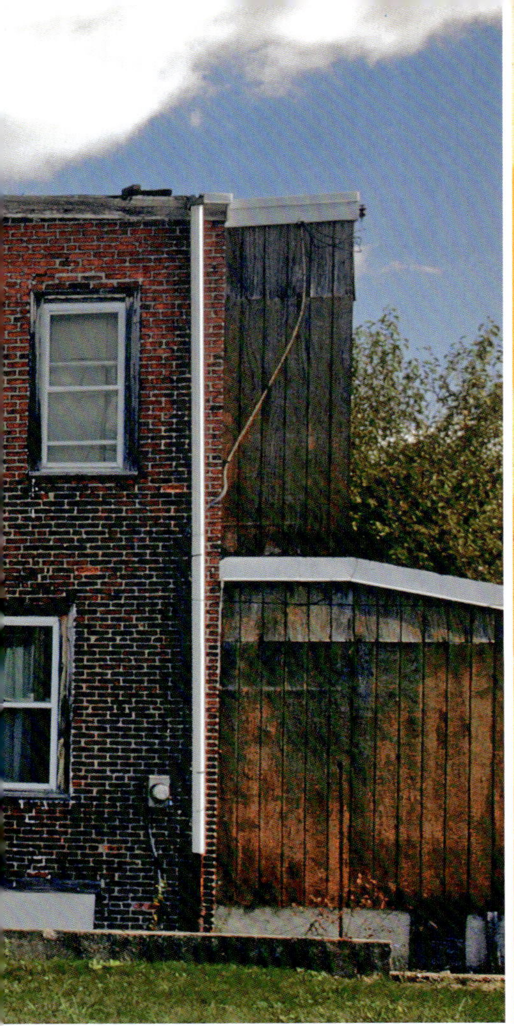

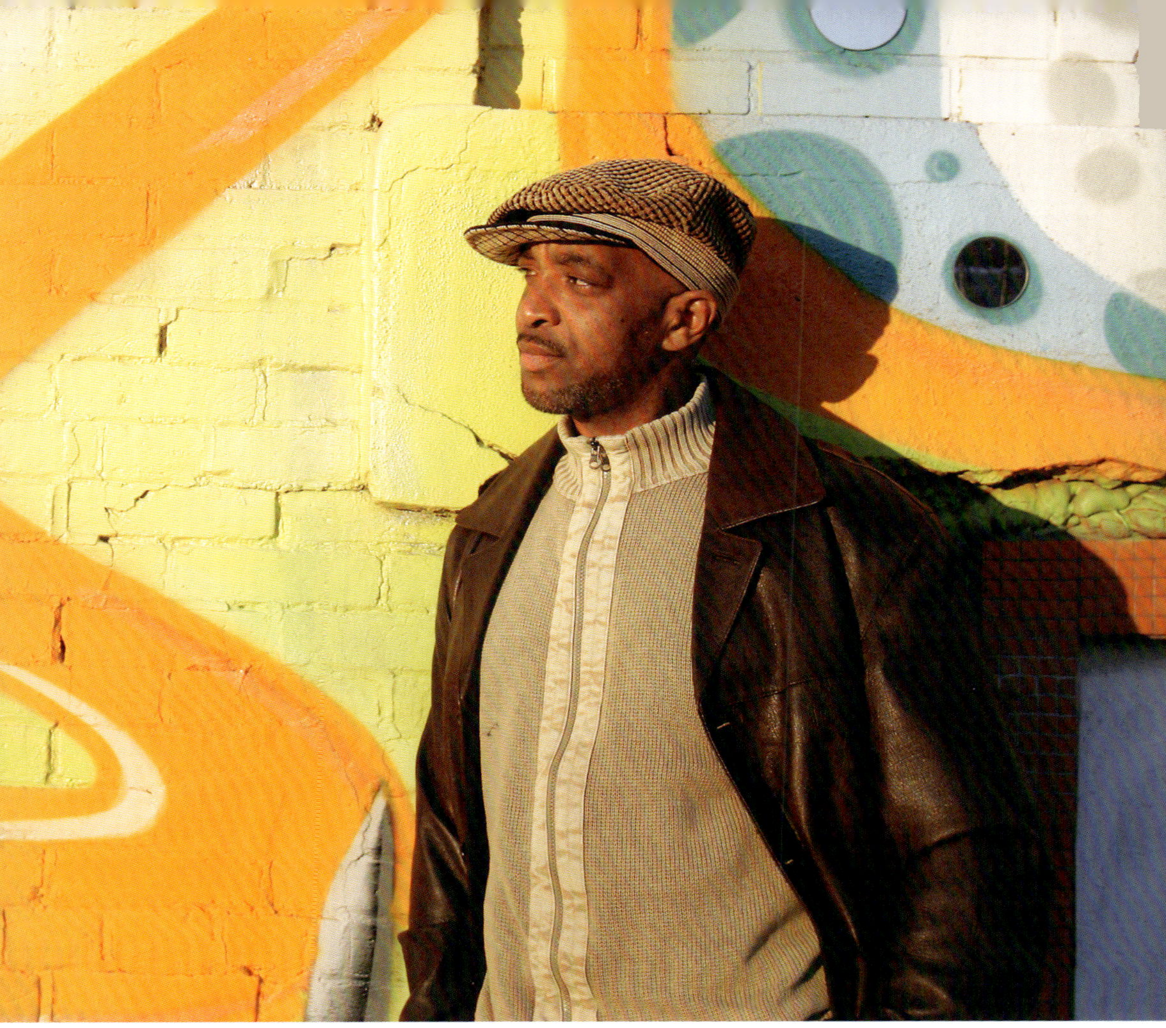

Reformed graffiti writer Pose II, a lead instructor at the Youth Study Center and ArtWORKS! art education programs.

Pose II had the street cred to win the young offenders over. His incarcerated students tell the correctional officers, "Man, you should bring around more people like him." In addition to the name—the tag he adopted when he was still a graffiti-spraying menace in New York—he's got the hair, the clothes, the reputation. He can talk the talk because he's walked the walk and his students know it. In his younger days, he ran wild, tagging trains and buildings, stealing spray paint and jumping subway turnstiles. He was arrested, paid for his crimes, but doesn't regret any of it. Graffiti, he says, isn't just about defacing property. The artists have something to say.

"It's not just about writing on the wall. These are people who want to have their voices heard and there's a whole creative process behind it. Even if they got rid of all the spray paint, all the ink, graffiti would still exist as an art form," he says. "Graffiti is the most alive art form in the world."

As a college student in upstate New York, Pose II tagged the Fine Arts building and a teacher pushed him into art classes. He learned history and perspective and how to mix colors. He learned that other art movements—like Impressionism—were hated in their earliest days. He learned to blend his formal learning with his natural talent and flair to develop a style all his own. That's what he takes into the classroom with him now—his talent and his history. He pushes his students to think as individuals and to seek inspiration, noting, "Yes, I teach art. But you have to get to the heart first."

"You have all these young cats from the streets who are locked up and you're able to reach them because their defenses are down. They're doing art and they're relaxed. It leads to conversations about why they're there and where they want to go," Pose II says.

Educational Outreach Coordinator Jason Slowik says that when the students show up for class, "They've just come from the low point in whatever happened. They got caught. They got in trouble. They got sentenced. But they come from this low point and they can actually be shown a new way. They've already been down the steps and now we can show them the way up."

Opposite
Brad Carney directing participants in the House of Correction art education program.

Below
A portrait being painted in the House of Correction.

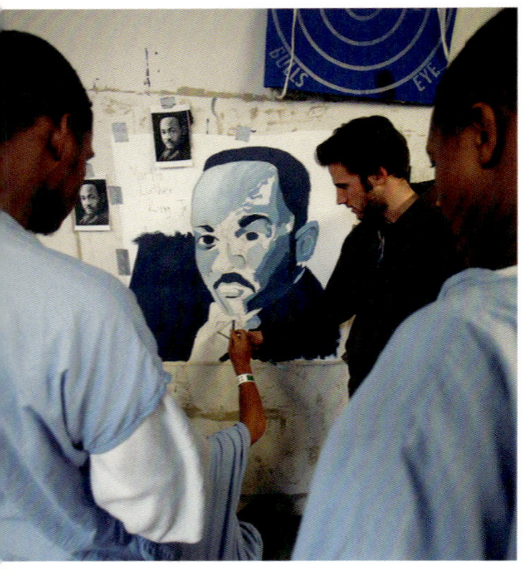

Working with professional artists shows them that real people can make a career in art. It gives them options, Slowik says: Make this drawing, give it to your mom, you'll get out of trouble; give it to a girl and she'll be your girlfriend; sell it to a friend and make $5.

The classes provide the students with new ways to express themselves. They can be a comfort, a constant, something stable and good in these troubled lives. Slowik has seen the positive effects: One student continues to come to after-school programs although his "sentence" is long done. This boy fills the pages of his MAP sketchbook when things are rough at home because "he knows everything is cool there," Slowik says.

Eric Gibbs, now nineteen, got caught using a marker on a high school locker and ended up arrested for vandalism and in ARTscape. "It was actually one of the best things that happened," he says. "Just being in that kind of environment with so many artists, you can't help but have them rub off on you." After he'd worked off his community service time, he joined Mural Corps, then went into the Mural Arts' internship program and became an assistant instructor. Now a student at Philadelphia's Tyler School of Art, Gibbs says his story really isn't that special. "I definitely see a change in a lot of kids. They come in stealing bikes or selling drugs but, by the end, they want to come back and make t-shirts and make murals. It really changes their lives."

One girl who struggled with truancy in high school took part in the creation of Don Gensler's "Symbols of Change" mural (see title page), her face prominently featured on a Center City wall. She is now a Community College student who enjoys bringing new friends to see her larger-than-life face.

Another youth, released from the House of Correction after an aggravated assault arrest, is now working with MAP. He came to them, Golden says, "symbolic of a young person who has talent or ability, but he has no ability to recognize his own gifts. He doesn't see himself as someone who can take a stand or who has a voice. He sort of just goes through life." The boy gained confidence through the art classes, but his struggle continues on the outside. "He's at a critical juncture right now and I don't know where he'll go," Golden says. "I hope he gets

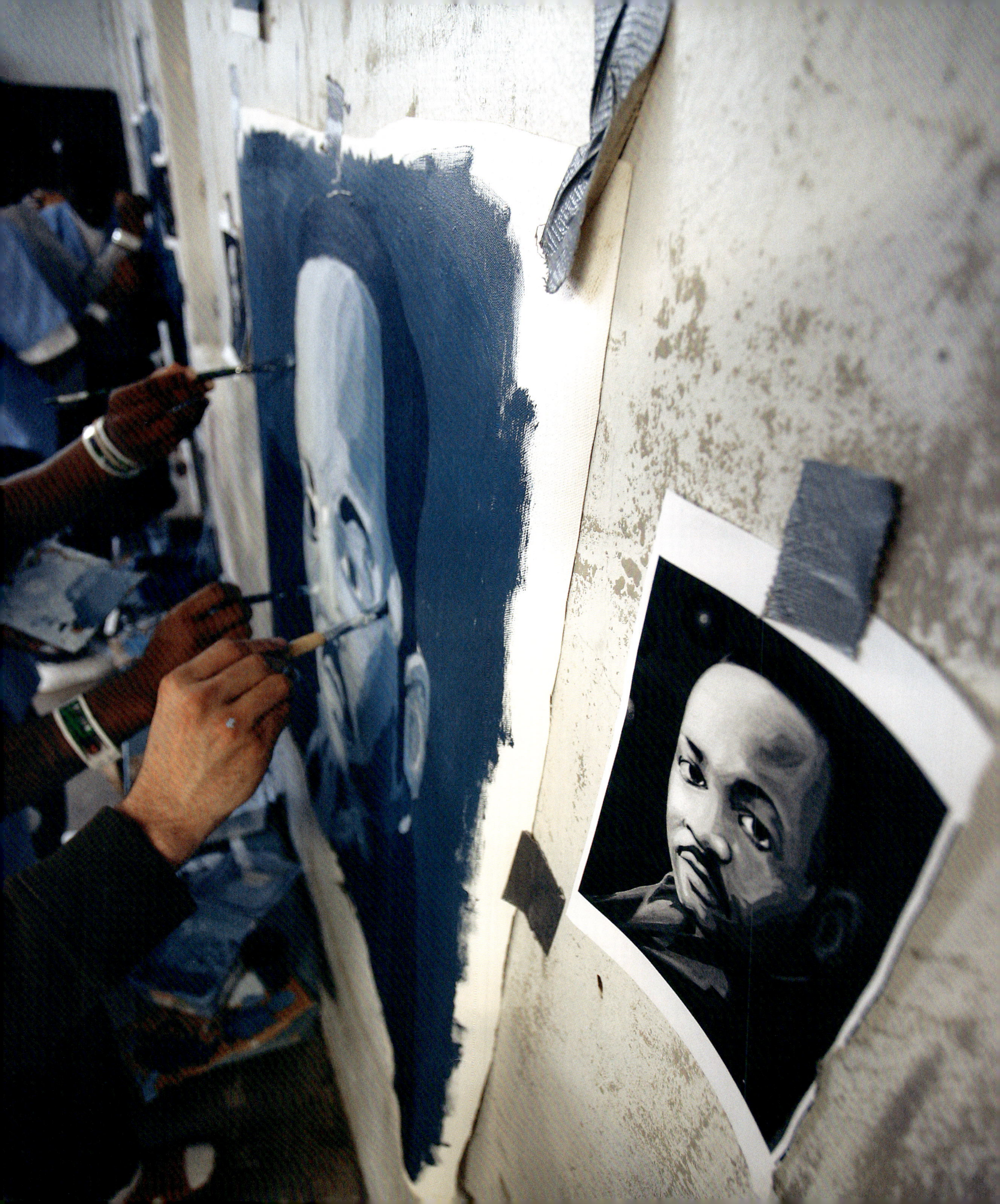

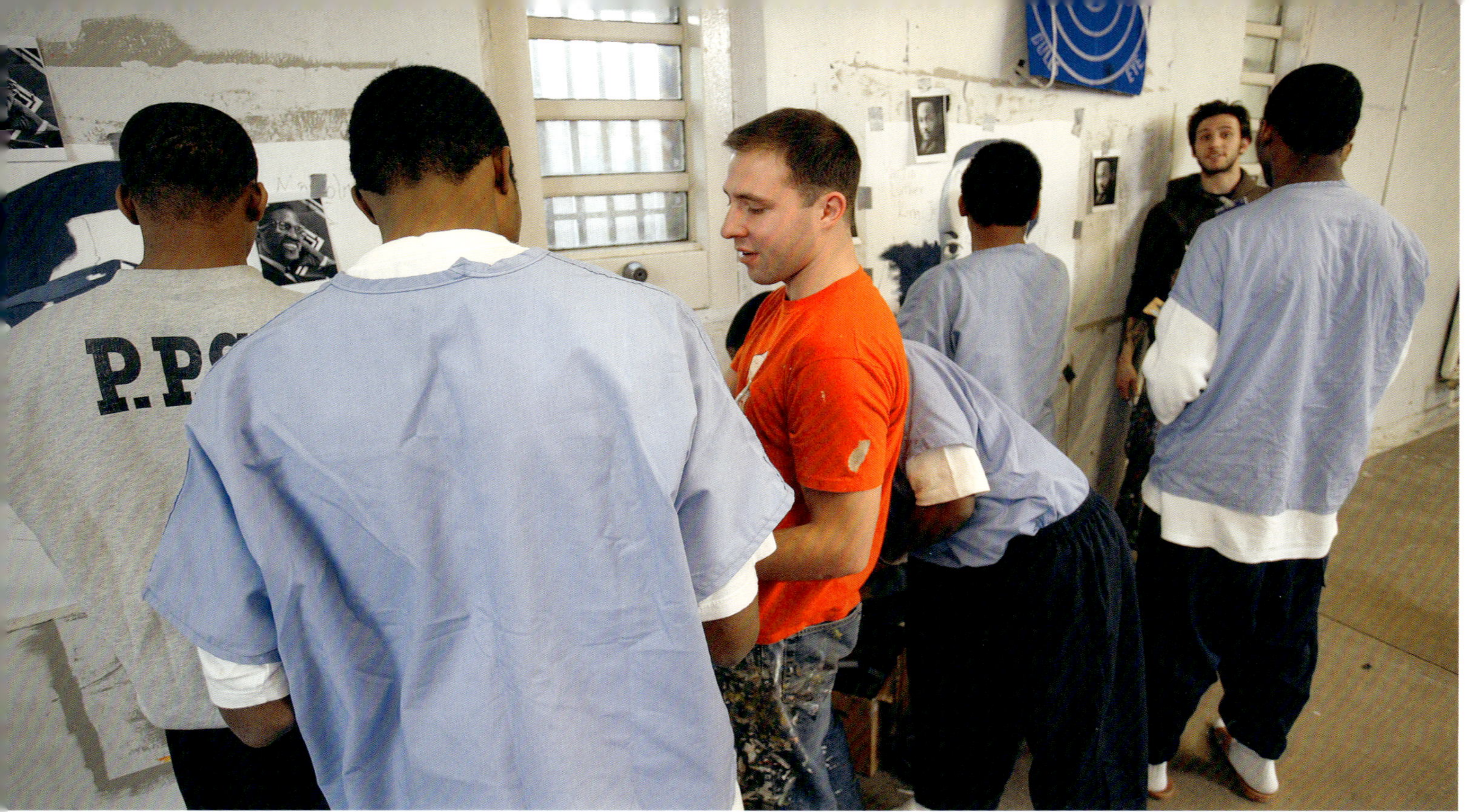

over whatever death wish he's had for the last few years and sees that so many people are pulling for him."

"We do a good job because we're there and we try to get the best out of them. Considering the obstacles and conditions put in front of us, the output has been astounding."

He could fail. Golden realizes that. There's always a percentage—she likes to think it's a small one—of children the program can't reach. "It's hard not to feel a real sense of failure when it happens. You can't help but personalize it," she says. "What I've learned over the years is to take the loss and somehow turn it into energy to keep moving forward or turn it into a lesson. Those of us who work with kids at risk have no choice to see it any way but that way or else we'd be immobilized."

Says Slowik, "We're not all social workers. The honest truth is we're doing the best we can until we can do better.'"

"The best we can" is what Traister has done for almost three years. "We do a good job because we're there and we try to get the best out of them. Considering the obstacles and conditions put in front of us, the output has been astounding. But then it becomes: Where do we go from here?" Traister says. "We can light a spark and get it going but we've got to have that follow through. We've got to figure out what the next step is."

For many of his students, his class is the first time they're getting attention in a positive way. Before, they got noticed when they did something wrong. Now, they're noticed when they work hard or produce something striking.

Opposite
Jason Slowik, coordinator and instructor, with a workshop at the House of Correction.

"It builds self-esteem and they realize they're not invisible," Traister says. "They realize that if you accomplish something positive, you can still be recognized."

His working conditions are harsh: The students work in an unventilated room, with no desks, with mice scurrying at their feet, under constant guard. His challenges are unique: Holidays are tough, as are family days, especially when visitors don't show up. Students miss lessons because of lockdowns or because they're being punished for something they did outside Traister's classroom.

Once, after counting his equipment, Traister found he was down one pencil sharpener. It could have fallen out of his bag on the train or on his walk to the building, but the fact that something with a blade in it was unaccounted for meant room searches and time wasted. During another routine room search, guards tore a piece of a student's art. The boy brought the remains to Traister and said, "I want you to keep it." It was the only way to save it.

"It made me feel good and it made me feel bad," Traister says. "It made me feel bad that he couldn't keep it and show it to his family but it was good that the spark was there. He did it and it was great and he was excited about it. He just couldn't keep it."

During one class, Traister asked his students for suggestions for a new antiviolence mural. Some of them scoffed at first—like a mural could do that, like a mural could change anything—but he persisted: "We're not saying murals are going to stop the violence, but we have to make people aware of what you guys see in the streets daily. It's not about stopping it. It's about making people stop and think."

The boys started offering stories, many of them featuring firearms: How picking up a gun—a "burner"—for the first time makes you "feel like you're Superman, like the way cops feel when they get their badge"; how those who are known not to carry guns are the most likely to get robbed; how the slain are considered "fallen soldiers." Drugs, they said, were forever. "The hustle" was life—one boy said his mother was the one who taught him how to deal drugs.

With only moments to go before the boys had to return to their cells, Traister asked them what war they were fighting in. He asked them how many people they knew had ended up like Tony Montana, the drug kingpin in the movie *Scarface.* "The hustle is a business and the overhead is high," he told them. "Think twice. You only have one life."

Then they left to be locked up again, and their teacher gathered his pencils and papers and walked out of the room.

"It's hard," Traister says. "Everything here is hard. But you have to try."

Artist Profile

Ernel Martinez

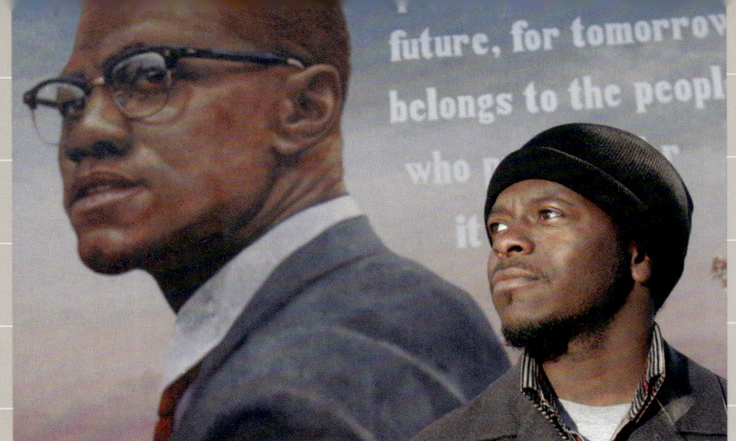

Although he was born in Belize, Ernel Martinez looks and sounds like an all-American young man, with a wife and a baby on the way. But his process-driven studio paintings that incorporate language into realistic representation suggest the inner complexity of this artist. His color choices and interest in narration and allegory reflect his Caribbean heritage. "There's a spiritualism and a mysticism that translated itself into my art," he says.

Martinez is serious about the students in his E^3 program. The Es are Encouragement. Empowerment. Employment. The Mural Arts program is "a safety net for kids that might have a problem in school or might be coming out of the judicial system." As a young black male not much older than the students, Martinez says, "I try to conduct myself as much as possible as a role model, something like a big brother. Most of the guys are between fifteen and twenty. One is actually twenty-two. I've had one or two girls in the program. All are black. I've shared some of the tribulations that they have and not so long ago, so its not too difficult for me to relate to them. It goes way beyond art. It's about life. We talk about surviving. How do you deal with this problem or that problem.

"I'm working with kids who don't have a particular interest in art. I am their first contact with art. I think my kids are sometimes amazed at what they are able to accomplish. We're doing these portraits right now. It's pretty complicated and they're doing great so far."

Although the students are paid a small stipend, Martinez is convinced, "The work we are doing there is what really keeps them coming. I try to be as positive as possible. Sometimes we have an all-day workshop where we do painting, poetry and we have food. It's fun."

Martinez grew up in South Central Los Angeles where, he says, "I was aware of murals but did not think of [art] as a career choice for an adult." Nevertheless, he made his first mural in grade school and claims to have painted at least one mural in all but one of the many schools he's attended. His mother, who worked in the school district for twenty years, made sure he attended good schools. As a child he was bussed from his neighborhood to a magnet school in a more affluent one. "It was a great benefit for me to be exposed to kids with different ethnic and cultural backgrounds," he says.

Martinez's true interest in art didn't begin until seventh grade, "when I took my first real class and met real artists through the teacher." Dyeing batik fabrics intrigued him, but it was mural work that really pulled him in. He believes he was predestined to be an artist. "I couldn't deny the natural gifts I was blessed with," he says.

When Martinez "started to run with the gangs in LA," his mother sent him to live with an aunt in Detroit, little realizing that Detroit had its own problems. "I think it was the murder capital at the time," he laughs, but "Aunt Jackie took me in and showed me patience and exposed me to things I might not have seen," including church and the good people associated with it.

At this time, Martinez partly defined his identity through artwork but, "It was a solitary life. My gifts were starting to show and positive reinforcement drove me to continue to make art." He even received portrait commissions and other jobs. He was recruited to apply to Pratt Institute which he attended for only a year before transferring to Kutztown University in Pennsylvania, an environment which he found "really nurturing."

For five or six years, Martinez did historical conservation in the state capitol building in Harrisburg, Pennsylvania. With the intention of continuing in this field, he applied to the University of Pennsylvania. While studying there, he audited the Big Picture course taught by Don Gensler and Jane Golden. In conservation, he had enjoyed repairing murals and restoring architectural elements originated by others; however, he soon realized that he wanted to paint more murals, murals of his own design. Fortunately, MAP welcomed his interest.

Unfortunately, community mural painting is not always straightforward. Once or twice, Martinez has found himself caught between clashing, although well-intentioned, agendas. "When a person decides to make public art, he's no longer a sole decision maker," Martinez says. "This means you will have to sacrifice [some of your ideas] and negotiate with the community and directors of programs. My approach to making a mural is that I'm typically the hands and eyes of the community without neglecting my own personal aesthetics."

Martinez enjoys working with young people as part of his job. "I've never wanted to be an artist and live the 'artist lifestyle.' I've wanted to make a living and make art, but becoming famous was never an intention. I'm most at peace doing large-scale work. Being an artist is a lonely career unless you do things like murals, which are community-involved, or teaching. Then you interact with others on a daily basis."

Opposite
Muralist Ernel Martinez.

Below
The new *Malcolm X*, 3211 Ridge Avenue, by Ernel Martinez—on the site of the mural by Cliff Hudson that also honored this world renowned human rights figure.

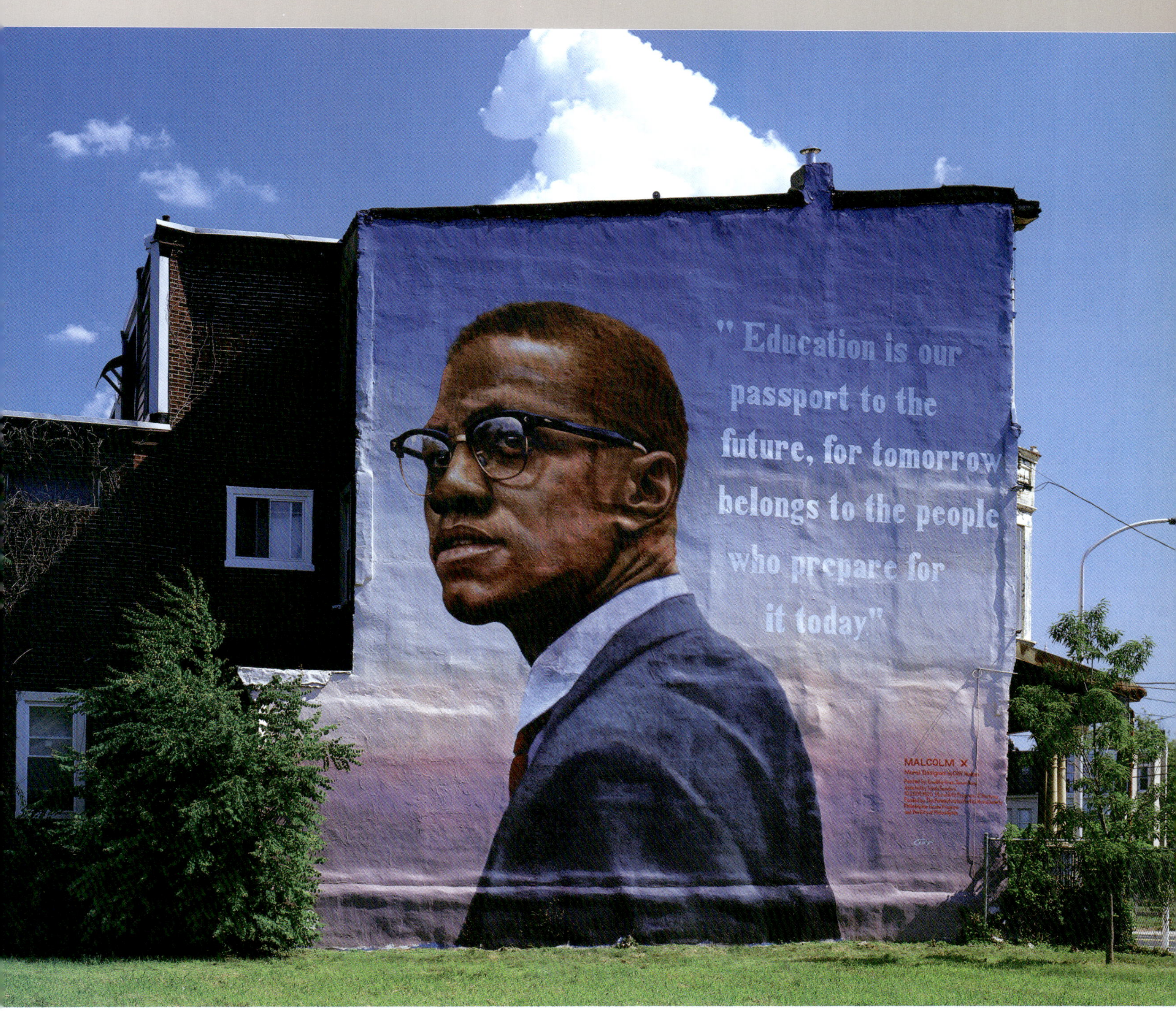

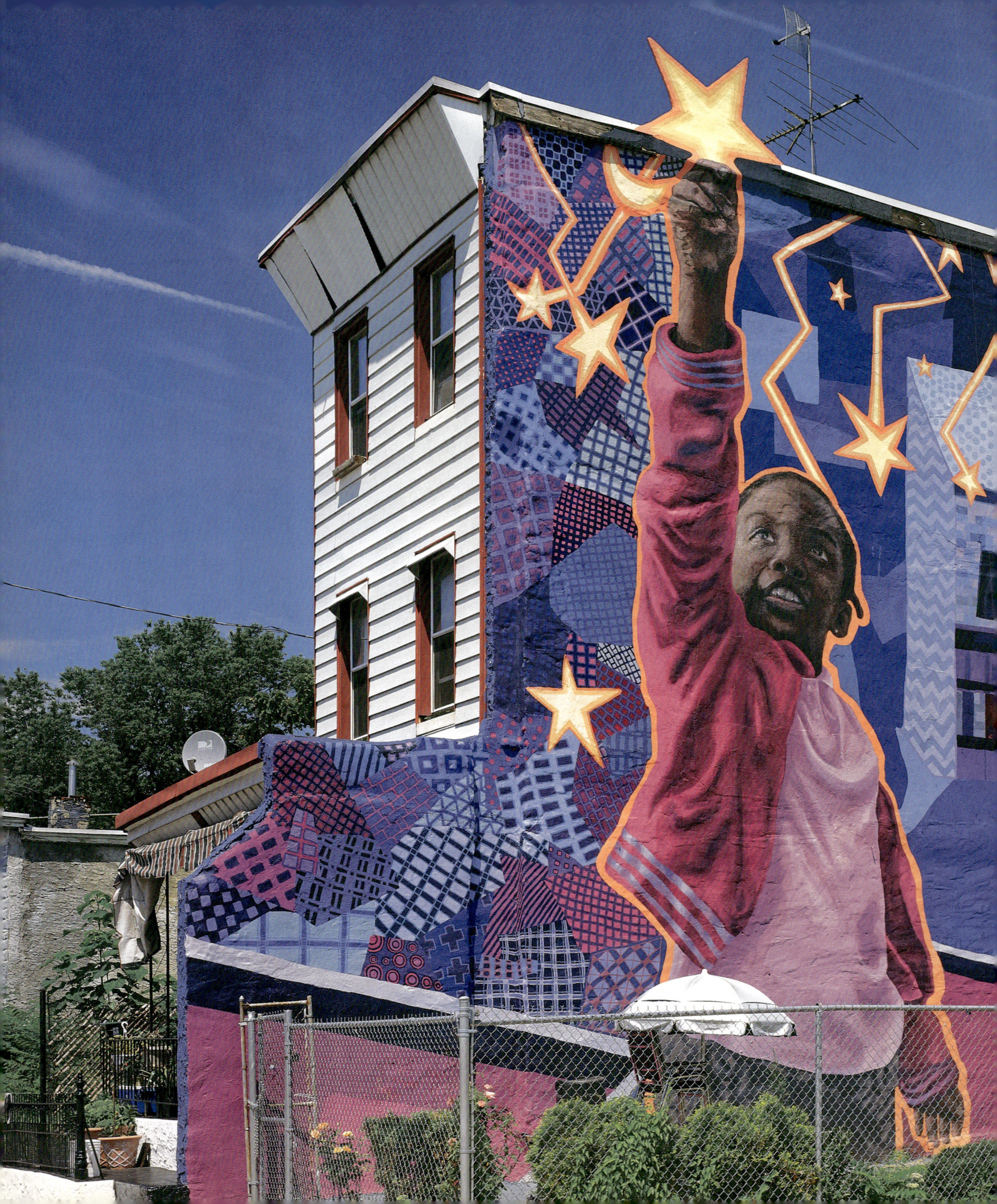

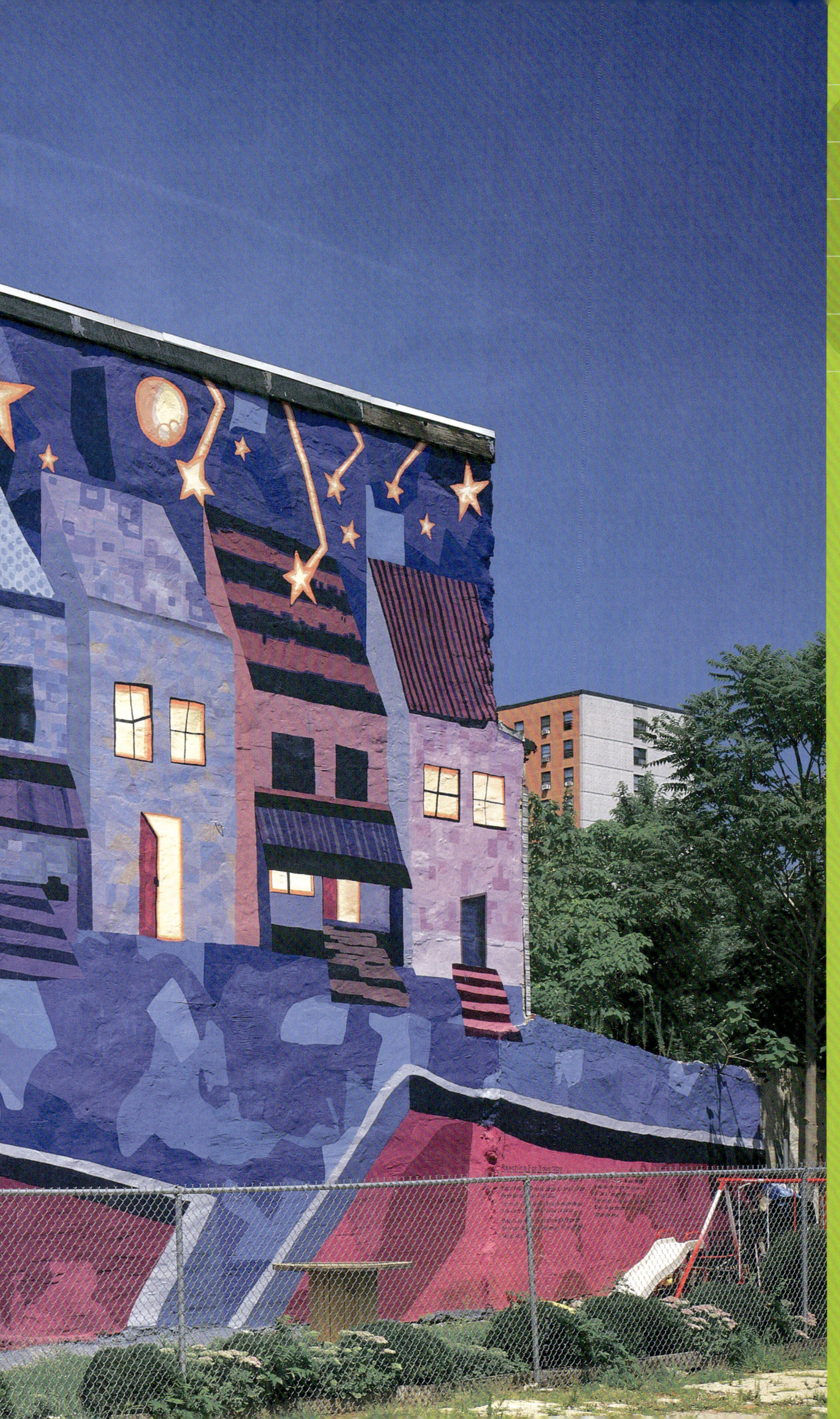

Chapter 4

Don Gensler's *Reaching for Your Star*, 37th and Mt. Vernon Streets. Created with the help of ArtWORKS! participants and students from nearby University of Pennsylvania.

Chapter 4

A Holistic Approach

It was the summer of 1984, and Jane Golden was told that if she could finish a mural over the graffiti-marred Spring Garden Street bridge in three weeks, she could have a job. The scene was Mantua, a community once known as "The Bottom," decimated by drugs and crime and blight.

Armed with house paint and assisted by a group of Mantua teens—some of whom had marked up the bridge in the first place—she made it happen, covering the two low walls with images important to that generation of Mantua youth: Malcolm X, kids on bikes, quotes from rap songs. The mural became a beacon for residents—home was only a short distance away—and it became the start of the mural boom—in Mantua and in the city of Philadelphia.

Since then, the Mural Arts Program had returned to this West Philadelphia neighborhood many times, reclaiming walls and, in most cases, the land around them. Of course, the murals are pretty. They brighten up the streets. But, of equal value, the colorful walls seem to start a domino effect of good things, Golden says. Empty lots have been converted into community gardens. Playgrounds have been repaired or restored. Long-term relationships between neighbors have formed and flourished.

"People seem to internalize that the mural is a sign that things can change and there's potential for the neighborhood," says Golden, who went on to become MAP's director. "And it doesn't just happen in neighborhoods where there have been struggles. There's a shift in attitudes that you discern."

What happens, she says, is the opposite of the so-called "broken windows" theory, which goes something like this: Don't fix a broken window and you'll get more shattered glass, maybe some graffiti, maybe some trash strewn on your property. But address a problem when it's small and it won't get bigger. Get new glass. Paint over the graffiti. Clean up the garbage. And it'll stay that way. For the last twenty years, MAP has been helping Mantua fix its broken windows.

Opposite
Community heroes Norman "Butch" Ellis and Richard Drain, in front of the west wall of Don Gensler's dynamic mural, *Holding Grandmother's Quilt*, 39th and Aspen Streets. The ArtWORKS! participants and students from the University of Pennsylvania's mural painting class assisted in the making of this mural.

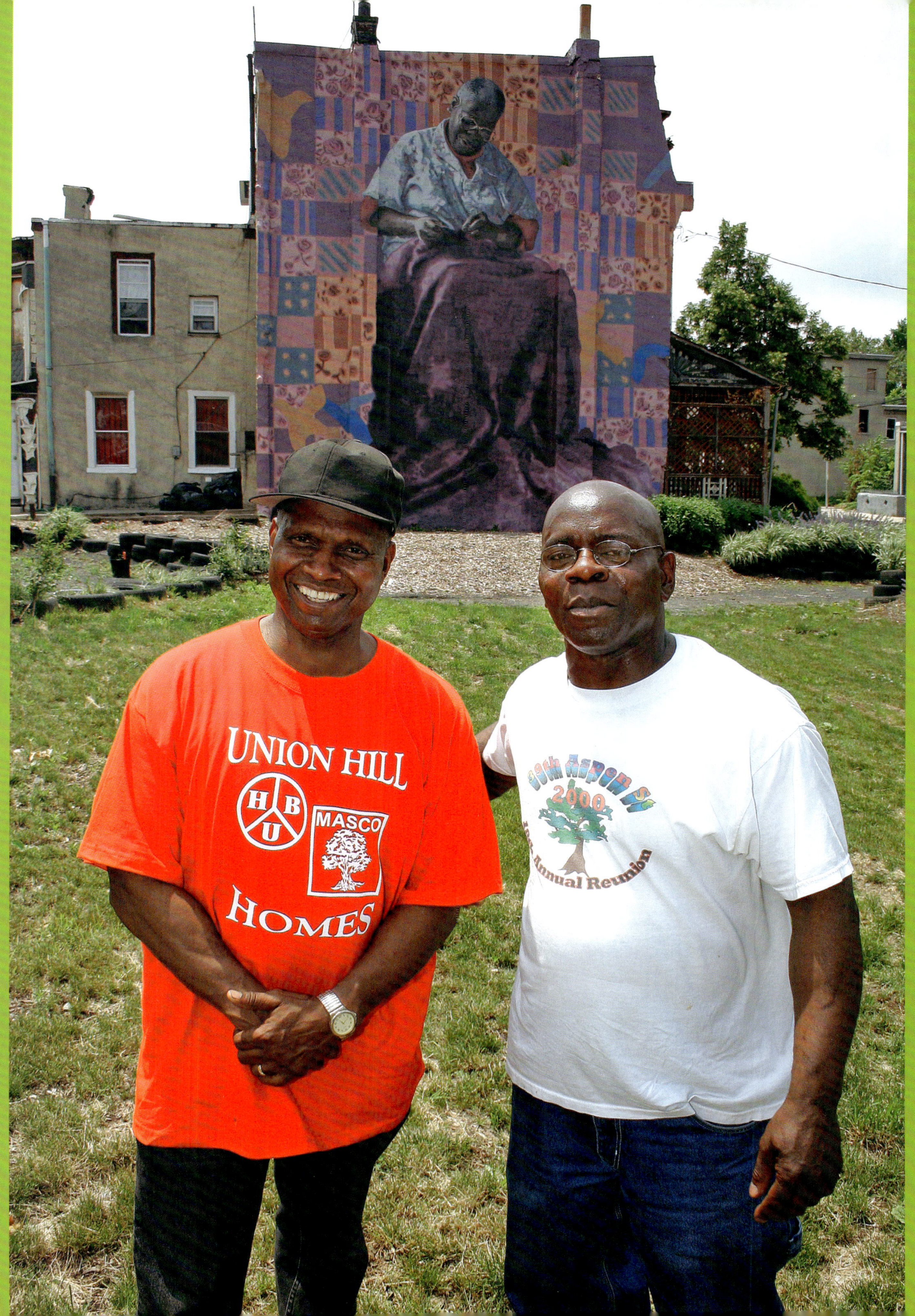
UNION HILL
H B U
MASCO
HOMES
2000
Annual Reunion

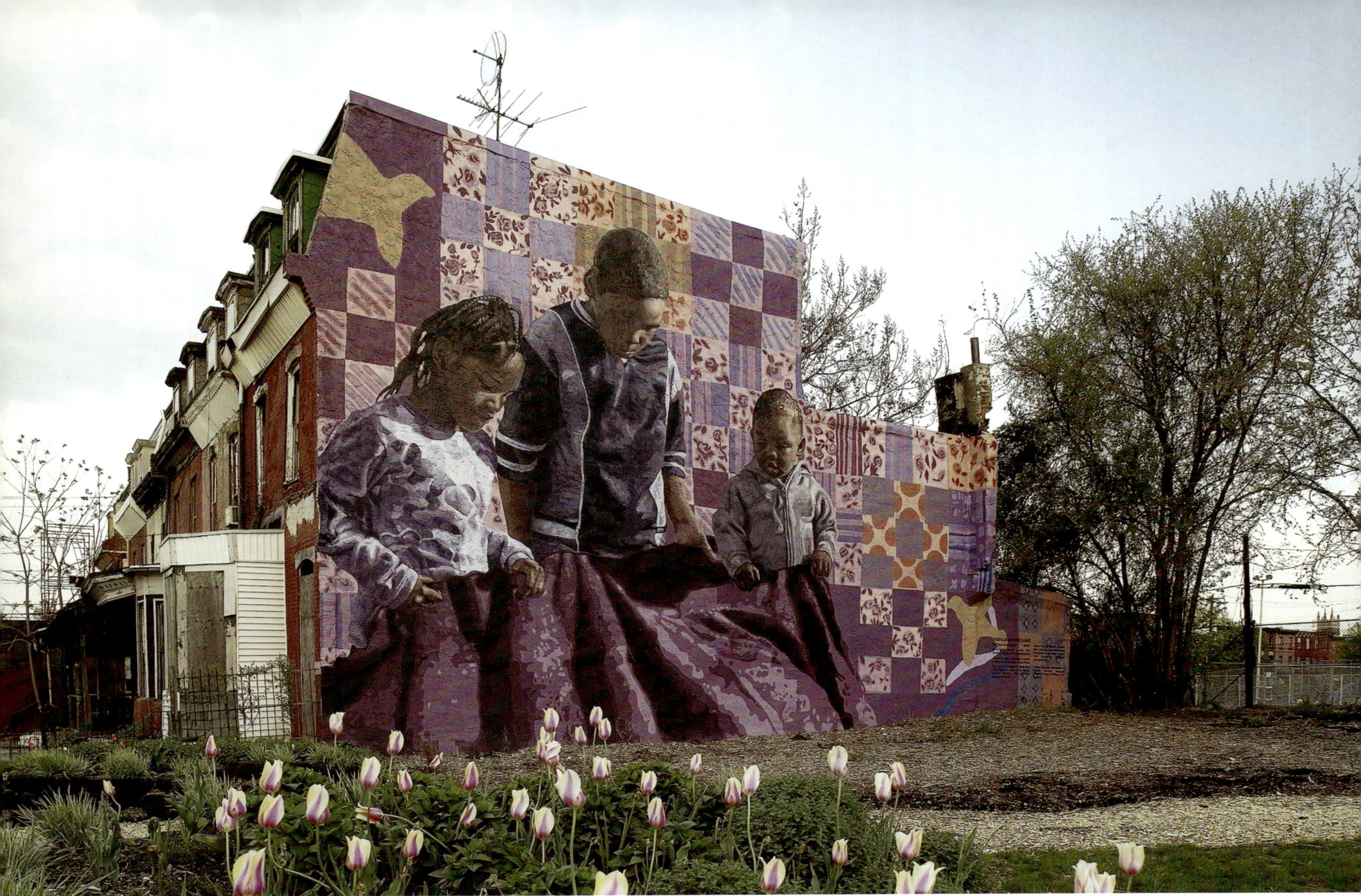

Thanks to the efforts of Mural Arts Staff, Philadelphia Green, and innumerable community members, an abandoned lot is transformed into a community garden and park in front of the east wall of the multiwalled *Holding Grandmother's Quilt,* 39th and Aspen Streets, by Don Gensler.

"We came in early, connected with block captains and community leaders and developed long term relationships," Golden says. "I've been really grateful we've had the opportunity to keep working there. People have a trust for us and a solidarity that working together over time can really make a difference."

Mantua really had nowhere to go but up. Once dangerous and defeated, this neighborhood was ruled by the city's toughest gangs, had open-air drug markets, and boasted a murder rate no one was proud of. Although it is within an easy walk from both the University of Pennsylvania and Drexel University, it never seemed to benefit from the money and attention poured into the universities. About one-third of all lots and buildings here are vacant, compared with about 10 percent citywide, as residents have fled. The population has decreased by more than 50 percent since 1960 and about half the families live below the poverty level.

But in more recent years, the city has poured money into Mantua's revitalization as part of Mayor John Street's Neighborhood Transformation Initiative, tearing down more than 110 blighted properties and planning new construction and parks. Mural Arts has been chipping away at the area for years, brightening individual pockets of this neighborhood one wall at a time.

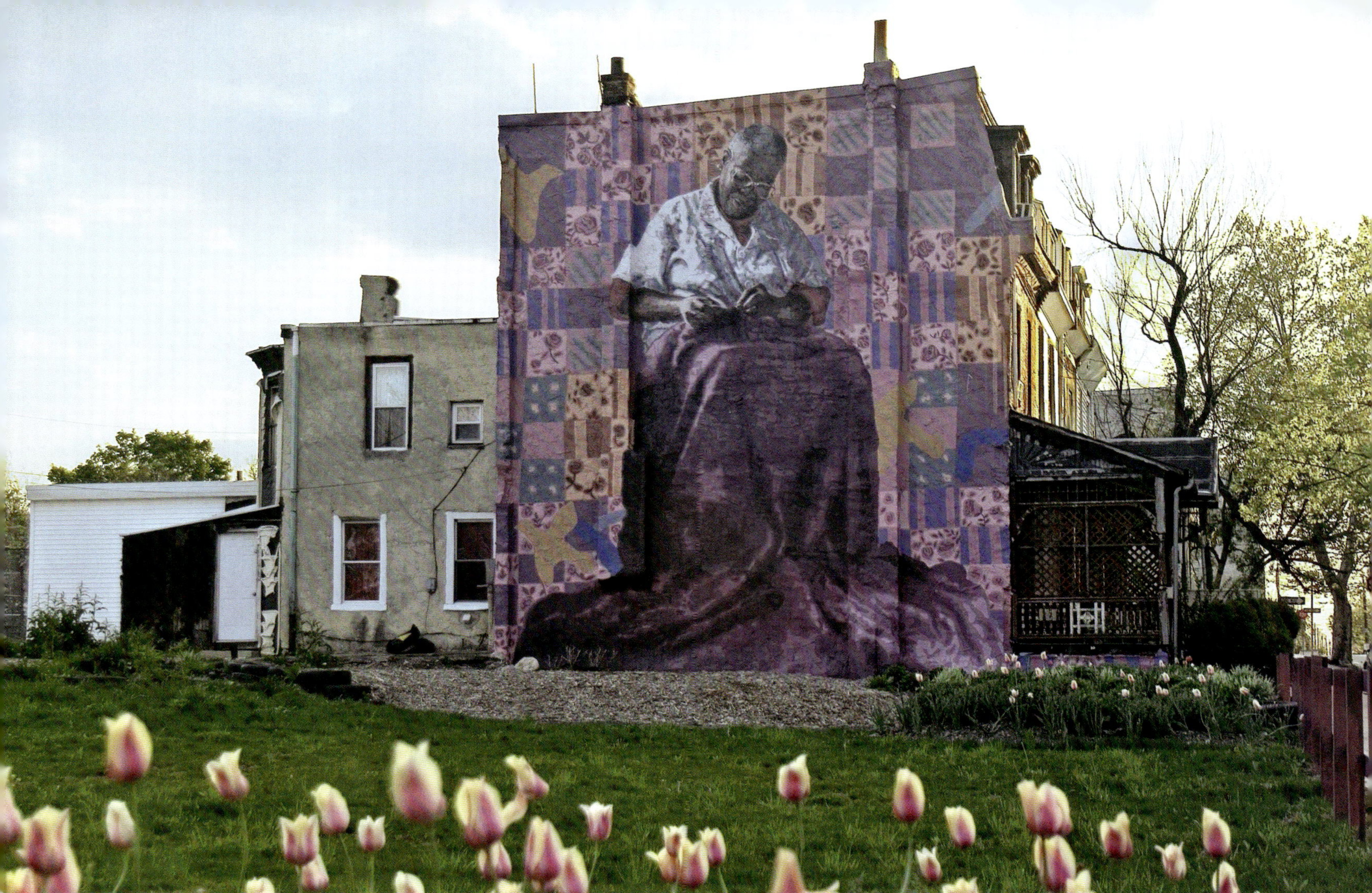

“The murals have made a huge difference in the renaissance of Mantua,” said Philadelphia City Councilwoman Jannie Blackwell, whose district includes the neighborhood. “People are included in the subject matter and the maintaining of them and they’re so vital to Mantua’s neighborhood improvement.”

Of course, murals are not a panacea, notes University of Pennsylvania professor and author Elijah Anderson. Mantua is still a neighborhood of concentrated urban poverty, with high unemployment and crime rates. Most residents, he says, “are decent people or trying to be decent, but there’s certain element that’s deep in the street.” But the murals “can show there’s a brighter day,” he says. “You can’t quantify the effects of wall art, but we can imagine that it brightens up the area, brightens up your little corner of the world, brightens you.”

“There’s something to the broken windows theory. If you have broken windows, it shows people don’t care. With Mural Arts, somebody’s paying attention. It’s like a theatrical production. People go by and say, ‘Oh, what are they doing? They must care about the community.’ It’s the opposite of letting the broken windows fester.”

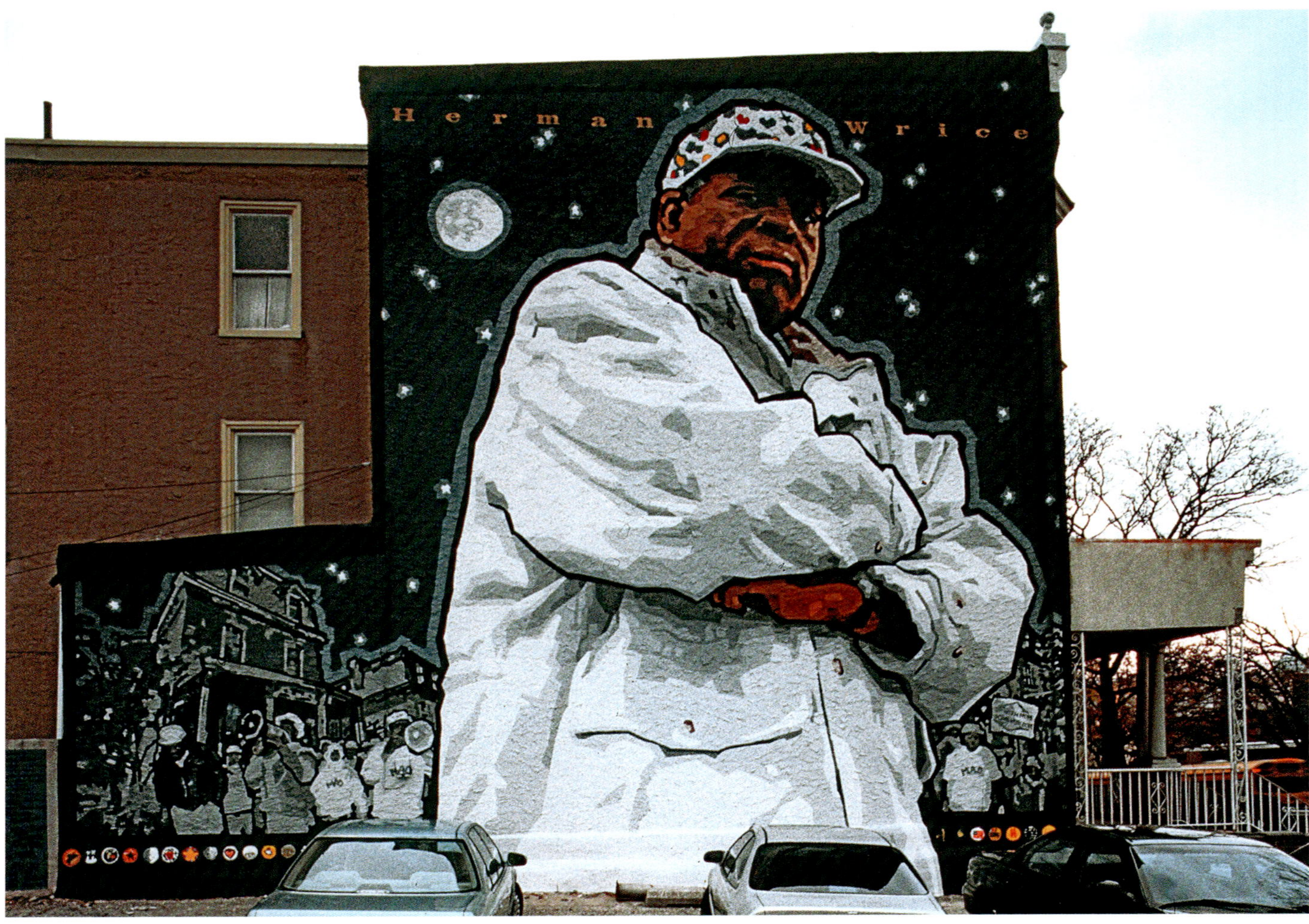

David McShane's as large as possible portrait of a beloved Mantua antidrug activist, *A Tribute to Herman Wrice,* 33rd and Spring Garden Streets.

One example of the power of murals is the scene on Aspen Street. At one time, the vacant lot between two houses here was overgrown and trash-strewn. Hidden inside, a criminal element was there, "smoking their reefer and doing their dirty stuff," says resident Norman "Butch" Ellis. Children steered clear. Most adults did, too.

Then, one hundred people showed up one weekend to clean it. Then, a local gardening group adopted it for planting. Then, the murals came.

What were once blank walls on either side of the lot is now *Holding Grandmother's Quilt* (2004; see page 64). The work by muralist Don Gensler covers two walls, one on each house. On the west wall, a gray-haired woman sits against a background of quilting squares as she works a needle through a flowing purple coverlet. On the east wall, three neighborhood children stand against the same background and hold that same coverlet, looking down at it as if in awe.

To complete the transformation of the area, MAP had help from the Pennsylvania Horticultural Society's Philadelphia Green Program and Skip Weiner of the Urban Tree

Connection. The land in between—neatly tended with flowers, shrubs, and benches—is slightly rippled, slightly hilly, to imply the wrinkles of a quilt. The programs have joined forces to maintain the area with the help of neighborhood youth.

The hoods that once hovered here are gone—or, at least, operating elsewhere. "We ran them out and we've kept them out. You may never get them out of Mantua, never get them out of the neighborhood completely, but we can keep them down," Ellis says. "Mural Arts has done a lot of work in Mantua, a lot of good work in Mantua."

Gensler, a muralist behind multiple works in the neighborhood, says that, at the very least, the murals bring people together. "Neighbors come out to discuss painting and then end up discussing other issues—and that's not a small thing," he says. "I like to think murals get people excited. Over the years I've worked here, I've seen a lot of Mantua grow and areas being fixed up and houses being rebuilt and restored and people getting grants to do different things and, all the while, murals are going up throughout the neighborhood."

That's what happened after the completion of *Holding Grandmother's Quilt:* The neighboring playground, once an eyesore, got new equipment and its supply building got a new coat of paint. The same ripple effect was felt on 35th Street between Melon and Wallace with *Holding the Past: A Window to the Future* (2002), a Gensler mural showing the hands of a ninety-year-old resident catching leaves from a tree. A trash-strewn park across the street that once had six-foot-tall weeds was cleaned, given a new gazebo and turned into a focal point with a public sculpture representing family.

The beauty of *Reaching for Your Star* (2003; see page 60) at 37th and Mt. Vernon Streets, another Gensler work that features a youngster doing just that, initially inspired neighbors to start taking care of a nearby play lot.

The hard part is maintaining that momentum. Once again, the 37th and Mt. Vernon Streets playground is deteriorating. Broken swings aren't being fixed, benches are looking shabby, and trash is allowed to linger. William Hodges, who lives in the house on which *Reaching for Your Star* is painted, says he does what he can, but five of the properties across the street are abandoned, meaning that there's no one there to help him maintain the area. He mows the grass in the empty lots on both sides of his house, plants a garden under the mural in the spring, and just keeps up the fight.

"This is the best corner around here. That mural is the best thing that's happened," Hodges says. "For twenty years, this neighborhood's been going down but when they came and put that mural up there on the wall, it kind of stood still. It stopped it from going down."

Gensler says the park's downswing saddens him, but he remembers how so many people came together and accomplished something, at least temporarily. It also reminds him that there's still work to be done. "That's the thing we have to realize about this work. It's got to continue to evolve and it takes time," he says.

It's easier when a group of neighbors or friends comes together and pledges to keep up the fight. *Holding Grandmother's Quilt* is looked after by the Mantua 39th and Aspen Street Community Organization (MASCO), an organization founded by Ellis and Richard Drain, two men who grew up in the neighborhood—and who once did their best to destroy it. Says Drain, now fifty, "We were the sociopaths of the past and now we're trying to instill social skills and socialization in the younger people." Both men have served time in prison. Both feel no one expected their organization to succeed.

It amazes him, he says, that this neighborhood, so ignored twenty years ago, is now featured on tourist tours of Philadelphia

They proved the naysayers wrong. MASCO is thriving, running clothing drives, offering tutoring classes, remodeling a shell of a home in a slowly rising neighborhood to turn into their offices. MAP has played a part in their success, the men say. The community—and the artwork—inspire them and show them that people care.

"Mural Arts gives people a lot of hope. When they first came to Mantua, they had meeting after meeting about the design and that's when I knew they took this stuff seriously. I thought they just came in and put them up," Drain says. "It's not an invasion of outsiders. They're good neighbors. You get used to seeing them and the murals. You see the love that goes into them."

Ellis, who has spent more than half of his fifty-seven years behind bars, says Mantua wants more murals, "as many as we can get." It amazes him, he says, that this neighborhood, so ignored two decades ago, is now featured on tourist tours of Philadelphia: "I can't believe it. Every day, they come driving through Mantua to see the murals."

Gensler says people are no longer just coming to Philadelphia to see the Liberty Bell or the Constitution Center. "They want to see the positive changes in the communities," he says. "Each year, the work is getting better and better and people are coming from all over to see it."

Locals, too, still stop to pay homage. Resident Jim Brown says he says a prayer every time he drives by the mural of Herman Wrice on the corner of 33rd and Spring Garden Streets (see page 66). Wrice, who died in 1990, was a community leader on an epic scale: He took in children who needed a home, founded after-school and sports programs, and led the fight against drugs with marches and the slogan, "Down with dope, up with hope!"

Brown was one of the boys who benefited from Wrice's largess. Now he's trying to give back, too, starting up his own sports league. "I see that mural and I whisper, 'Lord, I don't know what he threw me into, but I'm trying. Please help me,'" Brown says.

The mural is also epic: Based on a photo of Wrice, it shows him in a white tracksuit and hard hat, his arms crossed, his look stern. His figure is outlined in black with a shimmering light around him, as if he's a superhero. In the background, marchers with antidrug signs walk through the neighborhood, past the first drug house that Wrice and his supporters managed to shut down. Artist David McShane says he tried to paint Wrice as large as possible, as if he were still there, watching over the neighborhood.

"This was the mural that had the most positive response of any mural I've ever done," McShane says. "When I was painting, practically every single day someone came by and said, 'I knew Herman. I used to play on one of his teams.' Or 'He helped me start a business.' Or 'I used to go to his drug marches.' He was well respected and they were glad to have a mural of him."

The Community Paint days for the mural were wildly popular with residents, especially youth. McShane let them do some of their own designs on the bottom, creating replicas of the buttons Wrice used to wear or making up their own button designs. "There are a lot of people who have a stake in the murals. Because the community process is open to the neighbors, there's a lot of respect there and they look after it and take ownership. That's the key," McShane says.

Tony Wrice, Wrice's son, says the mural reminds community members to believe in themselves, to believe in their families, to believe in Mantua. That's what his father did. That's why he's still watching them, "standing tall and looking good."

"People have got to stand up for what's right," he says. "With murals come memories. We're inspired by this mural every day. We're going to take back the neighborhood."

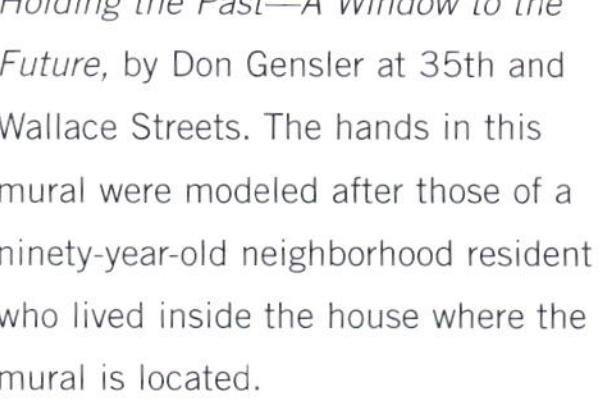

Holding the Past—A Window to the Future, by Don Gensler at 35th and Wallace Streets. The hands in this mural were modeled after those of a ninety-year-old neighborhood resident who lived inside the house where the mural is located.

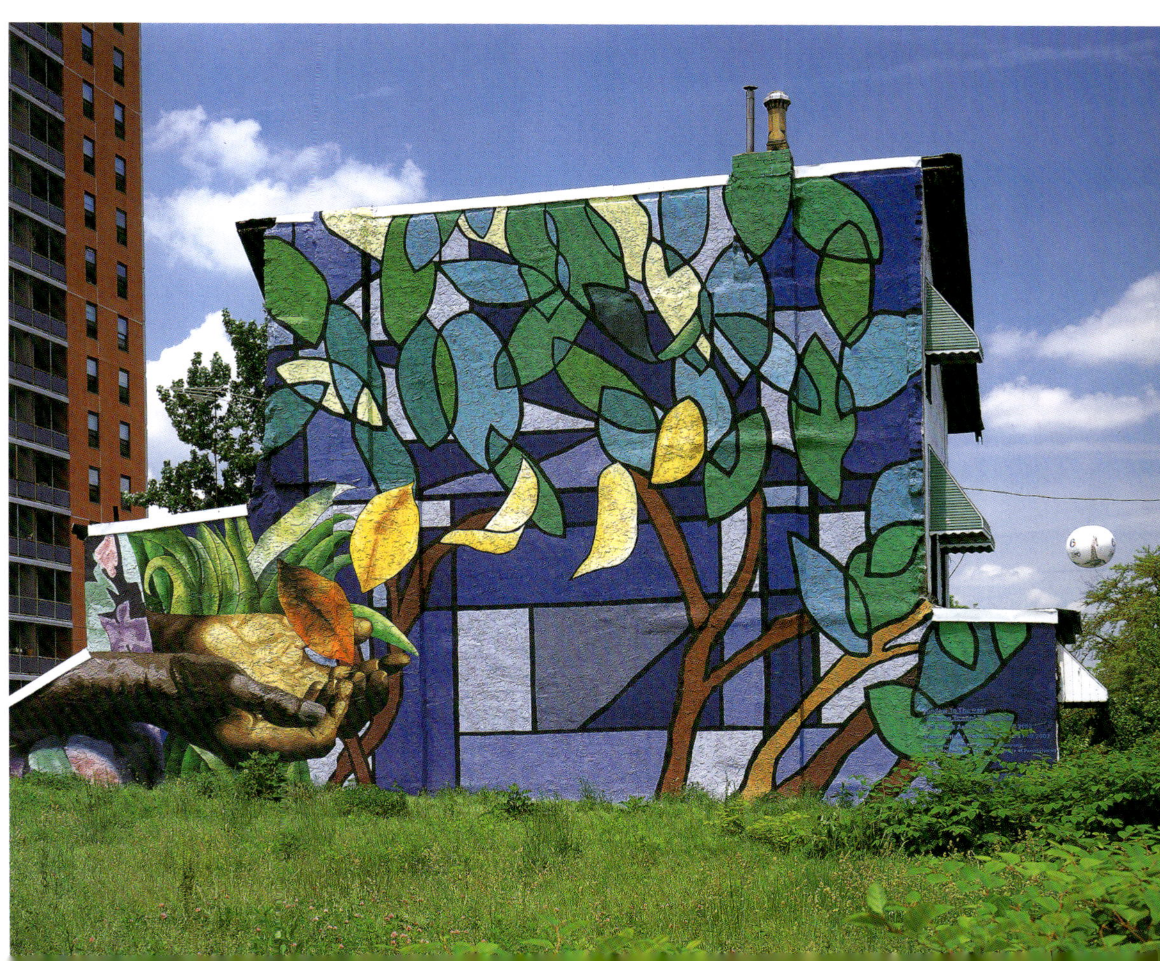

Artist Profile

Don Gensler

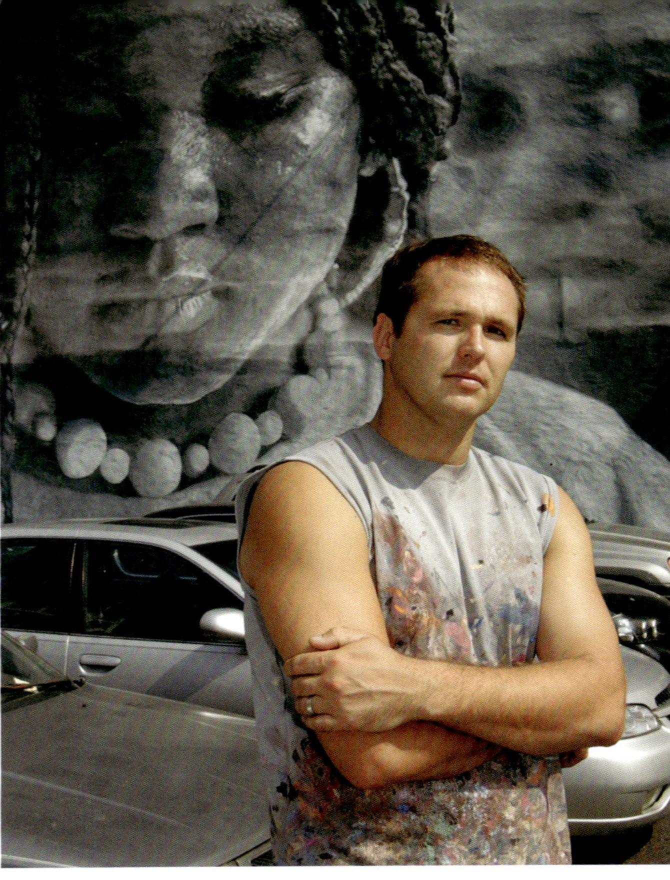

Every semester, Don Gensler and Mural Arts Program Director Jane Golden lead a class of nonart majors at the University of Pennsylvania through the demanding process of planning and painting a community mural. Although he generally has to put the finishing touches on the wall all by himself when students have completed the course and left for the holidays, the UPenn mural is only one of several that Gensler, unquestionably among the most innovative muralists working today, will be painting during those months.

Gensler's art experience is as eclectic as his painting skills. After attending Skidmore College, he had a broad variety of art-related jobs and residencies that no doubt developed his confidence in working with all sorts of people and led him to mural painting. He chose to earn his MFA at the University of Pennsylvania, "largely because I really wanted to work with Jane at MAP."

"I don't have any steadfast rules," he says. "The only parameter is that I need to spend some time with the mural stakeholders." Although Gensler uses high-tech tools from video to computer composition, it is his ability to see beyond the obvious, his willingness to recontextualize and engage conceptually, that makes his murals stand out. In 2004, he painted *Moving Toward Your Dreams* on the Eagles' stadium, Lincoln Financial Field. At 856 feet long, it's the third largest mural in the world. "My claim to fame," he jokes.

Gensler characterizes murals as "an installation within the city fabric," frequently incorporating images of real people, usually individuals directly connected with the making of the mural. This practice is not uncommon, but Gensler goes beyond simple portraiture to treat human figures as fluid pictorial metaphors. In *Moving Toward Your Dreams,* an eight-month project, the playful figure of a running child, one of the 250 kids who were involved in the project, is a repeated modular unit. Bright colored silhouettes of the boy are layered Doppler-like to suggest speed and complement images executed in naturalistic detail. The boy passes other children and finally leaps into the clouds and the future.

Another favorite ploy is to represent faces or figures in different scales of pixilation. "I see things as being filtered through different processes, whether it's my own hand or the camera or computers. I allow the design to change and evolve organically over time," he explains. "Proximity and resolution plays into my ideas: infinite pattern and repetition of, for example, the dots on a kid's jersey." Some images are simplified into large tonal squares. Others are composed of smaller or almost invisible squares. Does the contrast suggest degrees of visibility—spatial distance—or of understanding—psychic distance? Or perhaps it has to do with time and memory.

Gensler prepares through "immersion" in the topic or locale. He obsessively documents communities in video and still photographs. "Ideas come just from being there [in the neighborhood], being with the people. I allow myself to be consumed by the process."

Truancy was the subject of the horizontal *Symbols of Change* (21st and Market Streets, 2005; see title page), one of the city's most visible murals. Truancy hurts everyone. Direct participants in the mural included the Department of Human Services, police social workers, a school for truant kids run by Catholic Services, the School District of Philadelphia, parents, teachers, judges from Family Court, and, of course, truant kids, who are often sentenced to participate in after-school programs, including MAP. Gensler sat in on an unusual series of meetings, sometimes bringing together people who wouldn't ordinarily share a common goal. "We had a roundtable discussion with kids and social workers and then we brought in some judges. These are the same judges that may have sentenced the kids to boot camp or other things. It was an almost cathartic process in some ways—a great discussion for me to hear," he says

He decided to include a few kids from the group in his design and to ask all the kids to participate in "a visual conversation." Each one created a symbol "of where they are or of a positive direction they wanted to go." He wound up with one hundred pictogram-like symbols carved into Styrofoam.

Opposite

"Ideas come just from being there . . . being with the people. I allow myself to be consumed by the process," says Don Gensler, seen here in front of his antitruancy-themed mural, *Symbols of Change,* at 21st and Market Streets. This project was the culmination of eight months of work with judges, truancy officers, parents, and more than 250 ArtWORKS! participants.

Below

A detail from *Moving Toward Your Dreams,* 700 Pattison Avenue, by Don Gensler. Made possible by the Eagles Youth Partnership.

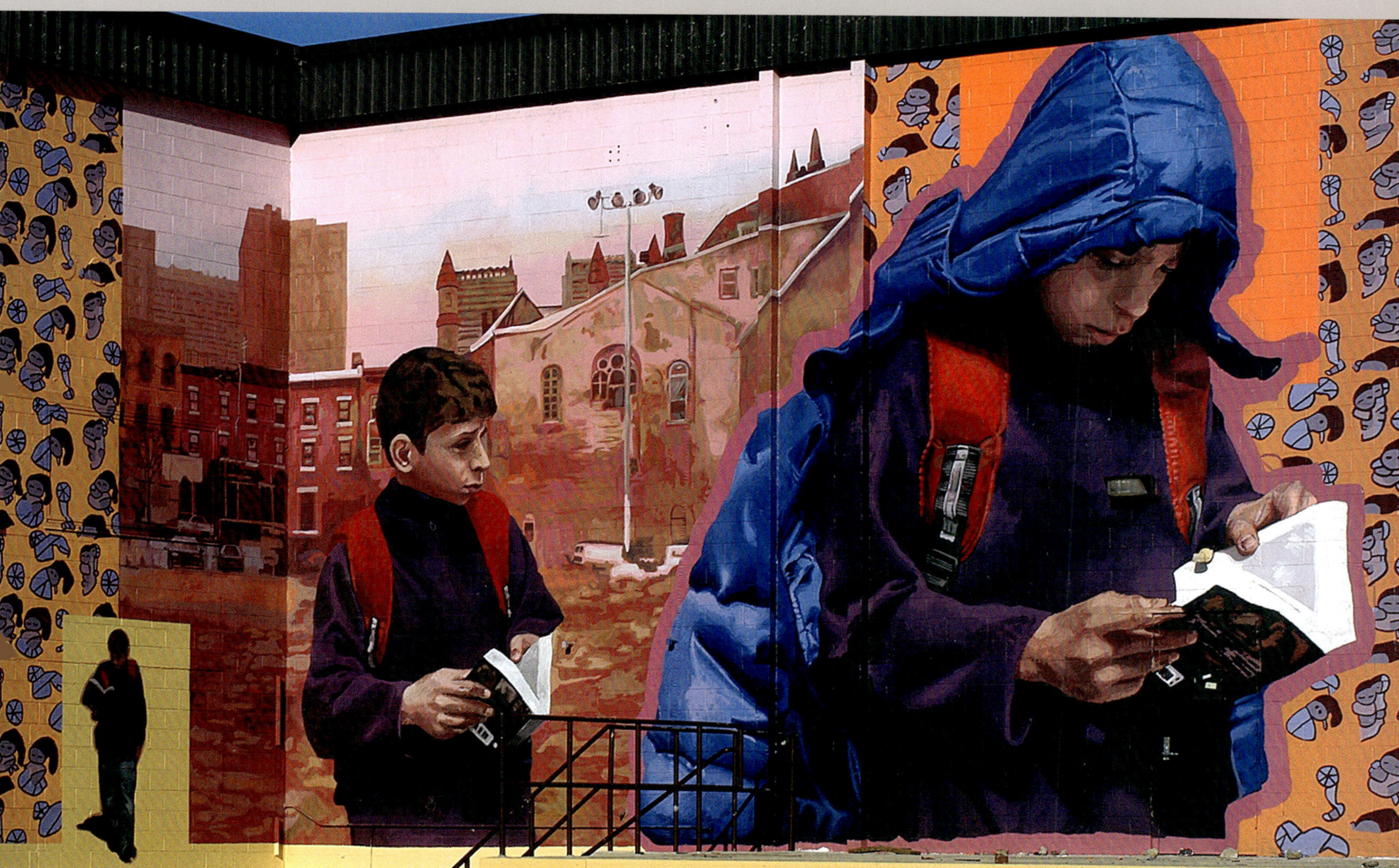

Reflecting the subject, the completed painting is serious. The primary images are enormous photograph-based portrait heads executed in somber tones of gray and black. The symbols of hope, painted in warm earthy Titian red or pale ochre, seem to float on the surface of the painting as if on a translucent curtain. The students painted the design Gensler drew on parachute cloth. He added the symbols after the cloth was sealed to the wall. "Most of the faces are slightly blurred and only the central figure is coming into focus. I wanted to lure you in with a kind of photographic process. One of the students told me, 'I'm so glad that my face is on the wall because I have a lot to accomplish in life and I'm really excited about that.'"

Something about Gensler's attention to light and dark, the silhouetting of one shape against the other, and the subtle blending of one into the other, makes the viewer conscious of the marvelous gift of sight, of visual experience as pure sensation. It might remind those who know him that Gensler once was an abstract painter. This heightened awareness of an internal experience, of looking and of seeing, imperceptibly becomes a metaphor for all kinds of insight, psychological as well as physical, into the people and relationships in Gensler's murals.

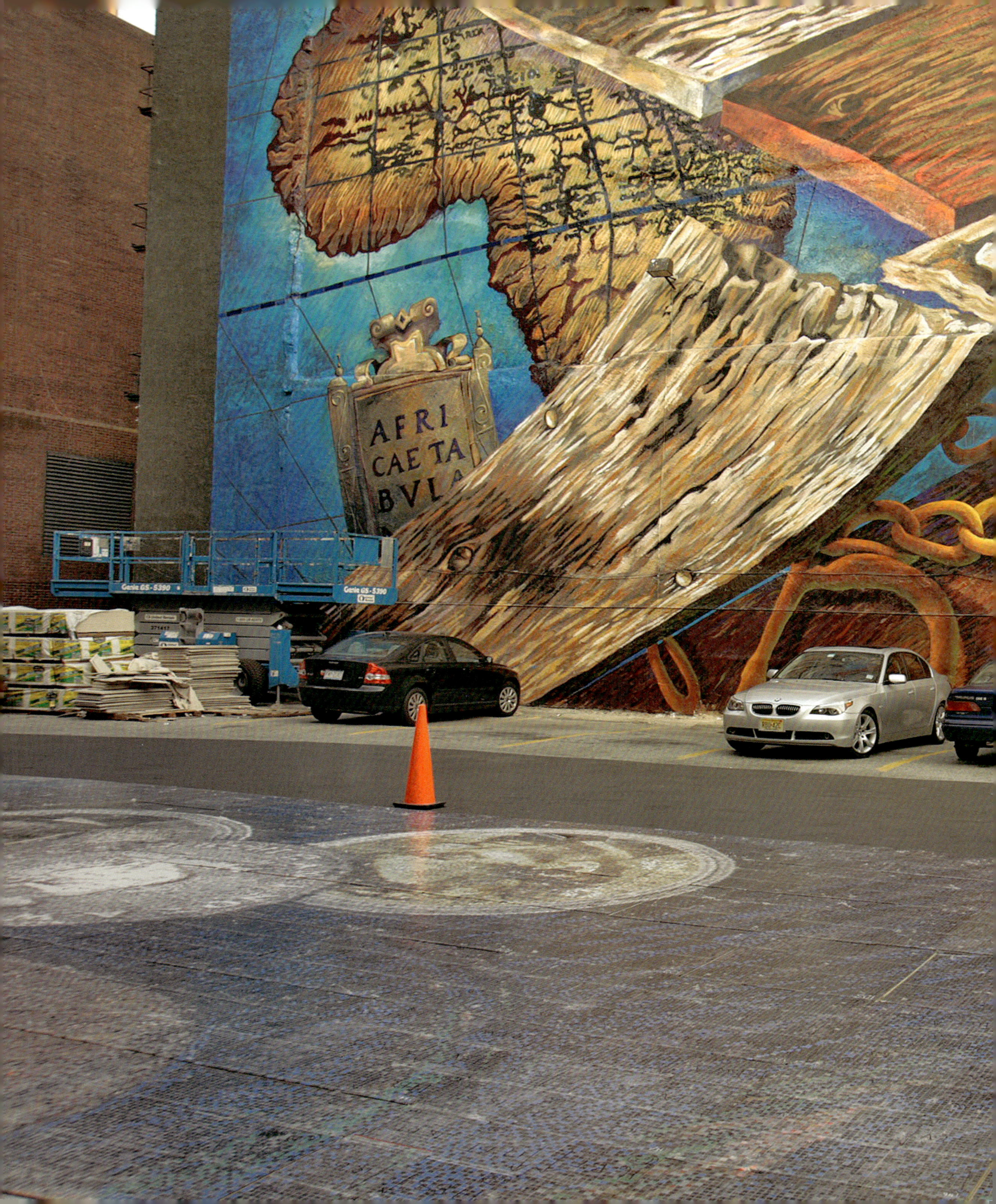
AFRI
CAE TA
BVLA

Chapter 5

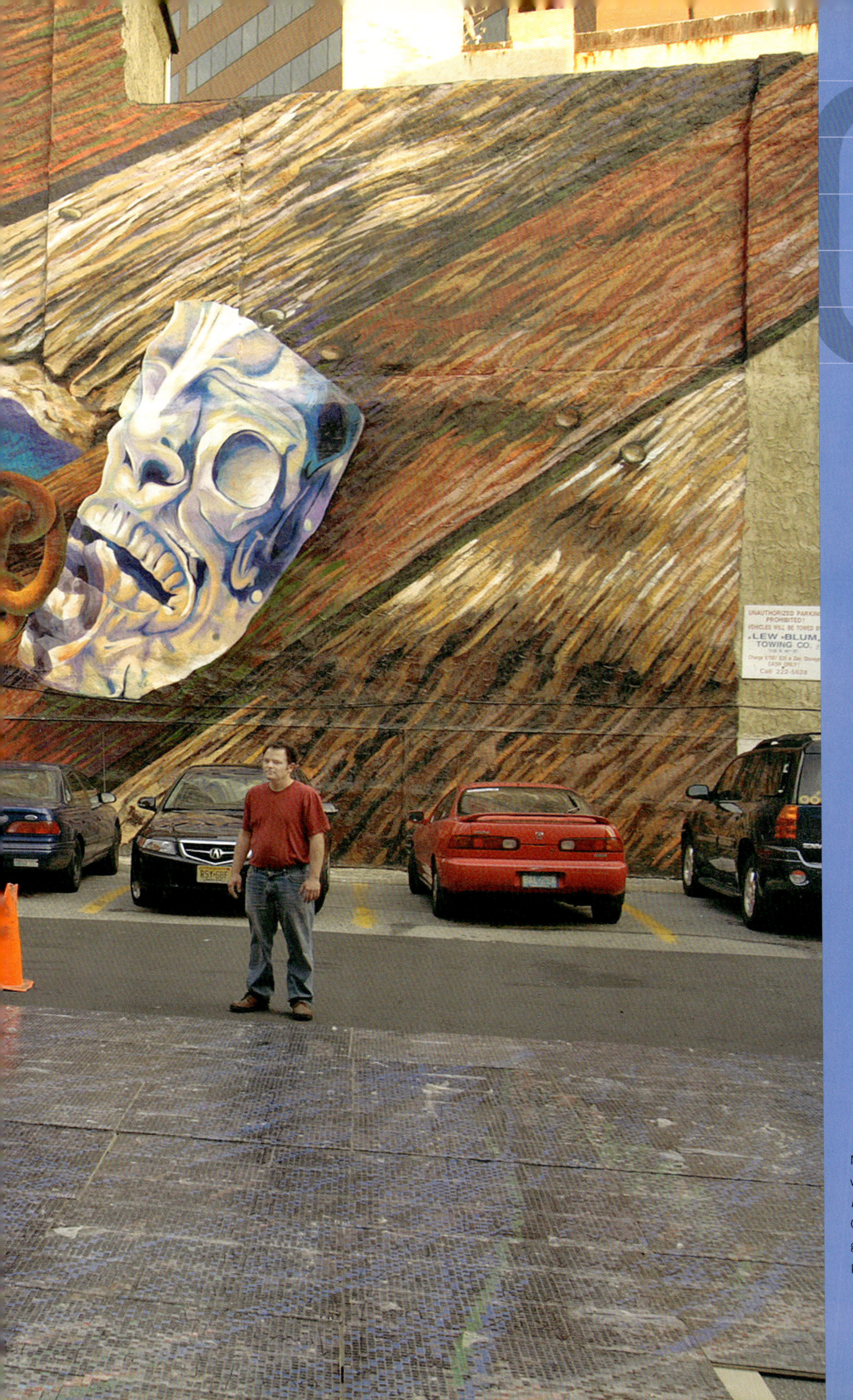

Muralist Josh Sarantitis reviews the tile work to be installed behind him at the *Lincoln Legacy* mural project, 707 Chestnut Street, the largest Venetian glass tile mural in the world and made possible by the Lincoln Financial Group.

Chapter 5 A Philadelphia Legacy

When Josh Sarantitis was asked to create a mural honoring the legacy of Abraham Lincoln, he knew a simple portrait of the man with the distinctive stovepipe hat and beard would not do. Lincoln means so much more than that: He led the nation through war, encouraged the development of the American West and, perhaps most important, signed the document that ended slavery in the United States. "That portrait's okay for the museums, but it's not really relevant to today's world," Sarantitis says. "It's rare to have the opportunity to do a piece that talks about the social state of the United States and [other] issues."

Like the best of the Mural Arts Program's projects, *Lincoln Legacy* combines art, community, and education. Through public meetings at the National Constitution Center, Sarantits was inspired to create a mural focused on slavery. It includes the struggles of those who endured slavery and that institution's lasting effects on the nation. With the help of area students and his *Tilepile* computer program (see Chapter 10 for more on *Tilepile*), Sarantitis translated his design into an eye-grabbing photo-based mosaic.

From a technical perspective, "It blows everything else away. It sets the standard for this type of work," Sarantitis said. Combining paint and Venetian glass mosaic, the luminous four-thousand-square-foot mural covers one side of a building (707 Chestnut Street) less than two blocks from the Liberty Bell. The central figure is not Lincoln but a contemporary African-American student in Philadelphia surrounded by images of slavery and abolition. The planks of a slave ship blend into the stripes of the American flag. An Abolitionist coin shows a woman in bondage and the words, "Am I not a woman and a sister." Shackles contrast with a figure dancing in celebration. Lincoln himself is seen only in penny profile—on a coin.

"It's an honor to do this type of work," Sarantitis says. Mosaics, he says, are four times as expensive as paint and are four times the amount of work. But funding from Lincoln Financial Group—and the help of those dedicated student workers—made this one possible. Children in Mural Arts programs and from five Philadelphia schools—Bache-Martin,

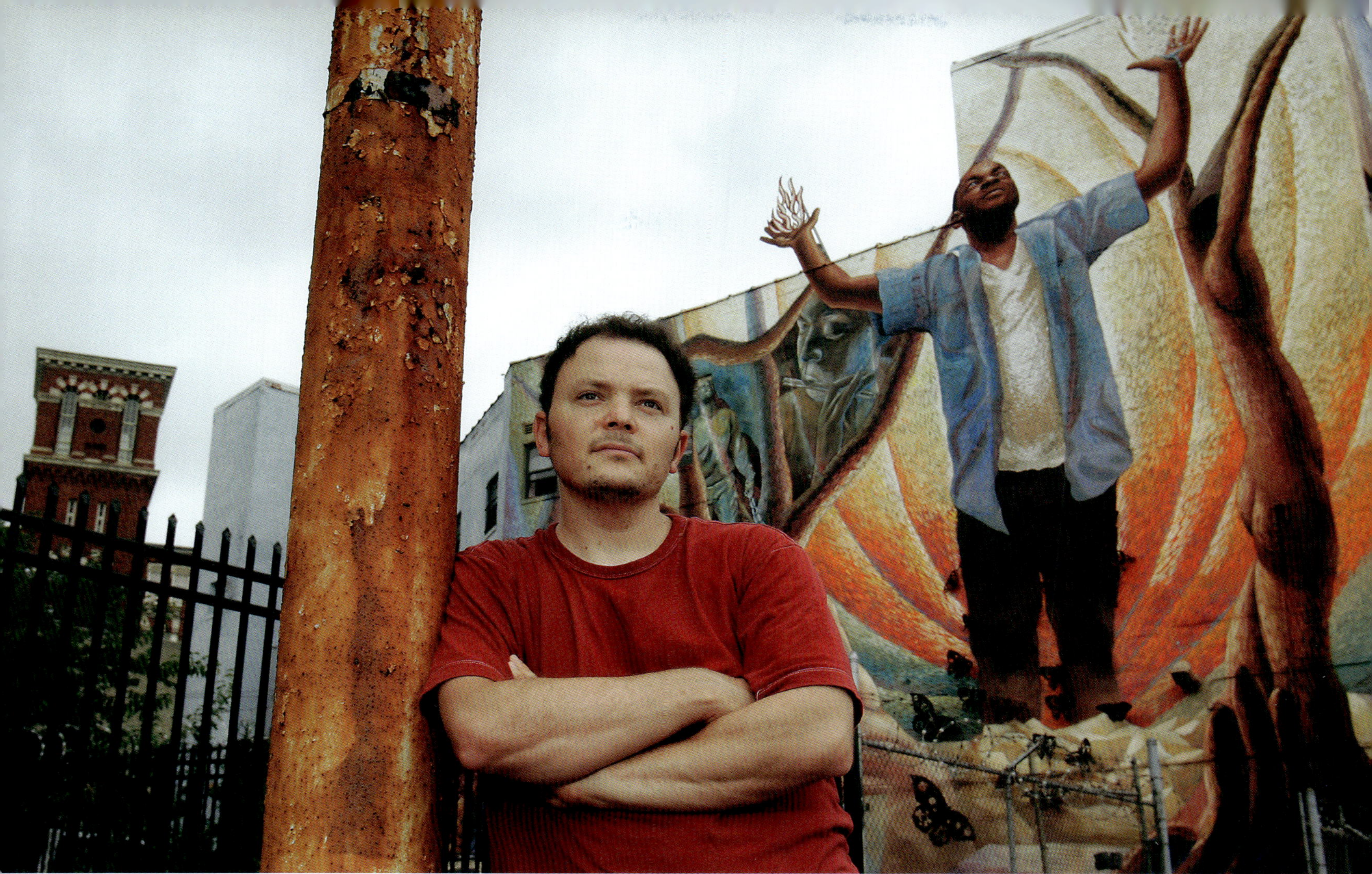

Josh Sarantitis incorporates metal sculpture, mosaic, plywood extensions, mural paint, and a wealth of symbolic imagery here at *Metamorphosis*, a mural painted with clients at the Ridge Avenue Shelter, 1360 Ridge Avenue.

George A. McCall, William M. Meredith, Albert M. Greenfield, and Philip Kearney—worked on the mural. With the help of his mosaic planning computer program, they turned one million tiny pieces of colored glass *(or smalti)* into the large panels that make up the finished work.

But the students used their heads as well as their hands. They studied a curriculum on Lincoln's life and accomplishments, sometimes translating that knowledge into smaller art projects. At Meredith School in Queen Village, the children decided they wanted to do paper mosaics of Lincoln as a human—and as someone from outer space. "They saw him as an alien, as someone who was bringing outsiders in," Principal Stuart Cooperstein says. "That's creativity and thinking and taking the research and working with it."

Cooperstein said his students loved the after-school program, noting, "They were thrilled to even be selected. The self esteem that goes with these kinds of things, I can't even talk about."

Says Mural Arts Director Jane Golden: "A project like *Lincoln* really taps into what we're trying to do: make beautiful art and have kids involved in every step."

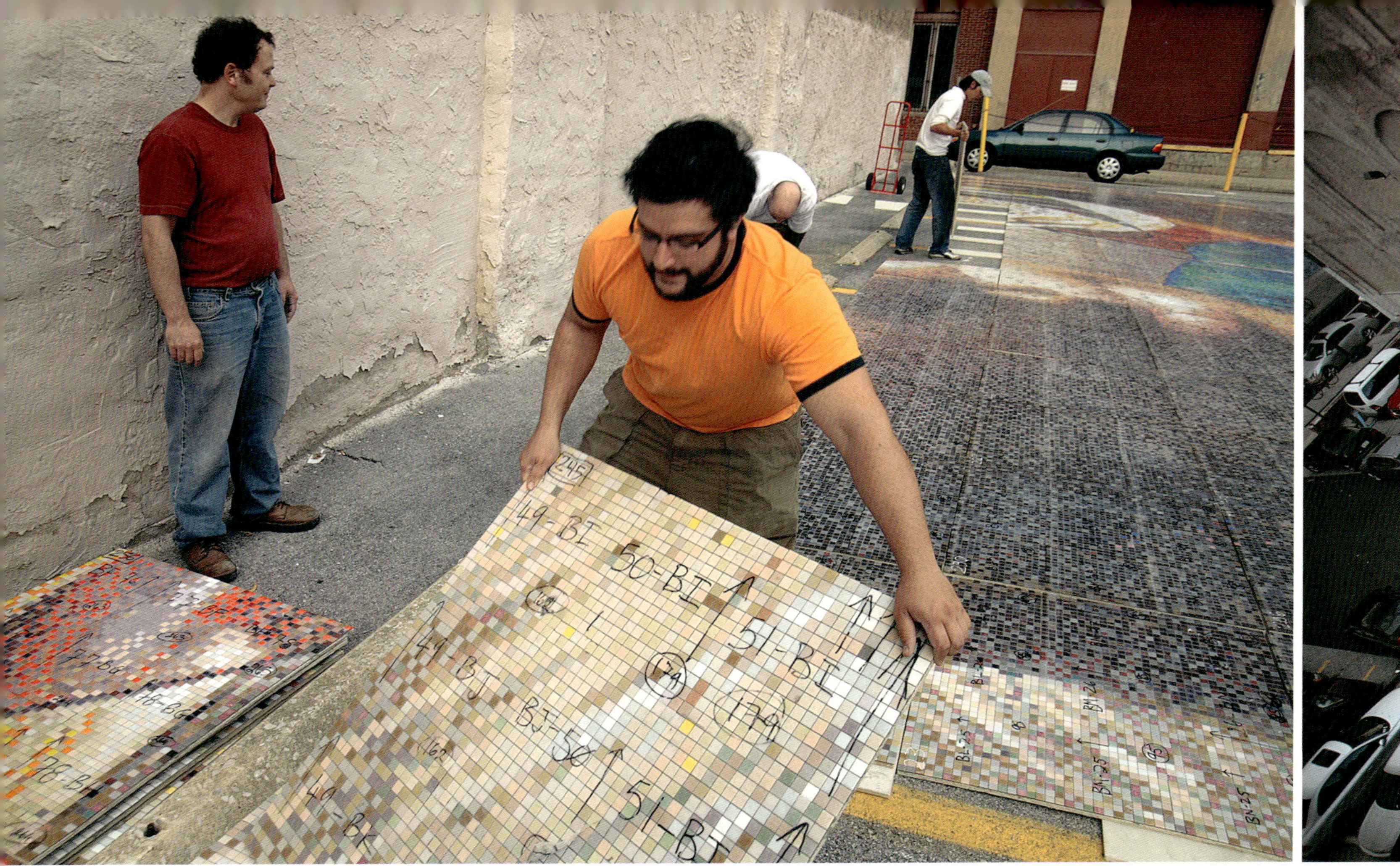

Fellow muralist Eric Okdeh assists Josh Sarantitis in laying out the tile for the *Lincoln Legacy* project, 707 Chestnut Street.

Sarantitis grew up with two seemingly competing interests: art and society. Unable to choose one, he majored in art at Oberlin College, where he concentrated on installation. After graduation, he took a break to travel with his then girlfriend, now wife, Julia Barton.

In 1989, Sarantitis and his wife took a mural of San Francisco tour led by Patricia Rose of Precita Eyes Mural Arts Center. It's possible to see eighty murals in the Mission district within the eight-block tour. Some were sponsored community murals, but most of these murals were the work of small groups or individuals. Sarantitis was transformed. "From that day forward," he says, "I knew murals were the perfect marriage between doing art and community organizing. I was interested in both.

"There's a history of community organizing in my family. My grandparents were Communists growing up in New York in the early part of the century." Sarantitis, who has visited many parts of the Soviet Union, has a different perspective: "I relate most to the idea that all the isms are the problem: communism, capitalism, church-based isms. Large scale institutions are a problem.

"I truly believe my work is political but it doesn't support any political agenda. My agenda is to show the importance of creativity for each of us, the importance for each of us to put our

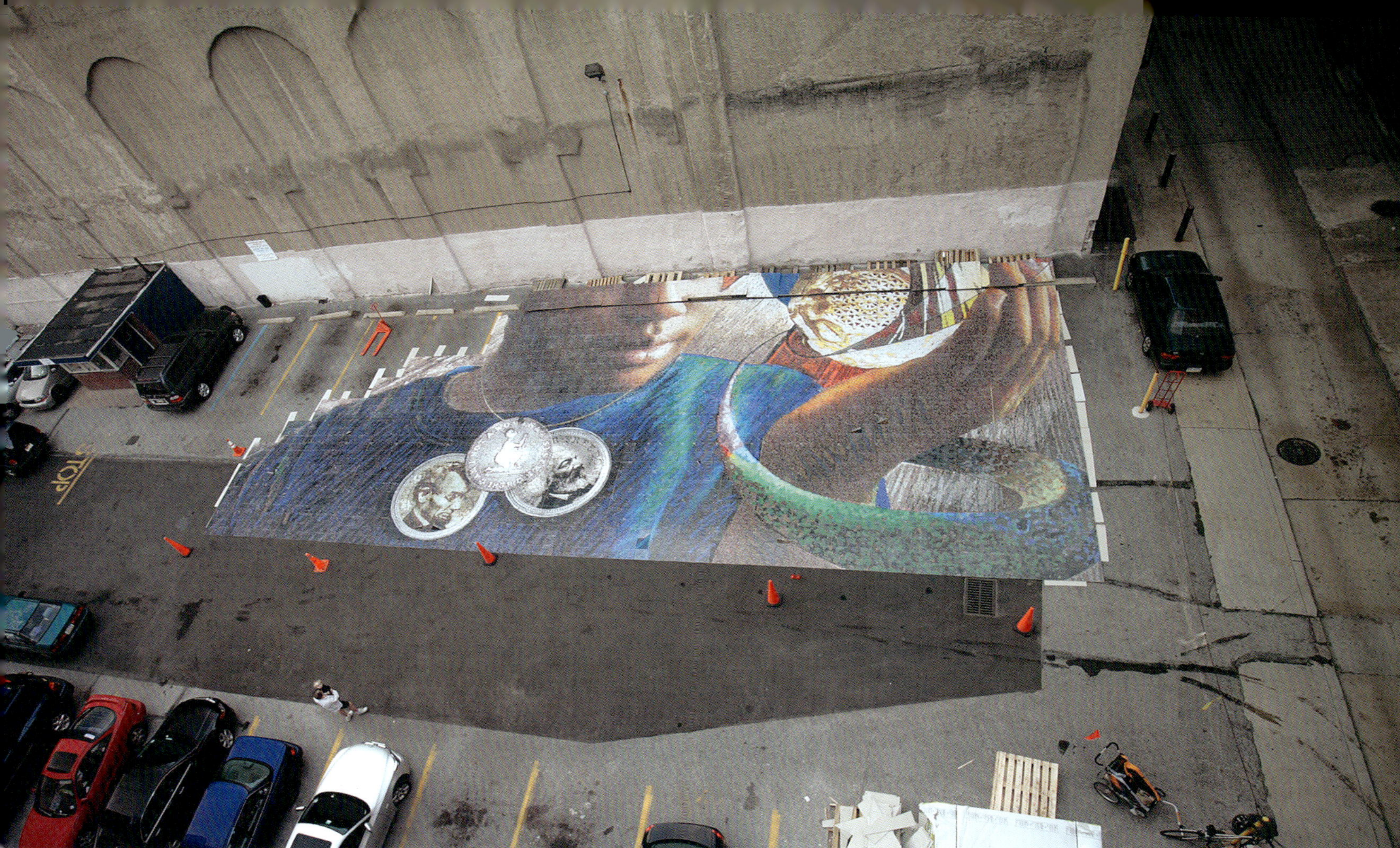

To get a clear view of the *Lincoln Legacy* tile design before application, artist Josh Sarantitis must raise himself in a lift to this bird's-eye vantage point.

mark on the world. In our society, most people don't have the tools or knowledge or belief that they can be creative. I mean it in the basic sense. People *can* use their hands again—without watching television or consuming in some other way.

"I want the murals to create a dialogue so people who pass by will think and question—even question their own beliefs—whether they pass by ten times or a hundred times—that they will think of a new idea. I'm into simple images and complex beliefs."

One of Josh's biggest projects both in scale, time, and interpersonal skills was the decoration of the exterior of 1360 Ridge Avenue, home to around one hundred men who participate in a "Clean and Sober" program. Over a seven-month period in 2001, Josh led workshops in photography, painting, collage, and mosaic for the men. The population and participation varied, but between fifty and seventy-five people contributed. "It's an alcohol and drug rehab program and the recidivism rate was very high," Sarantitis explains. "There were a lot of creative and talented people in there: artists, teachers, parents—people who had a lot to talk about but didn't have a place to talk, people who were willing to share their stories. The whole intention of all the workshops was to create an atmosphere for creativity and a venue for self-expression. The design brought out some intense personal story-telling."

The men chose personal subject matter for *Metamorphosis.* In planning the walls, Sarantitis used photographs taken by some of them. Sarantitis says the bright-colored narrative images have "many levels of meaning." A man lying in a fetal position seems to undergo a metamorphosis, partly suggested by flocks of welded steel butterflies attached to the wall. The three-dimensional butterflies were made by men at the shelter under the supervision of an instructor. Dark episodes in a person's life are illustrated in the shadowy monochromatic spaces between the limbs of trees in the mural. The butterflies, symbols of happiness to some people and of illusions or dreams to others, are guided by a giant pair of hands which represent the caring staff at the Ridge Avenue Shelter. Large and small, they cluster around the forty-foot-tall figure of a man who stands taller than the open offering hands.

This "self-realized individual" lifts up his own hands to the sky. In the right one, he holds fire and, in the left, water. Sarantitis constructed the flames and the rain clouds as mural extensions that rise above the roofline of the three-story building. These give the huge figure an overwhelming presence, although his posture is supplicant, prayerful—much like the orans figures from the Roman catacombs and in Coptic Egyptian and Jewish art. Two participants collaborated on a poem describing the narrative wrap-around design and this poem is executed in a mosaic panel. The public dedication of *Metamorphosis,* which was restored in 2005, is still remembered as exceptionally moving because of the testimony of the men who worked on the project.

"There's a lot of blood and sweat in a project like that. Some of the best artists I worked with [there] stole from me," Sarantitis says candidly. He knows it's naïve to believe that murals can instantly transform the lives of men who have struggled with drugs and alcohol for many years. "They would steal from their own mother. And they probably have in most cases. They're at Ridge for a reason—it's the end of the line; either that or a crack house. As long as what they are stealing is not going to derail the project, you go on. It's not so much ignoring it as trying to move forward. 'I'm not going to give you a lecture on morals,'" Sarantitis says, "'It's not my place.'

"That was the most difficult project I've done, [dealing with] the most raw or basic elements of human existence. I was there as a white guy. Most of them are black. I was there to earn trust and trust is a very expensive commodity. I think I learned as much as they learned."

Says Golden, "None of our muralists work harder than Josh."

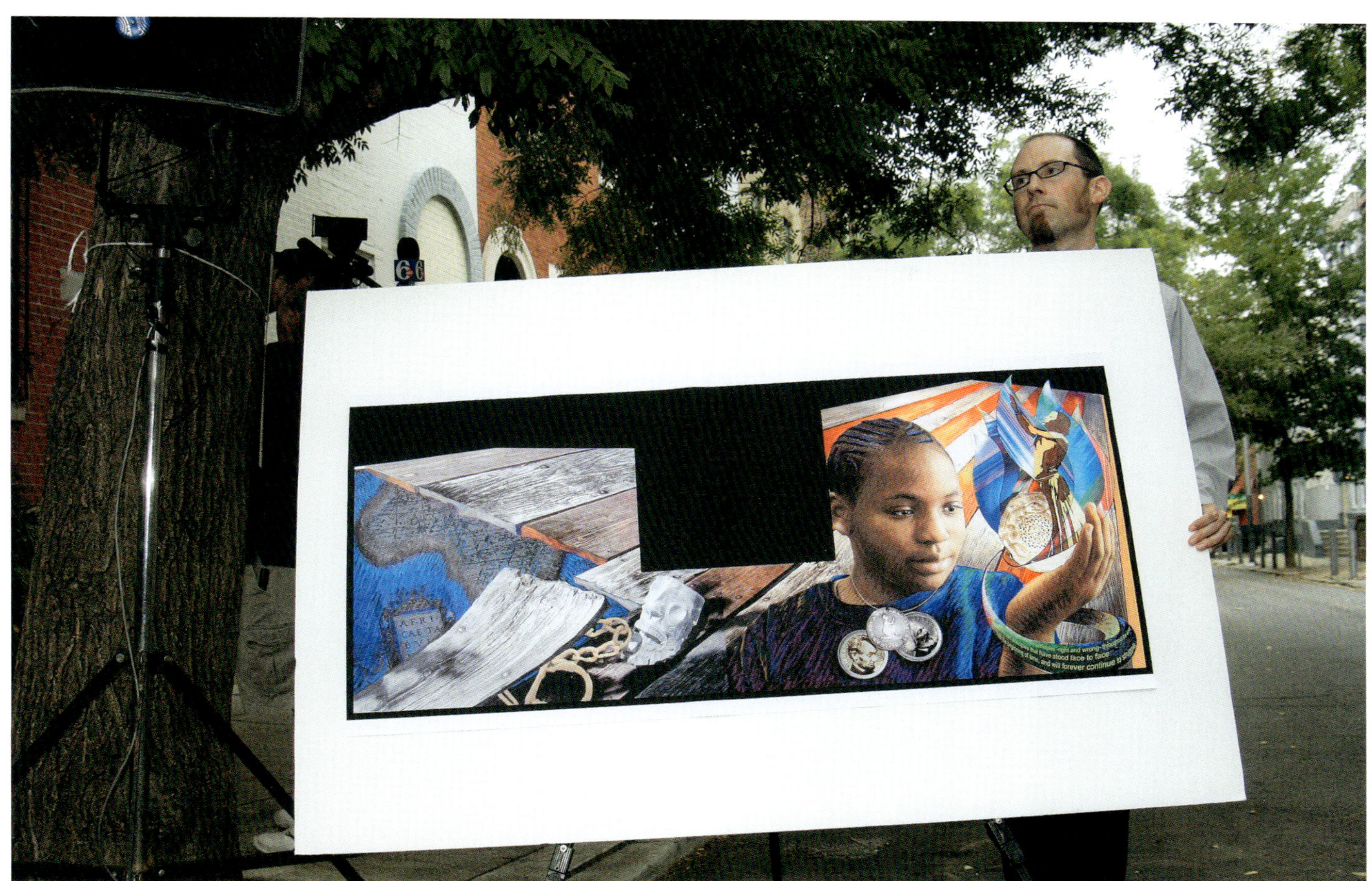

At a press conference, Tim Clair, MAP Director of Operations, holds the design for the *Lincoln Legacy* mural project, an innovative multimedia mural interweaving paint and Venetian glass mosaic.

Artist Profile

Gabriele Tiberino

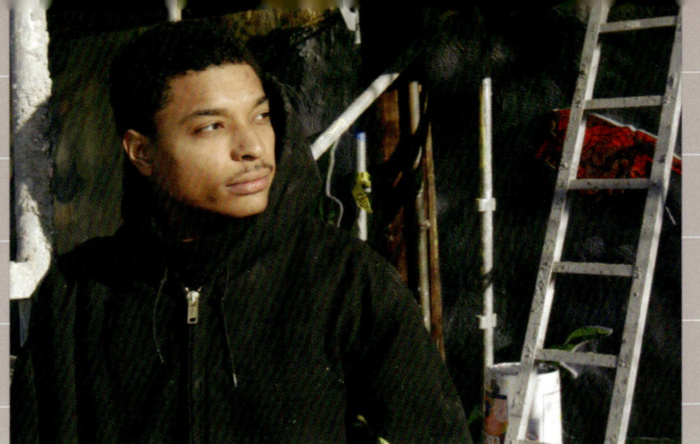

At sixteen, Gabriele Tiberino, scion of one of Philadelphia's best-known art families, was probably the youngest person in Philadelphia to be lead artist on a mural. By that ripe age, Tiberino had already spent half his life as a pro. At the age of eight, he had his first show in a South Street gallery. "The people from Channel 6 came in and put the camera on me," he remembers. "That was the only show where I sold out everything."

Tiberino can't recall when he began drawing. "My father was an artist and when I was little I just thought I had two moms." Tiberino's recently deceased birth mother, Laura Allen White, known to many as "Samirah," ran Mocha Gallery in Germantown. One of her contributions to Tiberino's development as an artist was to frame his early work for exhibition. Like Samirah, Tiberino's father and his wife Ellen inspired Gabe through encouragement and example. Surrounded by art and artists as he was, he says, "I almost had no choice. I knew that was what I wanted to do."

Before they became well-known painters, Joseph and Ellen met in New York, although both grew up in Philadelphia. Tiberino's father, Joseph, attended the school that is now the University of the Arts. His second mother, Ellen Powell, was born soon after her parents arrived in Philly from sharecropper days in Virginia. Ellen was a precocious artist who won a coveted travel scholarship while attending the Pennsylvania Academy of the Fine Arts.

Ellen Powell Tiberino's work is admired for its linear drama and often depicts aspects of the lives of women. Her drawings are in the collection of the Philadelphia Museum of Art. She died in 1992, following a long battle with cancer. In 1999, Mayor Ed Rendell proclaimed the family home and adjacent buildings a museum in her honor. The museum (3817 Hamilton Street) possesses a large private collection and exhibits work by Ellen Tiberino, and others. It is both ambitious and unpretentious, embracing nine properties, several belonging to members of the Tiberino family, and an enclosed courtyard decorated with murals painted by Tiberino, his father, and his older brother. Two more siblings do not make art full time.

Many artists in the city, including muralist Parris Stancell, owe a debt to Ellen Tiberino, an unfailingly generous and insightful mentor. And many still gather for classes in the courtyard to paint or draw when the weather is fine. Gabriele Tiberino, who graduated just this year from the Pennsylvania Academy of the Fine Arts, has living quarters above the museum with his father and about six to eight other artists and musicians. While attending the Academy, he painted murals in the summers and looks forward to becoming a full-time muralist. "I've done four murals by myself so far," he says, "and worked on around twenty." He began at MAP when he volunteered to work with a visiting Cuban artist, Salvador Gonzalez, who was making the mosaic mural *Butterflies of the Caribbean* (163 S. Susquehanna Avenue). "I didn't get paid," Tiberino notes, "but when Jane came down to see the mural, she said, 'Wow! You're doing all this work; we'll have to put you on the payroll next summer.' And ever since then, I've been working for Mural Arts." Gonzalez returned to paint another mural the next summer and Tiberino was right there working with him.

Tiberino's first solo effort for MAP was *Welcome to K&A!*, which he painted at the age of seventeen. It was part of a larger project called "Murals in Motion," murals intended to be viewed by riders of public transit. "It's up on a rooftop, about 24 feet high and 150 feet long. You can't see the whole thing unless you're on the El train. It's a picture of children, different children that I knew. That was pretty cool."

But Tiberino's favorite mural is indoors, in the Support Center for Child Advocates (1900 Cherry Street), a nonprofit association that provides legal and social support services for children. The center's lawyers represent children free of charge in custody, abuse, and other situations. They want their offices to be a welcoming environment for children who may not have a home. Tiberino's mural wraps around the walls of a large playroom.

"Portraits are pretty much my specialty," Tiberino says. "I've been drawing portraits all my life." He does a lot of private commissions. The Center gave him some photographs of kids aged about five to twelve to put in his mural and he added a niece and nephew of his own, all playing in an autumnal outdoor setting. "Kids are playing, blowing bubbles, playing hide and seek. On one wall, they're playing instruments. One's playing a flute. One's playing a violin and one is singing." Tiberino, who posed for his parents and their friends when he was a kid, also got some of the kids running around the playroom to pose for him. "Kids always like me for some reason," he acknowledges with a laugh. He has yet to try teaching, though he is considering it.

David Siqueiros and Diego Rivera are Tiberino's favorite muralists. "Their work is really strong and different from most people. If they had anything to express, they just let it all out in

Opposite
Muralist Gabriele Tiberino.

Below
The Child Advocates' Mural, painted by Gabriele Tiberino in 2003 in the visiting room at the Support Center for Child Advocates, located at 1900 Cherry Street.

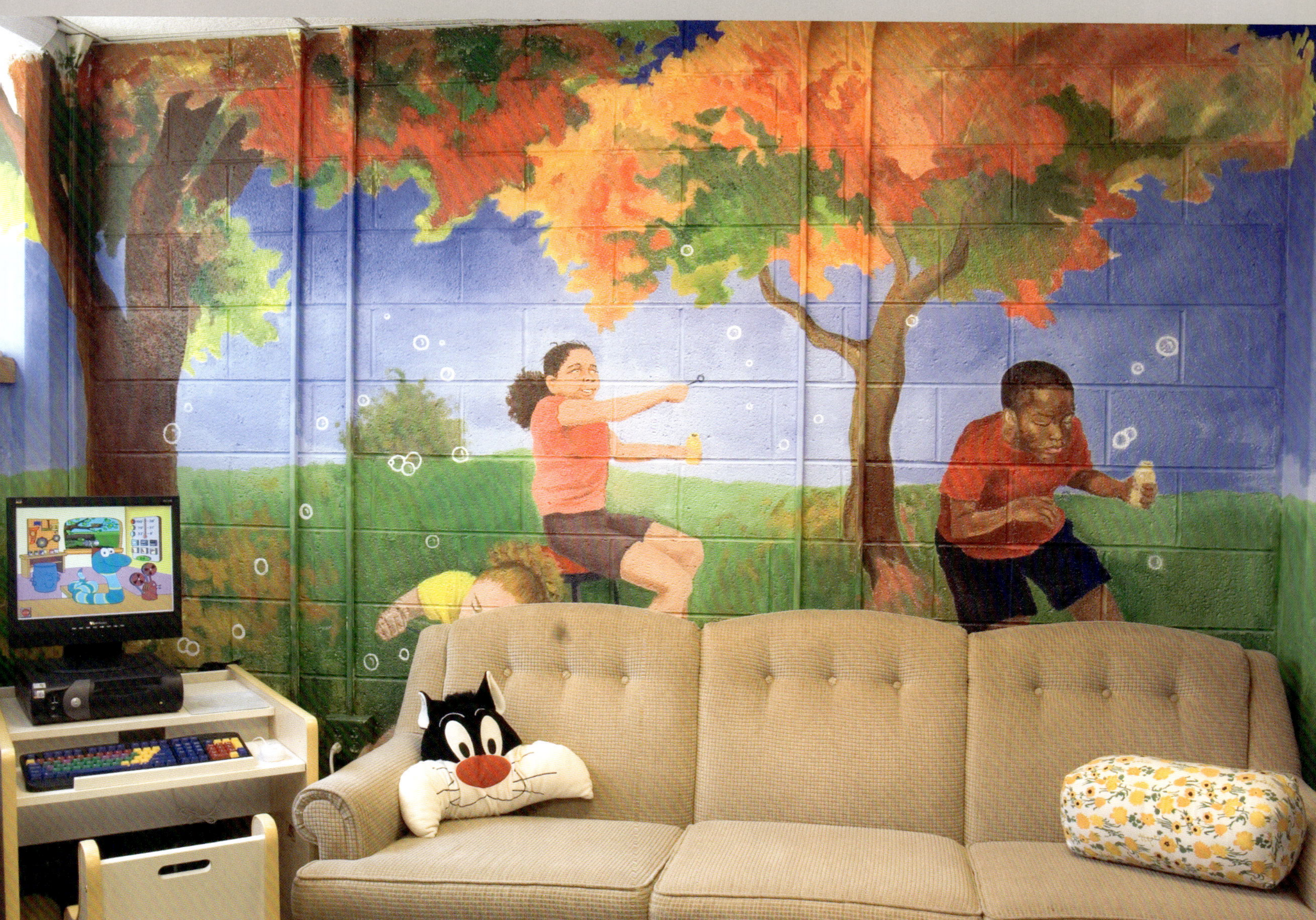

their murals. I don't like it when all the murals look like they were done by the same person." When asked to describe what he aims for in his own work, Tiberino thinks for a moment before he says, "honest . . . passionate . . . raw . . . alive."

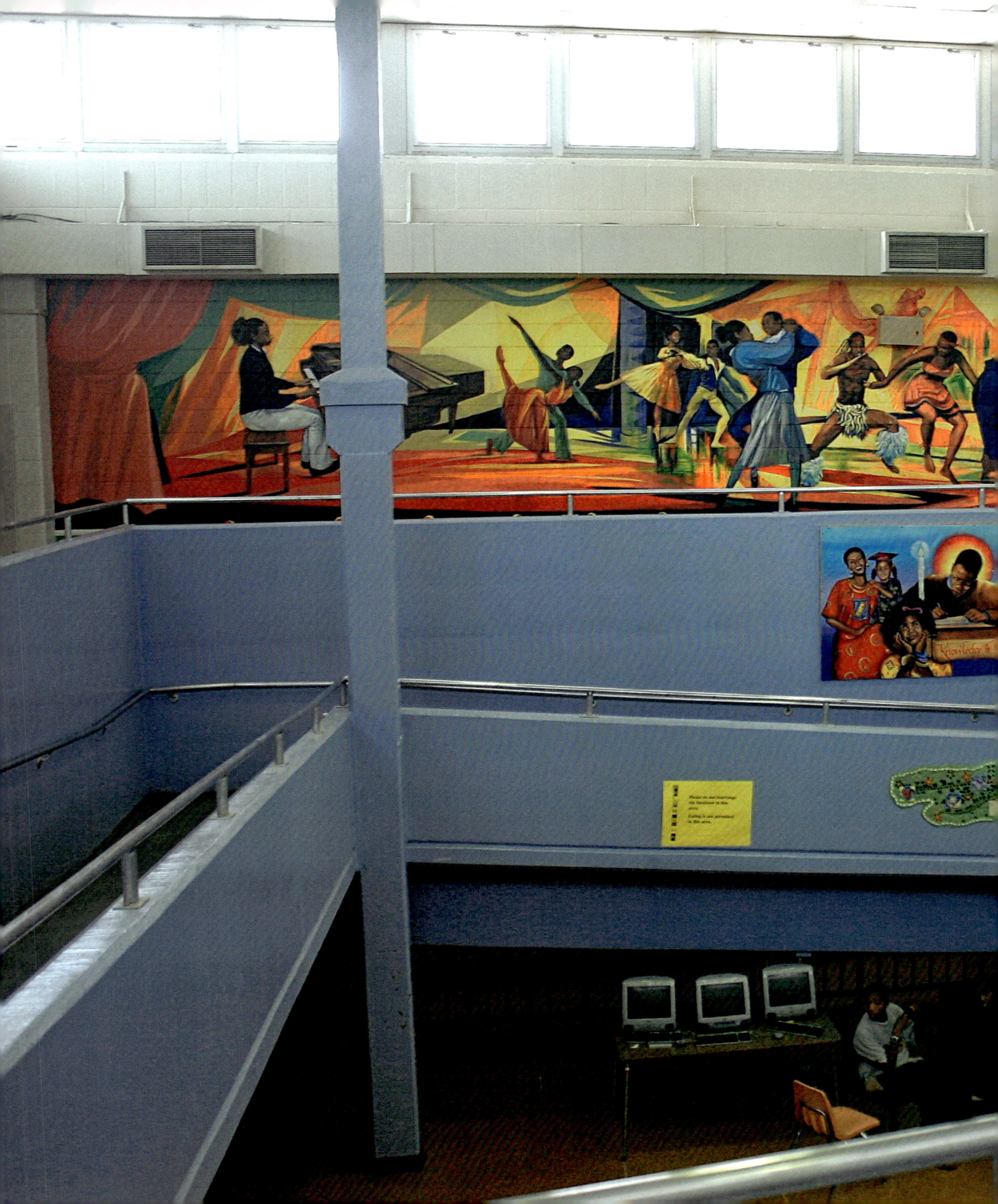

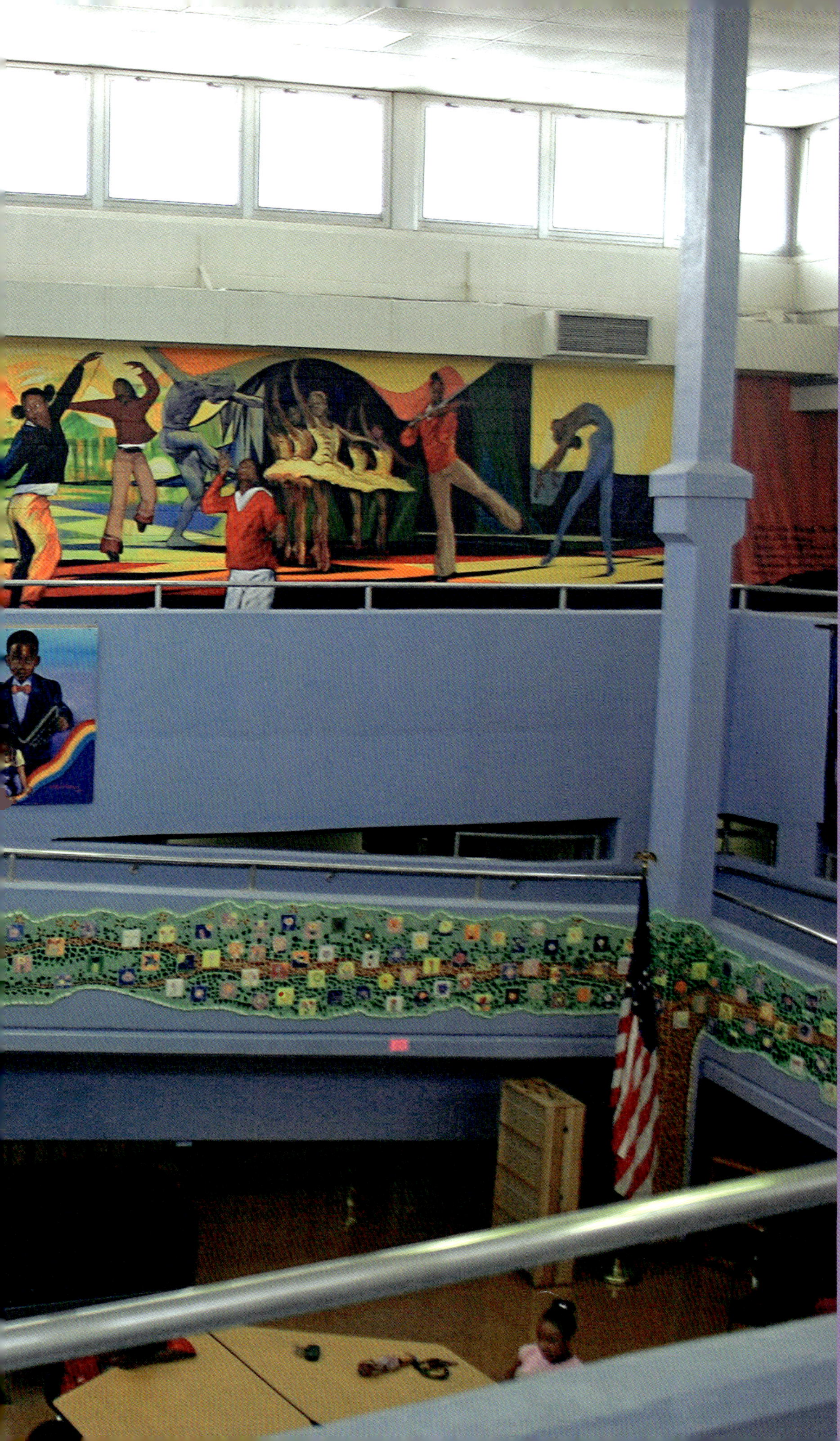

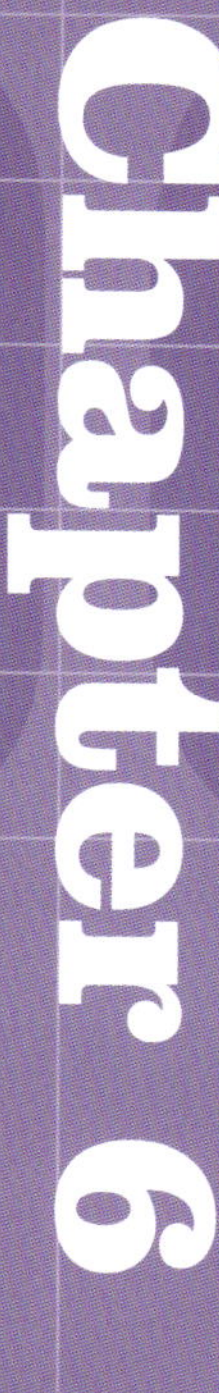

A History of Dance, a mural by Felix Osiemi at the Hill-Freedman Middle School, 6200 Crittenden Street.

Chapter 6

Environments for Learning

The students filling the hallways between classes at Hill-Freedman Middle School in Philadelphia's Mt. Airy neighborhood jostle each other as they rush by, book bags knocking against bodies and banisters. They are careless—no, carefree—not mindful of their bodies or of their pens and pencils, which sometimes leave stray marks on walls behind them like bread crumb trails.

Yet the wall with the mural remains unmarred. The students are careful not to brush against the paint. This is their gift to the school, they say, a part of their legacy.

"One of the seventh graders was walking by and said, "Dag, that's really nice. Who did that?' and I said, 'I did' and I was happy," says Jasmine Cherry, thirteen, who worked on the project. "It makes me feel good. I can look back some day and say, 'Wow. I did that.'"

A History of Dance—conceived by art teacher Valerie Van Pham and created by artist Felix Osiemi and a class of about two dozen students—stretches across the second floor corridor from one wing of the school to the other. Bright and bold, busy with reds and yellows and blues, the mural shows, among other things, a spinning ballerina, African dancers in native costume, modern youth grooving to unheard hip-hop music.

"It makes the students feel happy because it is happy. They respond to the color and the movement," says Osiemi, an artist who moved to Philadelphia from Nigeria in 1992. "This was a bare milk wall. Now it speaks to them. It is alive."

In 2005, the Philadelphia School District and the Mural Arts Program began a five-year collaboration that will create or restore one hundred murals in one hundred schools. Individual schools compete for the chance to get a mural, submitting ideas for themes and photos of available walls. In 2005, about fifty-five schools submitted applications and twenty were chosen.

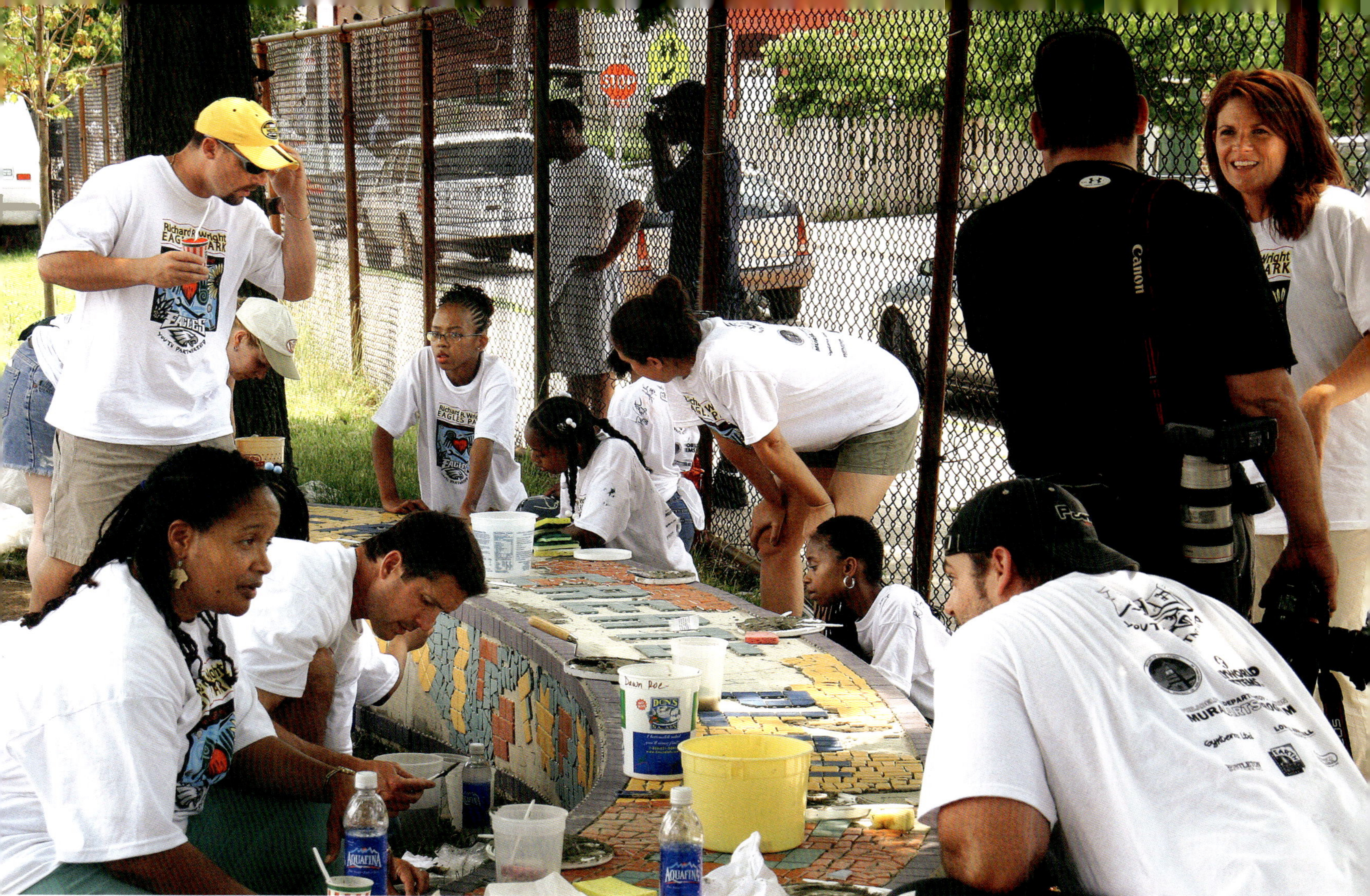

Students, Philadelphia Eagles players and administrators, and community activists enjoy a little water ice and help create a mosaic tile bench at Richard R. Wright Elementary—the public art revitalization of the entire school, inside and out, was sponsored by the Eagles Youth Partnership and the Philadelphia School District.

The program isn't cheap—costing the Philadelphia School District $355,000 each year—and it isn't easy—completing twenty murals a year with student input is an ambitious undertaking.

But outside funds from organizations like the Eagles Youth Partnership, the Neighborhood Transformation Initiative, and Philadelphia Green are a big help. The McKinley School project, a Campus Parks Initiative, was the first school to be entirely revitalized and the project that inspired Vallas to bring more murals to the system and to create the current partnership with the School District. McKinley was more than just an outside funded project—volunteers from the City, School District, Philadelphia Green, as well as the Philadelphia Eagles players, cheerleaders, and administrative staff all lent a hand to paint, construct, and restore the school. The finished works, which are inside and outside the school, include a U.S. map, the painted alphabet, even paintings of the teachers as children. McKinley has been transformed from "a prison into a paradise," Principal Deborah Carrera says.

More recently, the Eagles Youth Partnership worked at Richard Wright School in North Philadelphia. The summer of '05 project—*Do the Wright Thing*—included a new playground as well as painted and mosaic murals.

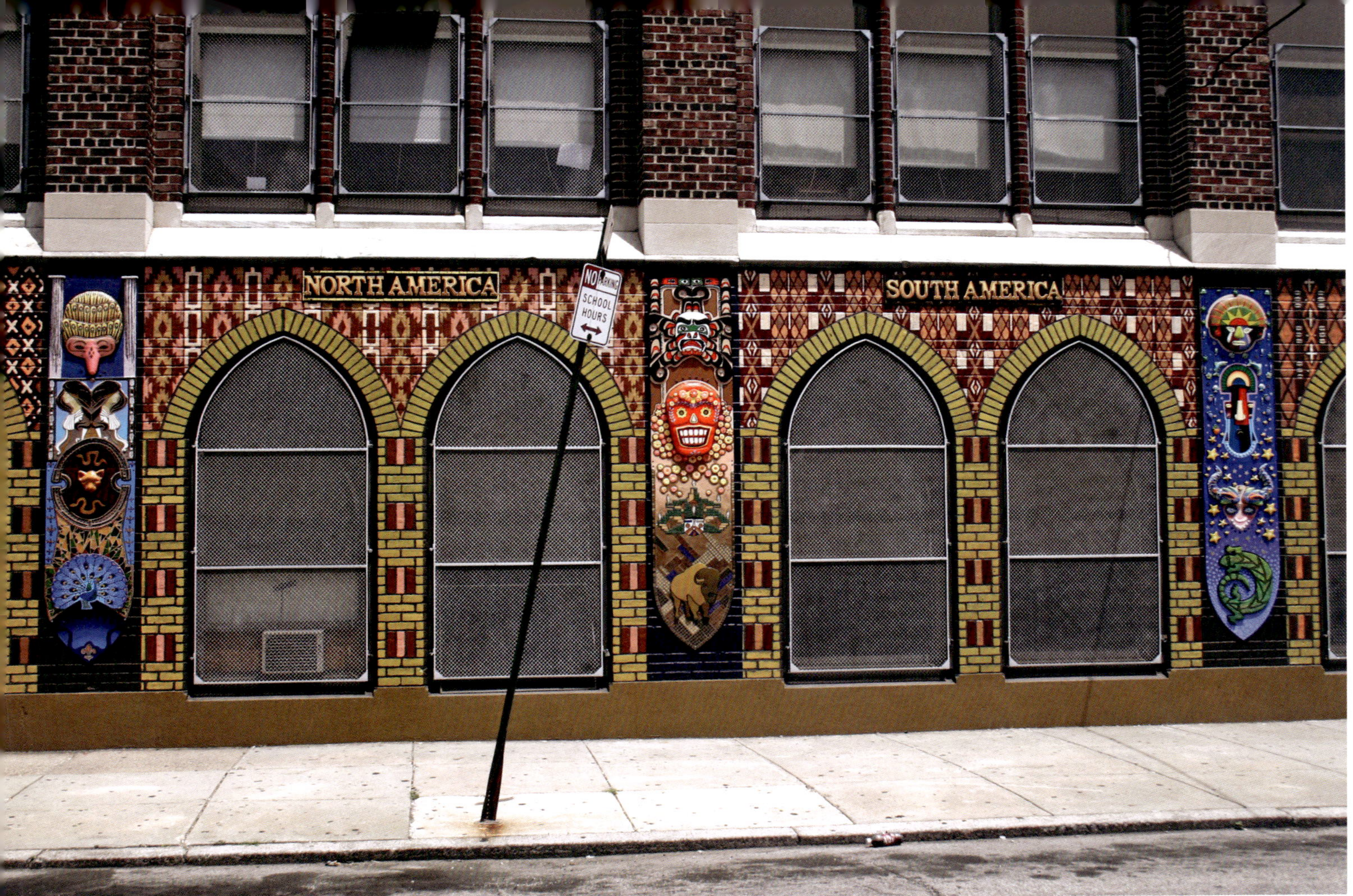

Three mosaic panels at Norris Barrett Middle School, created by Mike Smash and Jonny Buss along with students of the school, 16th and Wharton Streets.

"It makes the children understand there is a better world out there that they just can't see," Osiemi says. "Every soul appreciates beauty."

School officials agree that the benefits of the program far outweigh the expenses. Many of the city's school buildings are old, unattractive, "and pretty depressing places to be educated in," says school district CEO Paul Vallas. "Your school buildings should be your most majestic buildings. When you adorn them, it makes for a much more pleasant learning environment. Students feel differently. It affects their sense of self-worth and self-esteem."

"Equally beneficial is the mural-making process," says Dennis Creedon, the school district's administrator for creative and performing arts. For eight weeks, students work with a professional artist who serves as "coach, cheerleader and friend." They learn about the history of public art and the impact it can have on their lives. The actual "art part" is important—taking the sketchbooks home every night and recording the classes activities in diaries and in poetry form and painting the actual walls—but the intangible lessons are even more so.

Students learn responsibility as they follow the project through to the end. They experience the pride of ownership when the work is done and admired by all. They see, firsthand, that they can make a difference in their own lives and the lives of others.

"This teaches children they can be agents of change," Creedon says. "They don't have to be pawns in the game. They can move the pieces. They can have control of their lives."

And it gets students excited about coming to school. When the project was under way at Norris Barratt Middle School in South Philadelphia, the students "wanted to do anything to help with the murals. They'd run up to the artists or myself and beg, 'Please! We'll even help carry the buckets outside! Anything you need! Please!'" says Heather Messner, the teacher who oversaw the project. "They knew it was history and was going to be here for a long time and they wanted to be part of it. It was great to see such camaraderie among them and the enthusiasm from the entire school."

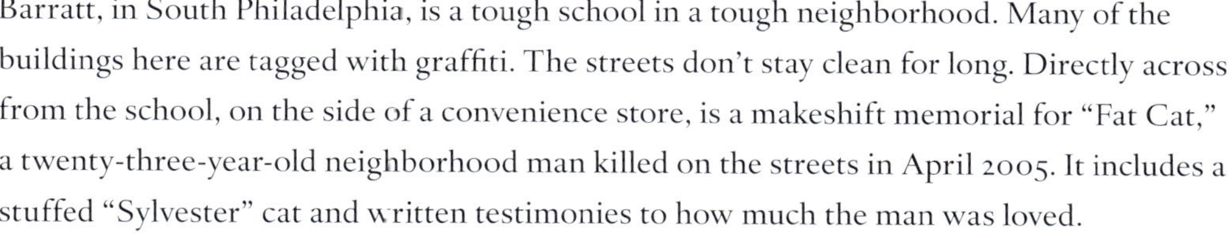

Barratt, in South Philadelphia, is a tough school in a tough neighborhood. Many of the buildings here are tagged with graffiti. The streets don't stay clean for long. Directly across from the school, on the side of a convenience store, is a makeshift memorial for "Fat Cat," a twenty-three-year-old neighborhood man killed on the streets in April 2005. It includes a stuffed "Sylvester" cat and written testimonies to how much the man was loved.

Asia, one of six continent-themed Venetian glass panels at Norris Barratt Middle School, designed along with the students of the school by Mike Smash and Jonny Buss, 16th and Wharton Streets.

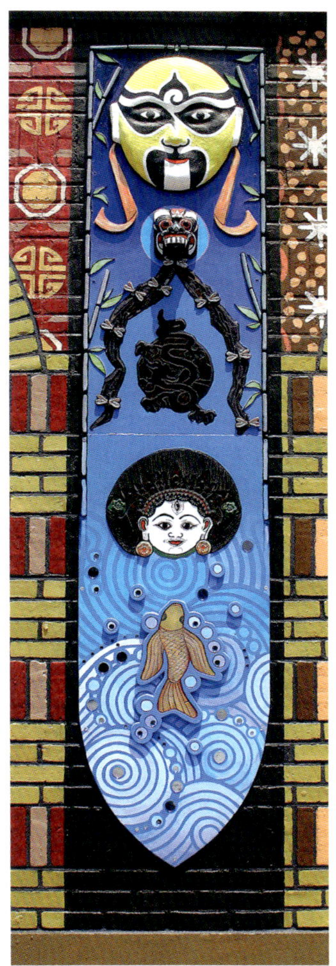

"He grew up here like these kids here," says store employee Mary Watson, gesturing to the students crowding the cash register with bags of chips and soda. "He went to school here like these kids."

The majority of Barratt's students are African American, but there are a growing number of Latino and Cambodian students. The school submitted the mural concept of *One World, Many Cultures,* a salute to its own diversity as well as recognition of other cultures. The underlying theme is "Knowledge is Power."

"It says we're accepting as a school environment and we tolerate and welcome differences and that's the hope we have for the world," Messner says.

Artists Mike Smash and Jonny Buss were assigned to work with the Barratt students. The students were enthralled by the pair: Both are informally trained. Buss is a former graffiti artist turned legit. Smash is a thirty-something who's a big kid inside, collecting *Star Wars* action figures, reading comic books, enjoying Japanese action movies. They'd show up covered in paint, with seemingly exotic tools and materials that allowed the kids to get messy. Says Messner, "They wanted Mike and Jonny to stay the whole year."

Smash wanted the students to have fun as well as learn. He wanted them to see that art can be an answer. "We try to communicate that once we're teaching, you could just be there for a nice memory or it could be a career, it's whatever you want it to be," he says. "But the point is people need to have art in their lives."

The first two weeks focused on general, introductory lessons: What does art give a community? What is the importance of public art? When it came to their specific project, because of the building's architecture, the group decided to create six panels, one for each of the continents—except Antarctica. It was left out, Messner says, "because nobody knew anybody or knew anybody who knew anybody who had been to Antarctica."

Then they dove right in. First the design and research time: What images—fruits, flora, fauna—would best represent each continent? What colors should be used? Which materials? "They got to see how art is a connection to different subjects and how it aids communication and bridges communication gaps. We talked about identity and how personal identity creates the community's identity," Messner says.

The hands-on portion came next. Because Smash and Buss use so many different materials, the students painted, poured molds, adhered pieces to the wall, talked about color choices and placement. "There were a lot of conversations going on," Smash says.

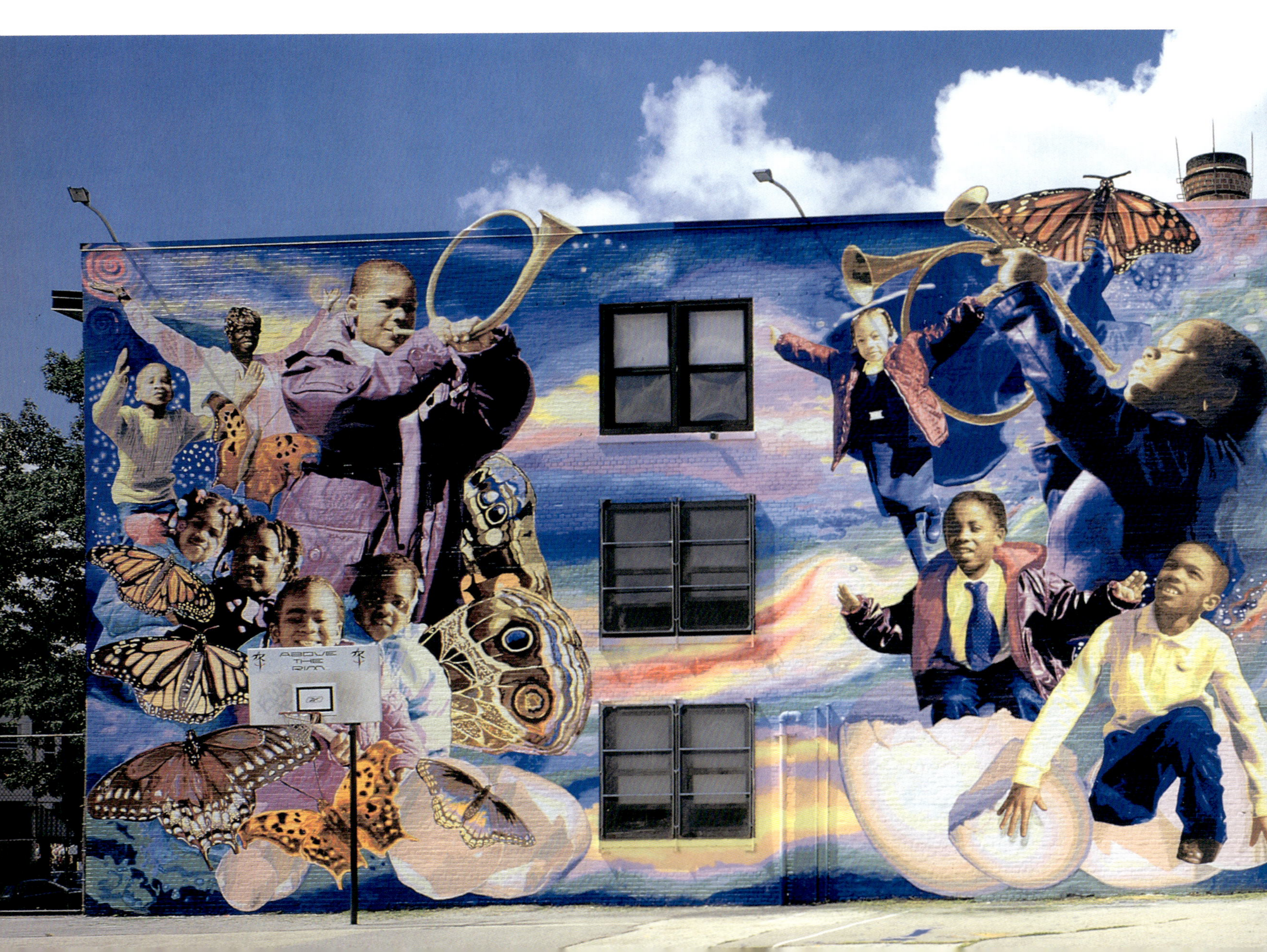

César Viveros's dramatic mural at the Gideon School, 2801 W. Glenwood Avenue.

There also was a lot of work to be done, and that didn't sit well with everyone. "Some kids didn't realize it was going to take a lot of time and thought. A few lost interest when they found it wasn't just painting outside," Messner says.

Messner says she finds something different to look at every time she looks at the wall. Neighbors who watched the mural's creation now watch over it.

But more stuck it out—and many others came to the art room regularly to be part of the project. One group of girls, the known divas of the school, settled down and got into research. At least two students showed real art talent. Even more students would go home and draw on their own time and show Messner their work the next morning. "Some of them were kids who normally acted up in art class who changed their behavior to be part of this," she says.

The six panels that comprise the completed work are eye-catching and exotic. They're composed of masks, carved wood, paint, Venetian glass, and tile. The symbols are both common —like Asia's dragon and bamboo—and rare—the same panel's Hindu temple. Europe has a group of *fleur-de-lis* designs, Africa has that continent's distinctive masks, North America has a buffalo.

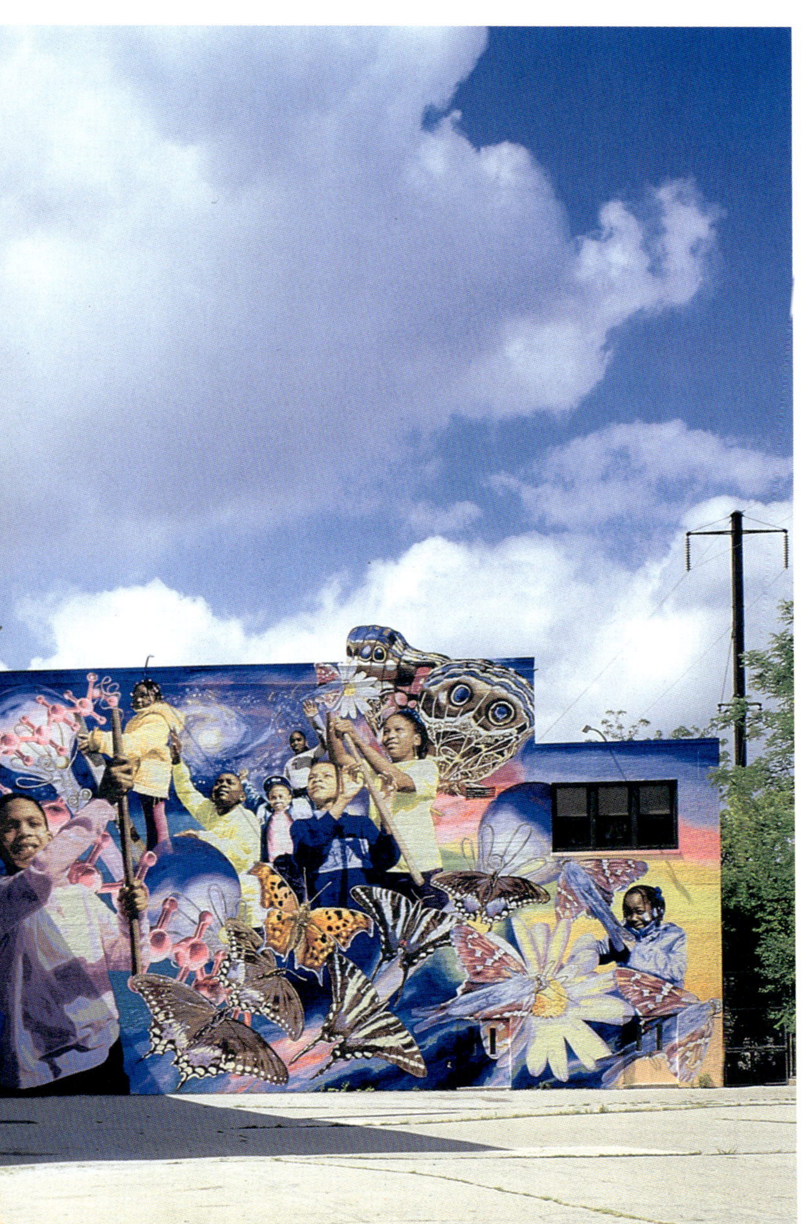

Messner says she finds something different to look at every time she looks at the wall. Neighbors who watched the mural's creation now watch over it. "We spread the word beforehand, to youth groups, the neighbors and churches, that we were trying to do something to beautify the neighborhood and spread tolerance," Messner says. "It's really brought the area together in a sense because nobody's disrespected it." Adds Watson: "They don't bother it because half the kids here were involved in it."

Other children have appointed themselves the mural's protectors. Deandre Stewart, twelve, helped paint the brick walls around the panels and he guards the finished work as a mother bear would her cubs. Anyone getting too close with a pen or marker has to deal with him.

"I'll be like, 'Hey, don't write on that. That's not respecting our school,'" Deandre says. "We made this so people can look at it and see how nice Barratt is."

When Smash and Buss were putting the finishing touches on the mural panels, they saw a woman watching them from across the street. She was upset. Smash asked Buss why he thought the woman was crying. Buss jokingly said it was because the mural was so beautiful.

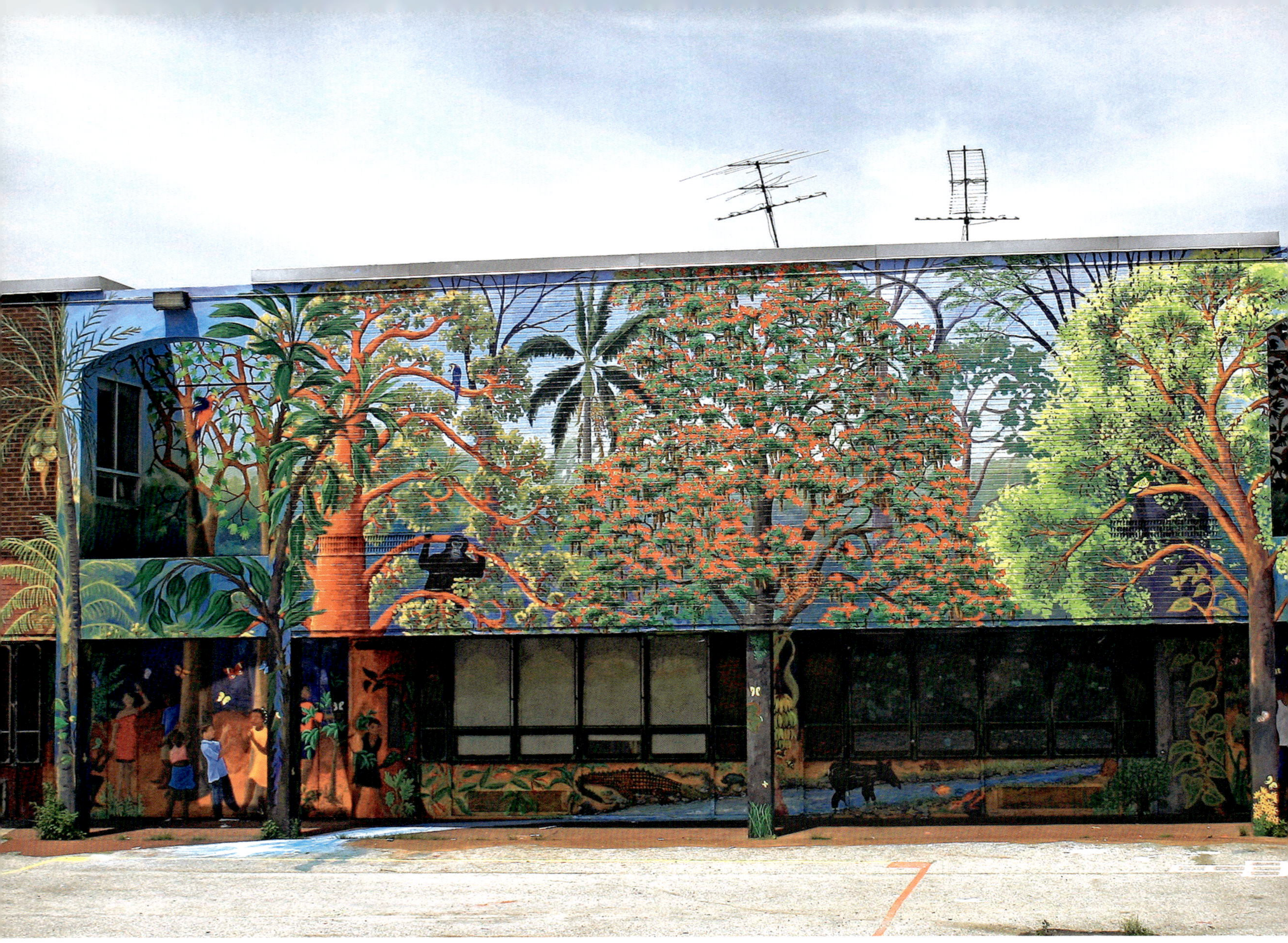

Ana Uribe takes the Potter-Thomas School's simple façade and transforms it into a tropical forest, 6th Street and Indiana Avenue.

He was right. Her tears, in this neighborhood where people are used to crying over loss, were for joy. Says Smash, "It was a really interesting thing. That was why she was really crying. Because she thought the mural was beautiful."

Of course, even if every wall in the city was graffiti-free and alive with color, the children would not be completely safe. During the creation of the Barratt mural, the mother of one of the boys involved in the project killed herself and his two younger siblings, ages ten and six. She left the older boy, age thirteen, alive so he could care for his grandmother.

The ten-year-old also had been a Barratt student. He was popular, always laughing, and with countless friends. He had loved art class, loved the mural, and loved watching his brother work on the panels. He was excited to join in when the group moved outside to paint the walls. He couldn't wait until spring to see the whole mural assembled.

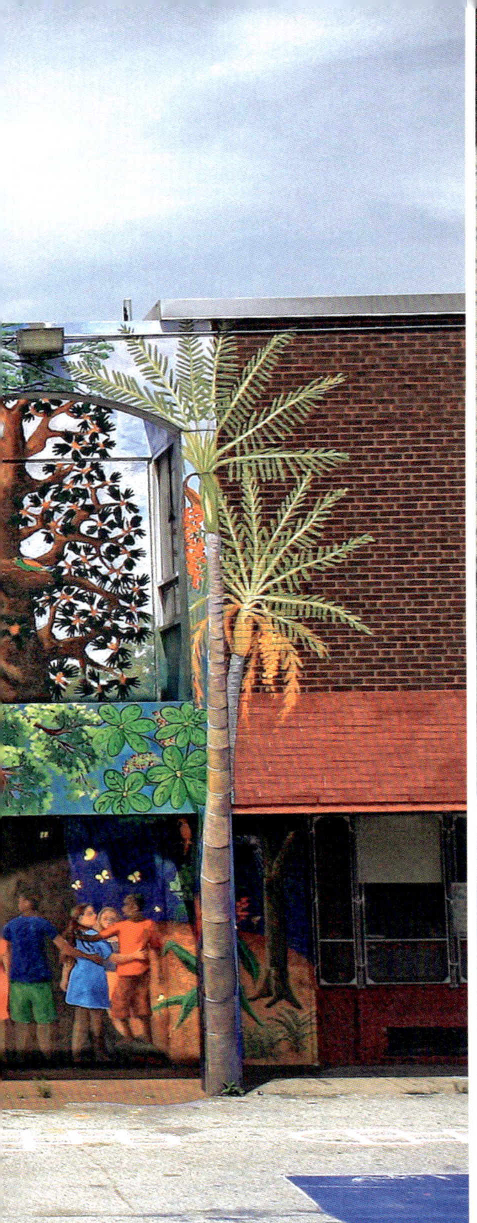

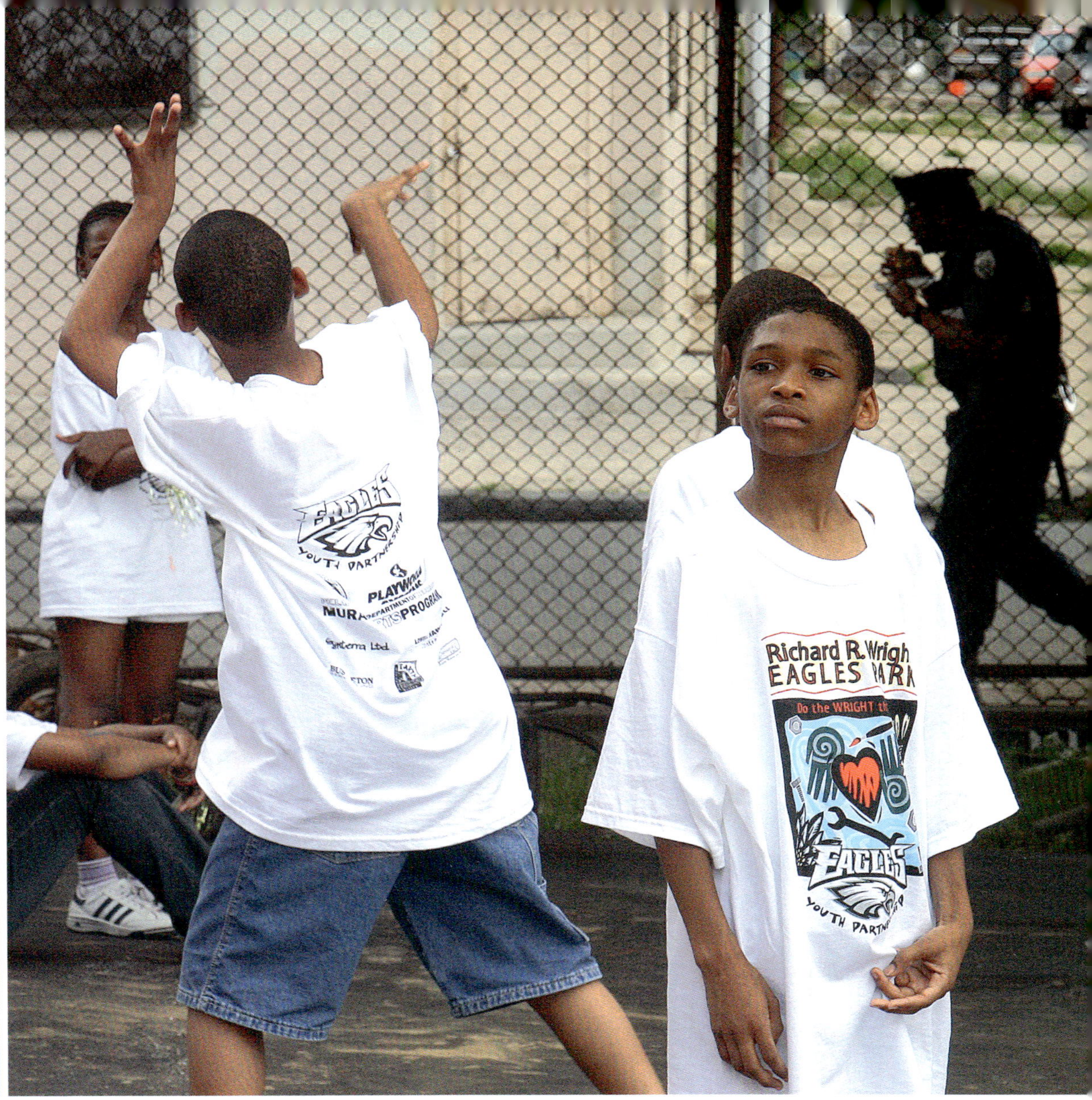

Students from Richard R. Wright Elementary, 28th and Dauphin Streets, taking a break from the June 8, 2005, paint day, sponsored by the Eagles Youth Partnership.

"It was hard. It devastated our whole community," Messner says of the tragedy. "We talked to the class and had grief counselors in and asked the kids what they wanted to do."

The students decided that they wanted to dedicate the panel representing Asia to their lost schoolmate. It was fitting, they said, as they had been working on that panel when the boy died and it symbolized his Vietnamese heritage.

At the mural dedication ceremony, the surviving brother was too upset to speak. But Messner told the crowd of students, parents, teachers, and community members that, just as the mural would last, so would the memory of the little boy.

"It just helped the kids and the whole Barratt family," she says, "knowing his spirit would be part of the school forever."

Artist Profile

Jennie Shanker

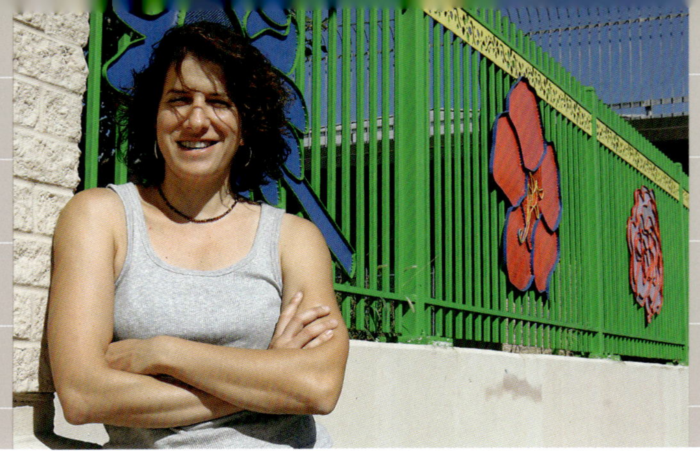

"In the two projects with MAP that I've done, I consider myself almost a choreographer," says sculptor Jennie Shanker "My hand is involved but not directly. It's more related to teaching than to my studio work and to impose my taste would be inappropriate."

Shanker, who has an MFA in sculpture from Yale University and usually works as an installation artist, teaches at the University of the Arts and Tyler School of Art at Temple University. She worked with high school students in the Mural Arts Program for the first time on the McKinley School project (summer 2004). The Mural Corps students were paid but they didn't necessarily have art experience. With the help of two assistants, Shanker taught the fifteen or sixteen students drawn from several schools design—and, to their surprise, welding. "It was a hot summer and I'm sure when those poor kids signed up, they didn't know what they would be doing." But, as Shanker says, "I've found that learning to weld is very empowering." Although some, especially the young women in the group, were initially dubious, "I've never seen kids more proud. They'd bring their parents or boy or girlfriends by to see them work in ninety-degree heat."

Murals, gardens, interactive games, and a general sprucing-up of the McKinley School and grounds involved a number of artists and volunteers, who were backed by the Eagles Youth Partnership, Philadelphia Green, and the School District. Shanker has nothing but praise for the football players from the Philadelphia Eagles Youth Partnership, who, in addition to giving financial support, devoted their "annual day of service" to working with neighborhood residents at McKinley School. "The Eagles got the community out in a way that no one else could have done. They painted the whole building. One reason that it doesn't get graffitied [now] is that the Eagles were there."

Shanker drives by McKinley (Orkney and Diamond Streets) almost daily on her way to work. Before MAP, the site was so chaotic and run down that she thought it was an abandoned parking lot for a trucking company. She soon learned that conditions on the school grounds were even worse than they appeared to a casual observer. The area was a popular location for drug use, sex, and other activities, which made it unsuitable for kids and demoralizing for the surrounding neighborhood.

Now Shanker loves the "fantastic" murals by Shira Walinsky that wrap the school walls with portraits, maps, and images of the solar system. And landscape architect Anna Forrester's Math Garden and Humanities Gardens are brilliantly designed as interactive teaching spaces, where igneous, sedimentary fossil-bearing, and metamorphic rocks provide seating. The plantings were chosen to attract birds and insects.

Bold floral silhouettes, four feet tall, on the garden fences are the first thing you notice as you approach the school. Shanker's Mural Corps kids had the challenge of defining and protecting school spaces in a way which welcomes the children and adults who belong there. The Mural Corps team developed and executed individual large-scale designs ranging from grapevines to daisies, then cut them from steel, welded them to 110 feet of stout fence, and painted them.

Shanker recalls: "When we started putting up the fences, kids from a nearby high school criticized: 'This looks just like a prison.' Then, when we began putting up the flowers and painting them, another group of high school kids came by and said, 'Why didn't you do this when we were here?'" Brightly painted surfaces now face out to the neighborhood. A series of interactive learning games for teachers and students are inside the garden, on the backs of the flowers. They include chalk board surfaces and counting grids.

"The principal of this school is stellar," says Shanker. "Deborah Carrera was key to the success."

The Mural Corps students did their welding in the metal shop at the University of the Arts. When Shanker discovered "that most of them had never set foot on a college campus before and had no idea of going to college, I gave them a tour of the school and answered as many questions as I could." She also arranged for an admissions person from the University to come and talk to the whole class. "It was a surprise how important that was. There isn't anything in their home environments that says they should consider college, but these are smart, motivated kids. They want more. I know that at least two are in college now and maybe a couple more [who will soon graduate from high school] are applying. The work on McKinley helps the whole community but this is an additional level of growth."

"Part of my interest working with MAP is wanting to have a more political component in my work," she adds. People sometimes discount the power that artists have in society or in culture; but [MAP] is one existing model where art's really making a difference for people in a concrete way—not just for individual kids but for neighborhoods; it's affecting the whole city. I'd like to do

Opposite
Jennie Shankar stands in front of her gates at the McKinley School, Orkney and Diamond Streets.

Below
This magnificent project brought together Mural Arts, the Neighborhood Transformation Initiative, Philadelphia Green, and the Eagles Youth Partnership to make a lasting transformation to a North Philadelphia neighborhood.

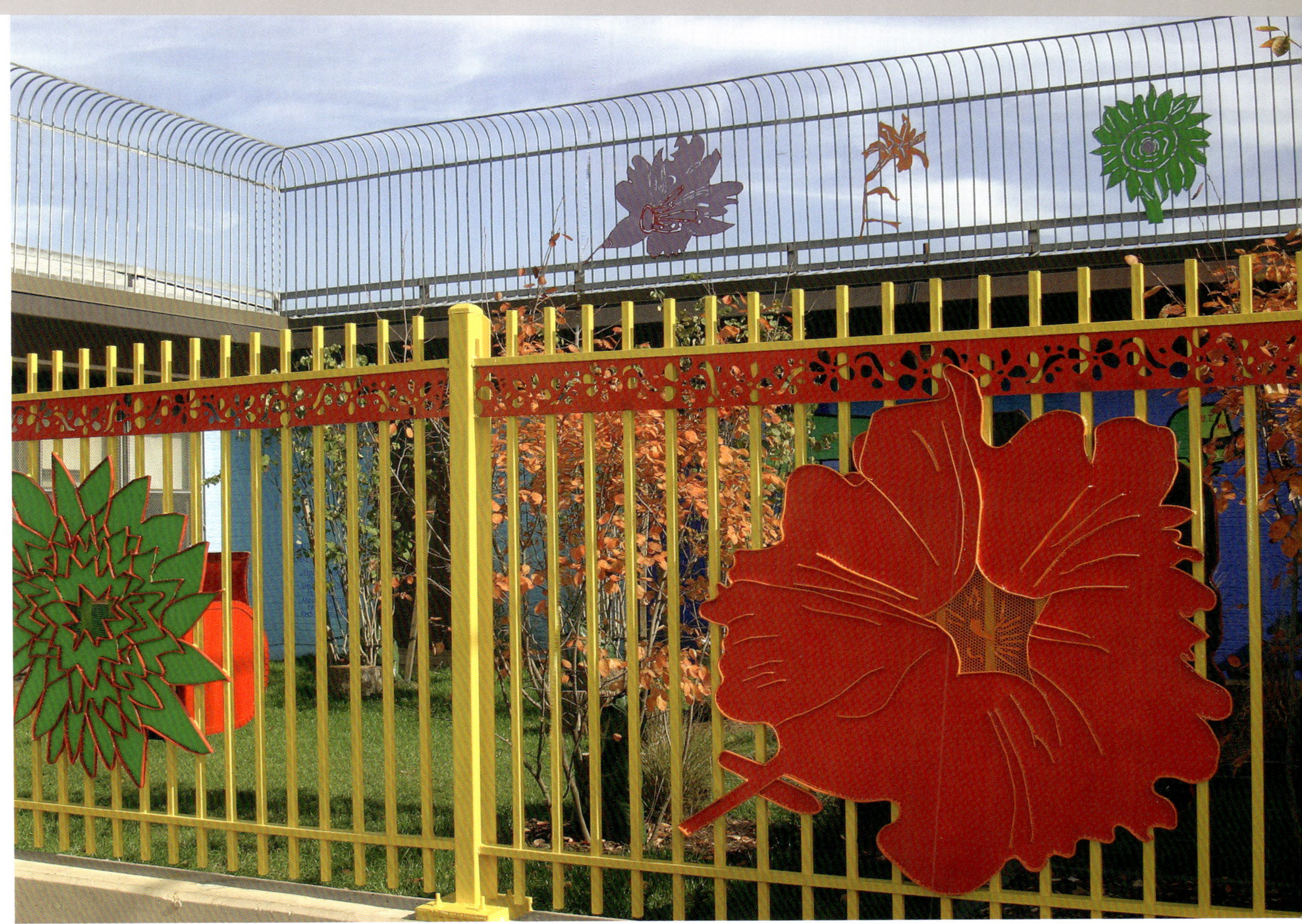

one of these projects every two years. It's a good way to step outside [my studio] for a little while and use what I've learned in a way that I know is really productive."

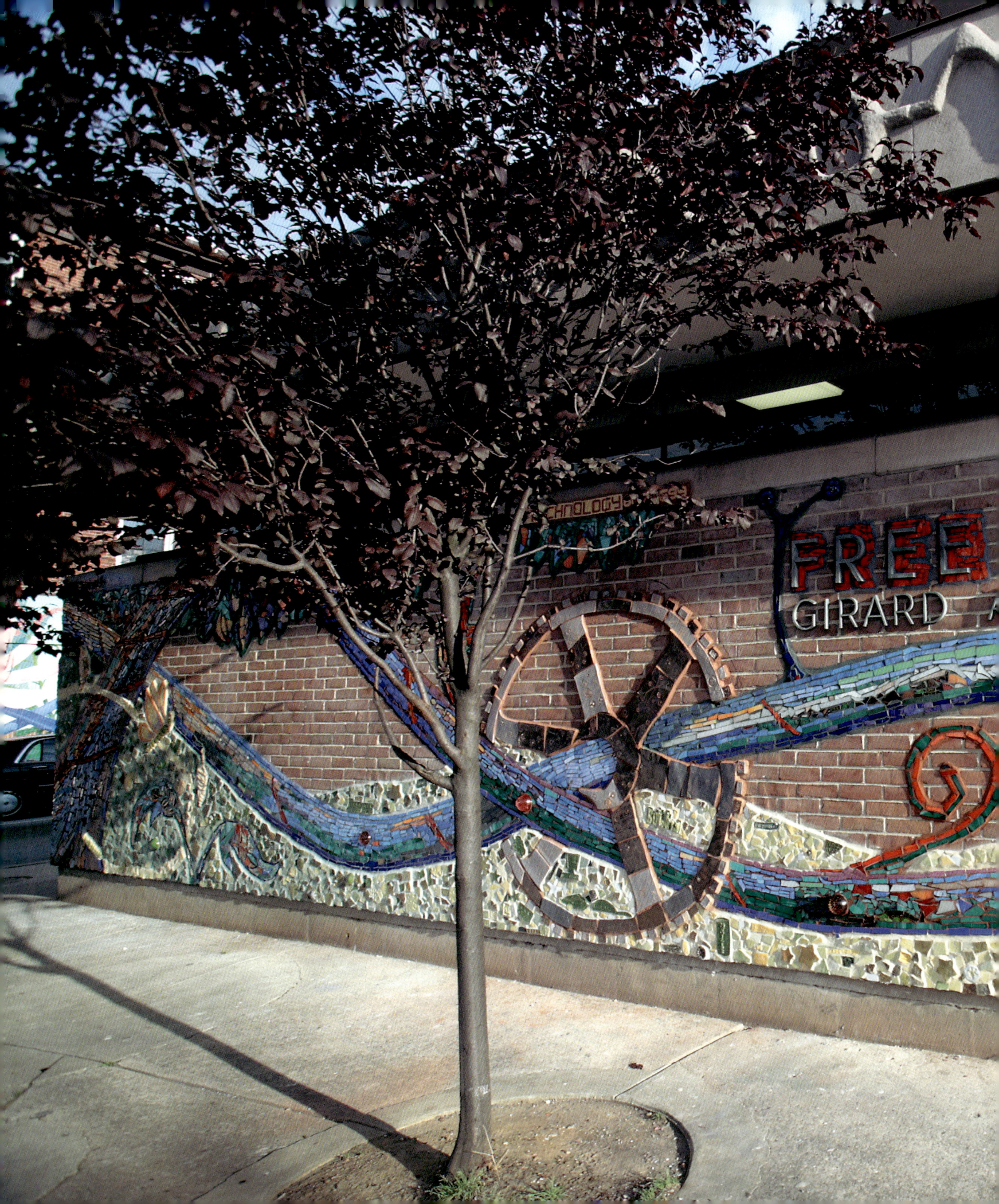
FREE
GIRARD

Chapter 7

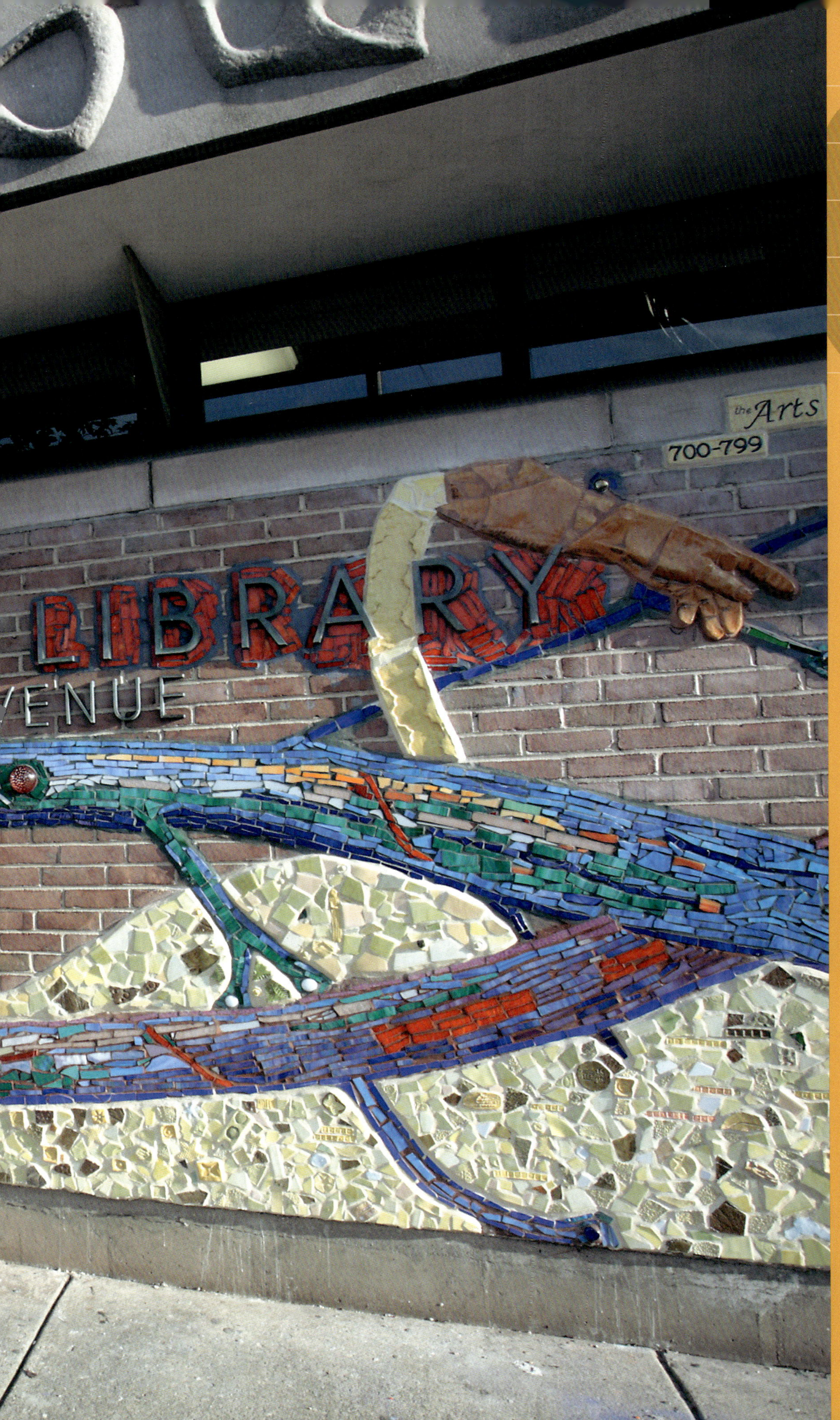

Dewey's World, in process, at the Ramonita G. de Rodriguez Branch of the Free Library of Philadelphia, 6th Street and Girard Avenue.

Chapter 7

Mosaics and More

Mike Mash's professional name, *Mike Smash,* dates back to his days in a punk rock band. He still likes to say, "If there's a check, I'm Mike Mash. If it's cash, it's Smash." But nowadays, "Smash" reflects the artist's predilection for breaking tiles for mosaics. Smash is brilliant at adapting the most contemporary materials to wall art. And he never forgets that "public outdoor murals are challenging terrain. You can use great materials but if your design ain't happening, it ain't happening."

Smash gained much of his knowledge of tile setting while working for an uncle who is "an amazing talent in the old way of creating an environment for the tile." However, after a year and a half of mixing cement for "white tile Jacuzzis in million dollar homes," Smash broke away to do original mosaics. Mosaic expanded into relief sculptures incorporating both carving and casting. In this chapter, Smash and others will discuss a variety of processes. Experts recommend that novice artists seek knowledgeable advice before attempting any project, especially if it's large, outdoors, or involves new material.

Opposite
Cavin Jones and Colleen Kane creating a mosaic with Big Picture participants at the Discovery Charter School, 5070 Parkside Avenue.

Below
Mosaic artist Mike Smash demonstrates the preparation of a mosaic tile piece.

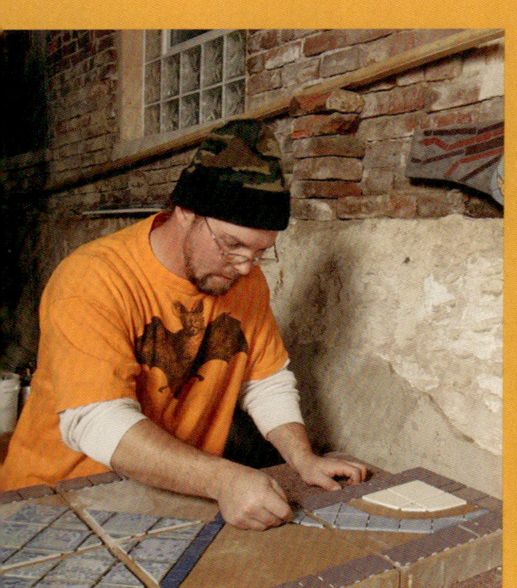

Indoor Mosaics

Perhaps the primary advantage of mosaic over painted murals is durability. The life expectancy of an exterior painted wall is measured in decades. The colors of mosaic can stay true for centuries outdoors and underfoot. Tesserae mosaic might be described as the oldest form of pixilation, although, of course, in ancient times the arrangement of colors was an approximation. An impressive approximation, however—ancient Romans composed dazzling illusionistic pictures from tiny square tesserae of colored marbles, slate, onyx, or other semiprecious stones. They also pieced designs in cutout shapes of stone, bone, or mother-of-pearl.

Byzantine mosaic was usually assembled from stone and translucent colored glass tesserae backed with gold. Each tile is subtly angled to catch the flickering light of candles or lamps. *Smalti,* colored Italian-style glass tiles, are about half an inch square, although they can be cut. They are suitable for indoor and outdoor environments and appear opaque but gain rich-

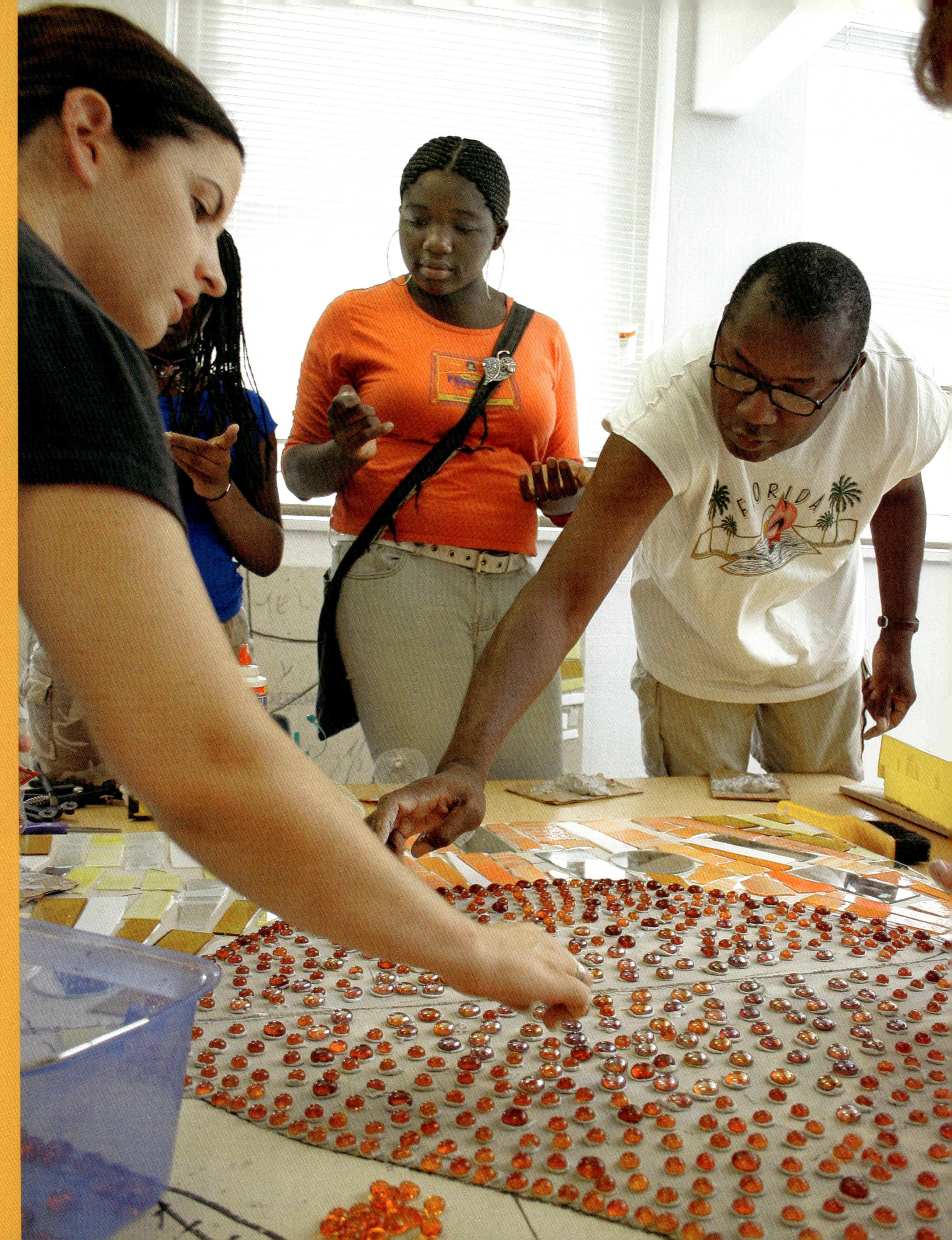

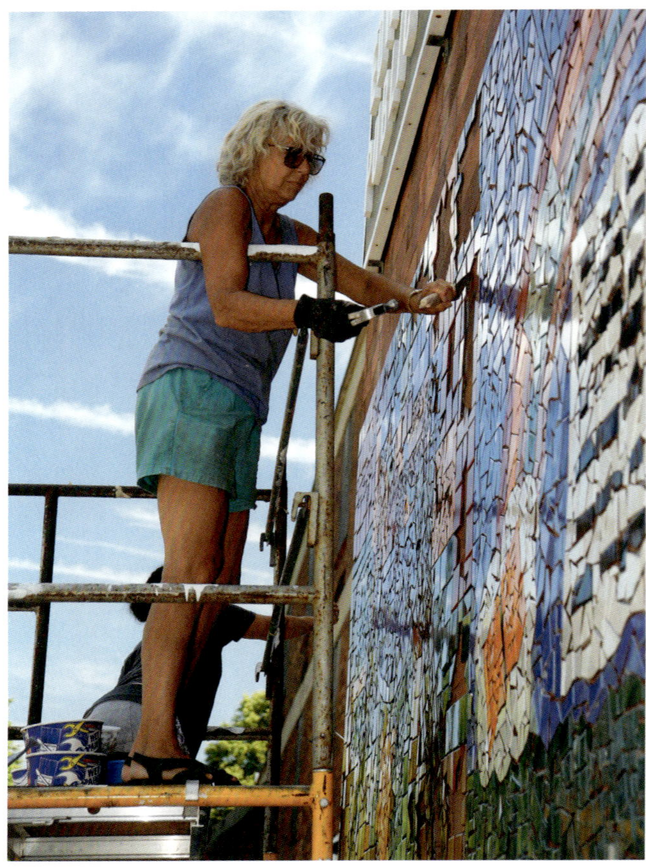

Mosaic artist Lynn Denton at work at the Edward Heston School, 54th Street and Lancaster Avenue. This mosaic is part of a school revitalization project sponsored by the Eagles Youth Partnership and the School District of Philadelphia.

ness from the slight penetration of light. Stone and glass mosaics stand up to wear because color runs through the whole tile and abrasion can't easily destroy the image.

Glazed ceramic tile is perhaps the most common contemporary mosaic material, but today's indoor mosaic artists are not limited to it. It's possible to attach almost any reasonably durable material to a wall with mastic or less flexible adhesives. Bathroom tiles and broken china are now popular mosaic elements. Colored glass over a white cement-based adhesive like Thinset can almost rival Byzantine mosaic. The minute commercial colored glass tiles, which come mounted on paper-faced sheets, certainly glitter. Separated into individual pieces, they are applied with silicone or mastic.

Outdoor Mosaics

Materials used outdoors must be frost-proof, which means they must be impermeable to water. Low-fired clay, for example, absorbs water. If it then freezes, it will spall or fragment. The American National Standards Institute (ANSI) calls tiles with a water absorption rate of 0.5 percent or less "impervious," but the practical reality is that mosaicists often must use materials that are not ANSI rated. High-fired clay (porcelain or stoneware, or industrial tile) can be used outdoors, but those terms on a label are imprecise. *Porcellanato,* Italian for porcelain, stamped on the back of a tile usually means it is impervious to water absorption. Not only must outdoor tile be impervious, any cracks in which water collects can be damaged by repeated freeze/thaw cycles. Careful grouting fills cracks and protects mosaic.

Some mosaic artists make and fire their own tiles. Lynn Denton sometimes asks each member of a group she is working with to make an individual tile on a theme. She fires the tiles and then places them in a mosaic in which each one functions as a unique relief image. She and other Philadelphia mosaicists often use an even simpler technique in which they invite participants to paint a picture or design in colored glazes on a plain industrial tile. The glaze is then fired-on at a relatively low temperature, forming a permanent surface on an impervious tile.

Individually glazed tiles can "frame" a painted wall. The big central picture is designed and executed by professional muralists. The bordering tiles on a related theme are decorated by kids and set by a mosaicist.

Mirror fragments are a virtual signature of prolific Philly mosaicist Isaiah Zagar. According to Betsy Augustine's small, abundantly illustrated book on him, *Philadelphia's Magic Gardens,*

Zagar is fascinated with mirrors partly because he is dyslexic. He also often places mirror writing (backward words composed of backward letters) in his murals. Betsy Augustine quotes him, "The mirror is endless energy, reflecting everything." Perhaps because Zagar's mosaics—he calls them "poems"—are so appealing and every Philadelphian has seen them, mirror is especially popular here.

Smash notes, "There are so many colors and textures of mirror. Every job I do, people want it, but mirror is never going to last outdoors." Smash uses a special mirror mastic; nevertheless, he says, "Even the best stuff will not prevent desilvering. I can't make mirror sparkly forever, but I can control the amount I use." He restricts it to half-inch strips so, "when it loses its luster, it will not destroy the whole piece."

Outdoor mosaic tiles are usually applied with cement-based adhesive—not mastic. The ideal surface for the adhesive is cement or stucco or cement backer board. This surface must be clean and somewhat textured. The mortar is applied with a trowel. Pieces of tile or glass or whatever the artist chooses are squished into it or slathered with it before being placed into the design.

After the mosaic has dried and set, the finishing step is the application of grout, a cement mixture which is forced into the cracks between tiles or tesserae to make a smooth exterior surface. All excess is scrupulously wiped away so that it will not dull the tile colors. Grout can be tinted any number of colors. Zagar effectively uses colored grout in his mosaics. Smash warns, however, that not all colored grouts are UV-resistant. Because of this, he generally sticks with white.

MAP frequently works with the Pennsylvania Horticultural Society by making murals which complement gardens, while, at the request of neighborhood groups, PHS often designs plantings relating to murals. MAP and PHS are currently working with People's Emergency Center to complete the Lancaster Avenue Beautification Project. The goal of this partnership is to use art, tree planting, and community and business development to foster community empowerment and bring about neighborhood beautification. Smash will be a lead artist in designing the mosaic work surrounding the tree plantings.

"Tilepile": Mosaic Pictures

Josh Sarantitis (see Chapter 5 for more on Josh Sarantitis) makes mosaics and murals all over the world, although he's probably made more in Philadelphia than anywhere else. He and his brother-in-law, Greg Barton, spent a couple of years developing *Tilepile,* a "pretty simple computer program that allows us to take any digital file and pixilate it into a color palette that would be defined by the tiles that we are using. We are copyrighting the idea and letting anyone use it." The program based on the RGB value (red, green, blue components of each color expressed as a hexadecimal number) of each tile and color planned for the mural currently runs only on Windows systems. Sarantitis plans to adapt it for Mac users. A Web site with the Java program is available on the Internet. Eric Okdeh uses the *Tilepile* program to organize tiles of forty-one colors into designs.

Sarantitis's ultimate goal is to design a robot that can place the *smalti* according to the design programmed into it. So far, this is mostly theory, but don't be surprised when he's done it.

Relief Sculpture

Smash builds relief sculpture for exterior walls from expanded polypropylene foam. The foam blocks, which were designed to decorate and insulate building exteriors, have a relatively soft texture and can be easily carved with a hacksaw or even sandpaper. The foam is not suited to a high level of detail, but details can be added later. Smash covers the simple shapes with water-resistant, alkali-resistant fiberglass mesh tape. Then he trowels on two or three layers of cement-based adhesive. In commercial settings, the foam is typically covered with stucco. Smash's use of adhesive, although unconventional, seals and stabilizes the surface with an impervious hard shell for future embellishment in paint or mosaic.

Dewey's World at the Ramonita G. de Rodriguez Branch of the Free Library of Philadelphia, 6th Street and Girard Avenue. This unique project, led by artists Jennie Shanker and Paul Santoleri, is the result of a collaboration between Mural Corps youth and the Ceramics Workshop class at Temple University's Tyler School of Art.

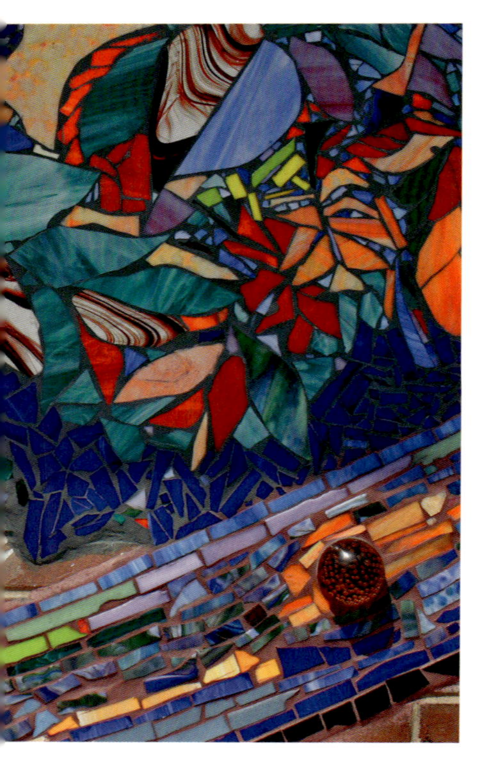

The sculptural chunks are attached to the wall with concrete anchors that go through the foam and screw into the wall. Smash says, "I always try to use the most durable and strongest materials and instead of putting one screw in, I'll put in four." Mosaic of different types can be set into an additional layer of Thinset or the relief can be painted. Smash notes that surface painting can increase the sense of three dimensions or flatten it.

At the Ramonita G. de Rodriguez Branch of the Free Library (6th Street and Girard Avenue, 2005), Paul Santoleri traced a rounded almost Celtic vine–like relief over the modern brick walls, leaving most of the brick surface visible (see pages 94, this page). He covered the relief with iridescent stained glass mosaic with colored glass spheres as accents.

Smash will sculpt with synthetic mortars such as Dryvit and "soft carve" concrete before it hardens, using a mixture of Portland cement and fine sand. In addition, he says, "I make some concrete tiles in molds that I make or find—any mold that looks cool. Say it's a ladybug; I'll sculpt a flower in concrete and as it's drying, attach the ladybug with Thinset cement."

For some elements—perhaps the ladybug—he uses a cement that is intended for casting garden stepping stones. These quick-cast tiles are about a quarter of an inch thick. "They can't be carved because it sets up fast, in about an hour, but it's really hard, like steel."

Collaborating with painter Harvey Weinreich, Smash made the *Four Seasons* theme for the Hawthorne Recreation Center at 12th and Carpenter Streets (2005). The long, low horizontal relief is broken into four sections, each featuring traditional seasonal motifs and a variety of casting, carving, mosaic, and painting techniques. Fall is represented by a moon and a pumpkin. Winter is a wind spirit blowing through the clouds. Flowers symbolize spring, and summer is a sun carved and then covered with stained glass mosaic.

New Approaches to Paint

Muralists traditionally have superimposed a grid over a drawing and then enlarged each unit to transfer the drawing to a larger, but identically proportioned, grid on the wall. A recent variation on that technique involves painting on accurately proportioned sections of tough synthetic material, commonly called "parachute cloth." Each section is adhered to the wall with acrylic gel. Both sides of painted fabric are thickly coated so that it is literally embedded in the tough waterproof gel. Artists use the traditional technique of scale enlargement to trace color areas onto rectangular sections of cloth. An accurate enlargement can be achieved mechanically by projecting the image onto the cloth and then tracing. The artist can label areas indicating which color goes where. Anyone with normal hand-eye coordination can fill in the color areas. Once the painted sections are installed, the muralist blends and matches transitions, adding highlights and other touches to pull the work together and make it sparkle.

The acrylic gel system, commonly called the "parachute cloth" method, has several advantages:

- The painting can be done by unskilled workers.
- Young muralists may have the thrill of seeing their contributions on a huge wall.
- Paintings embedded in gel have proved to be more weather-resistant than paintings executed directly on the wall.
- It's possible to make almost an entire mural in bad weather and without the expense of renting or using scaffolding for extended periods of time.
- It's possible to make a mural for a distant location.

This system is especially suited to illusionistic subjects and to artists who prefer to plan carefully. Not everyone likes it. Smash, for example, says, "I think that gridding the wall is necessary for some designs, but for the kinds of things I do a grid is almost a waste of time." Muralist Sam Byrd even tries to avoid committing to a detailed drawing. "I don't have a set way of painting," he says. "I might do it one day one way and the other day differently. I like to experiment. I don't like sketches."

Byrd is the exception, not the rule, although for some muralists the more direct methods have advantages:

- The artist's skill and imagination take flight in response to the act of painting.
- The mural develops as it is being painted.
- The unique expressions of participants can be preserved in other ways: for example, when each participant paints an individual tile of his or her own composition.

But the size of the wall is a factor. When scaffolding is involved, muralists can't step back to see what passers-by see. Then, it's good to have a plan on paper.

Casañas's Collaged Fabric Technique

Betsy Casañas has developed a unique way of using the "parachute cloth" and gel technique as a form of collage, which she describes as "a complete collaboration between the children and the muralist." Casañas asks kids to make paintings or writings on a subject related to the mural directly on the cloth.

When she makes this assignment, she's already developed her design and identified large areas of color, for example, the red of a dancer's skirt, which she will collage into the mural. The students' contribution "ends up being more of a color workshop than a drawing workshop. The kids I'm working with usually have no art background. I have them mix as many colors of red [or whatever is needed] as they can, so the color is not straight from the tube." Casañas freely rips up the painted fabric into vaguely suitable shapes.

Before the workshop, she has already planned, gridded, and drawn her mural on the wall. She attaches the children's work with gel, placing colors in suitable spots—anywhere there is a large area of color. She paints details like faces and hands herself. Next she returns to the areas of cloth collaged in gel and layers on shadows in translucent glazes of color, fusing the many contributions of children into a whole. "You have this massive image that's controlled and if you come close, you see all the other images by the children." Casañas's daughter participated in making a mural like this at the age of four. "I think it's a good technique to make the kids proud that they actually contributed in a really helpful way," Casañas says.

Templates

Diane Pieri's murals are not completely abstract but they are abstracted—flat and patterned. She says, "Since my murals are not figurative, it's not critical to have them in perfect proportion." Pieri always makes a very precise preliminary painting on paper, but, when she begins to paint, she simply divides the wall with a series of vertical lines which she uses as points of reference to keep her finished design proportioned to it.

Because repetition is typical of Pieri's flat designs, she cuts templates of important images or lines that will be repeated. For her garden wall at Starr Garden recreation center (6th and Lombard Streets, 2001), she asked each child in a Big Picture class led by Erika Matyok to design a flower. Pieri then cut the silhouettes of the flowers from foam core board and traced around each flower pattern with light sienna paint, which was painted over in bright colors in the finished work. Using the template, Pieri could easily repeat each child's fantasy flower several times throughout the design. The adult staff at the center were so delighted with the flowers that Pieri invited each of them to contribute one to the garden.

Mural Extensions

The shape of a building no longer determines the shape of a mural. Just as they sometimes build out from a wall in reliefs, artists today can break the contours of the building with shaped plywood extensions to the roof and occasionally to the sides. Others may have tried it before, but possibly Sarantitis made the first mural extension in Philadelphia (*Colors of Light*, 12th and Vine Streets, 2000). Certainly, he has constructed as many extensions as anyone. He likes the way they "break the surface of the wall, lift the restraints placed by a rectangular wall and, physically, create the feeling of an environment."

"Basically it's a way of combining sculpture, engineering, and painting to make the mural an interactive and effective work of public art," Sarantitis explains. He cuts the shape to be painted from an exterior grade of MDO paper-faced plywood and supports it with angles of galvanized steel. Ideally, Sarantitis says, the extension structure should be approved by an engineer. The plywood must be carefully sealed on both sides against moisture and the extension should be inspected regularly to be sure it is sound. Whenever he's near a wall he's painted, Sarantitis tries to check the roof to see how the extensions are faring.

When Sarantitis says that each extension project is getting "better and better," he's speaking not only of durability but of design. The sense of a more sophisticated future for murals can't be ignored.

Parachute cloth, a versatile and transportable support for acrylic paint, being painted by participants from St. Gabriel's Hall at a Balanced and Restorative Justice workshop within SCI Graterford's visitors' waiting room.

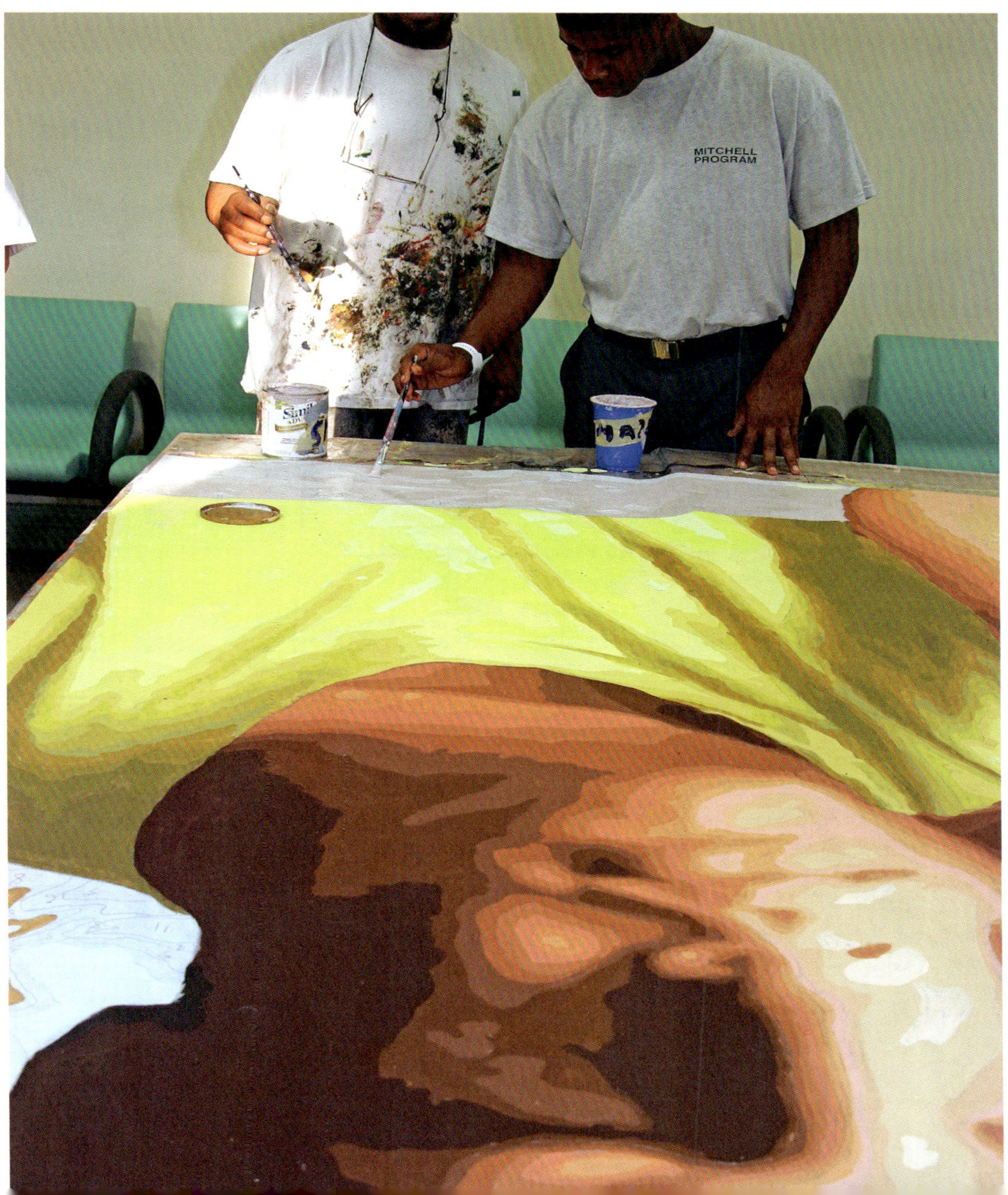

Artist Profile

Betsy Casañas

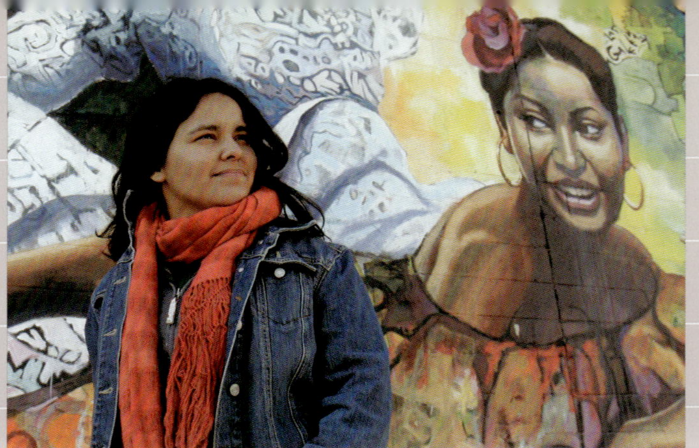

Lots of color—that's a phrase you're sure to hear when Betsy Casañas talks about her art. "I love color!" she says. But Casañas doesn't like anything straight from the tube, she wants variety—even in a single color. That's why she often gives her students the assignment of mixing as many versions of a single color as they can.

Variety is another word required to describe the work of this young Latina artist who enjoys using so many mediums. She's worked on over thirty murals for a variety of organizations in Philadelphia, including the Mural Arts Program. At one time, she felt restricted by the photographic style which is so popular in city neighborhoods. "I felt I was stuck," she says. But since then she's developed a method of using collaged paintings and writings by students to build up her compositions. "I love collaborative pieces," Casañas says, "I think it's so much richer.

"I get bored easily," she explains. "I like switching off and I really like where I'm working." Casañas is a full-time teacher at Philadelphia's Charter High School of Architecture and Design where she teaches fine arts, including a class in mural painting. Before that, she taught classes at the Taller Puertorriqueño and other city organizations. In 2004, she visited Ireland and taught teenagers and painted a mural there. "I had my students write about themselves, and their writings were used as background in the mural," she says.

Casañas's murals are a provocative mixture of traditional and nontraditional, just like she is. Like many muralists, she often works on parachute cloth, but she uses it in a completely original way. The mural *Bomba y Plena* is an example of her unique technique. She begins by asking her young collaborators to make individual designs on the cloth, working in a specific color range, which will be part of the finished mural. "I have the [students] do free-form drawings or use text." For one mural, she had kids do rubbings of textures and intriguing objects that they found in their own neighborhood.

Meanwhile, Casañas has scanned the entire mural design and now projects it onto the mural wall. "You take the cloth (decorated by the children) and you rip it and are very free in applying it." When Casañas has freely collaged in areas of color, like the background or large areas of clothing, she paints details of hands and faces and other areas composed of shapes too small to collage. The projected image guides her painting, which includes highlights and layers of translucent glaze to build shadows—all orchestrating the collaged sections into a unified whole.

"The work is very painterly, very impressionistic. You're always pleased with the end result. From a distance, it is an image of dancers, but when you come up close, it's children's drawings. It's a complete collaboration between the children and the muralist."

Bomba y Plena is based on two uniquely Puerto Rican folkloric dances. "When you say 'bomba y plena,' you are talking about everything that dance has: music and singing and the form of the instruments." Casañas points out, "*Bomba* is totally a dance of the drums." *Bomba,* which can have one of several rhythms, is played on percussion instruments brought from West Africa by slaves. *La bomba* is an event, always featuring dance as well as vocal and percussive music. It may have developed in coastal plantations. Although Africans were forbidden to worship their gods, they translated some of their customs into the festival of St. James.

Plena is a distinctive Puerto Rican dance associated with coastal areas, although it has become an informal urban entertainment. "It's a mesh of the musical instruments and of African, Spanish dances and the dances of the Taino Indians (the indigenous people who were almost wiped out by the Spanish)," Casañas says. "My great-grandmother was Taino. It was only five hundred years ago. You could see it in the structure of the faces. My mother's parents are very dark-skinned and Indian-looking." Casañas sometimes paints the images of her family and other members of the community as "familiar faces" in her murals.

La plena is a narrative song that describes, sometimes ironically, the lives of the people. Sometimes it was used to communicate to those who could not read, to satirize or detail scandalous stories, intrigues, or political events. *La plena* was called *"el periodico cantado,"* the newspaper of song. The guitar, a Spanish instrument, typically accompanies it. "Every day, they would learn a new song and go around and teach it to other people." Although the plena can be danced, the lyrics and music are more important.

"I'm used to running around," Casañas says. "When things settle down, it doesn't seem normal." In addition to teaching and painting, Casañas is a member of an interdisciplinary performance group. It performs in many venues. Members include Michelle Ortiz and Julia Lopez. Las Gallas—a play on *gallo* (rooster)—is "a made-up name

Opposite
Betsy Casañas in front of her free collage mural *Bomba y Plena*.

Below
Bomba y Plena, Mascher Street and Lehigh Avenue.

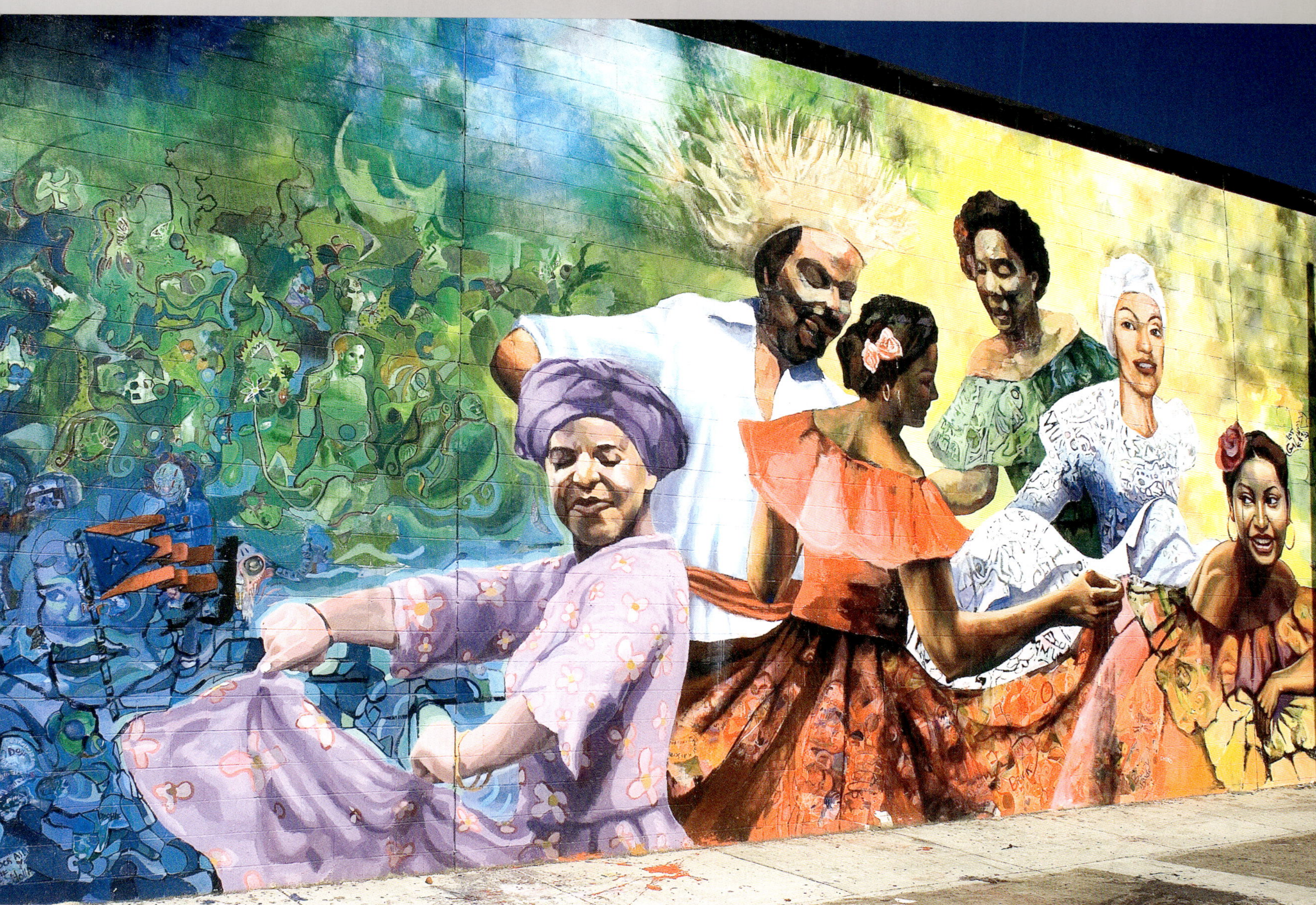

which came out of a conversation in a workshop. It means cocky. The whole purpose of the group is to get out of your comfort zone and step into somebody else's."

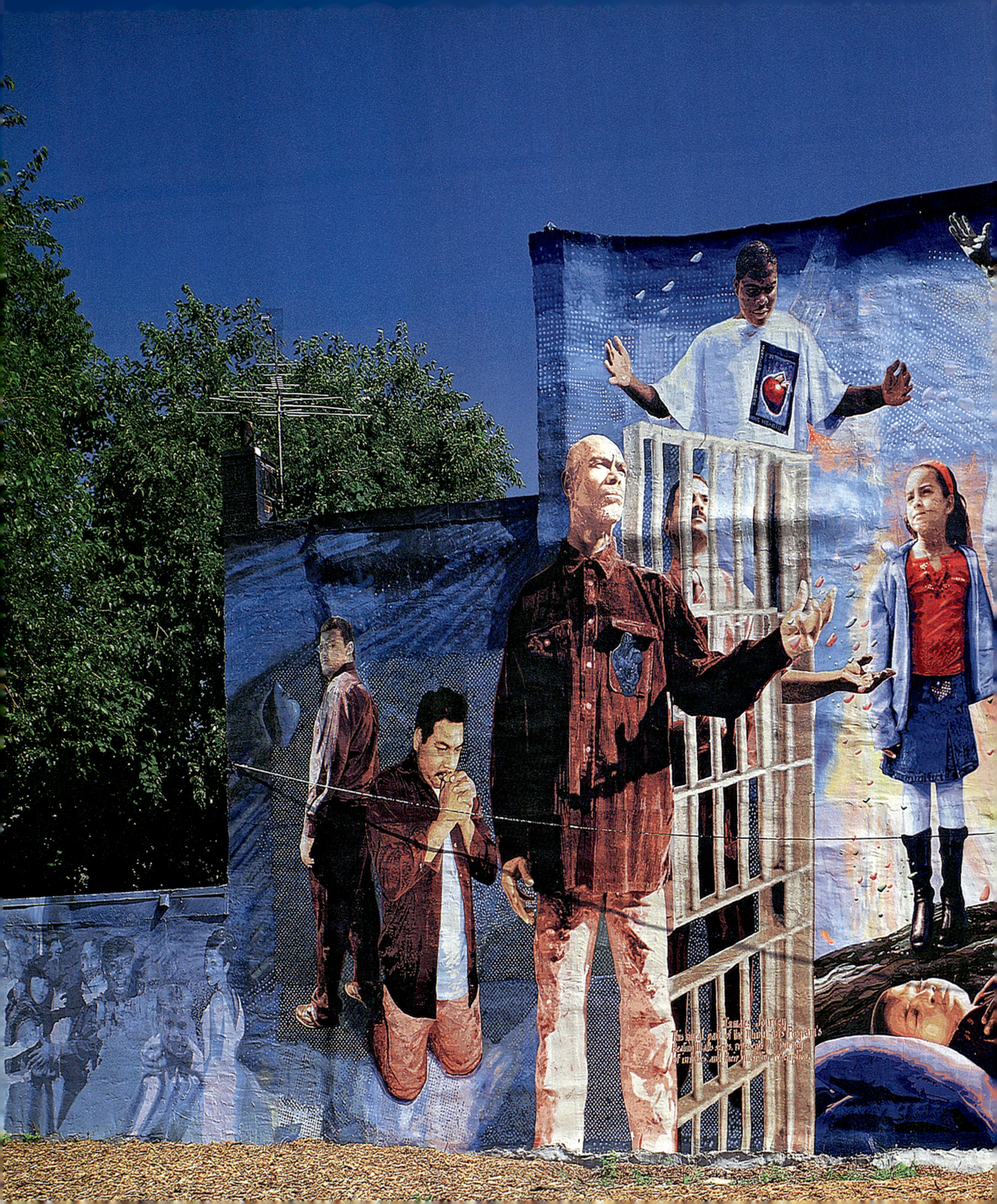

Chapter 8

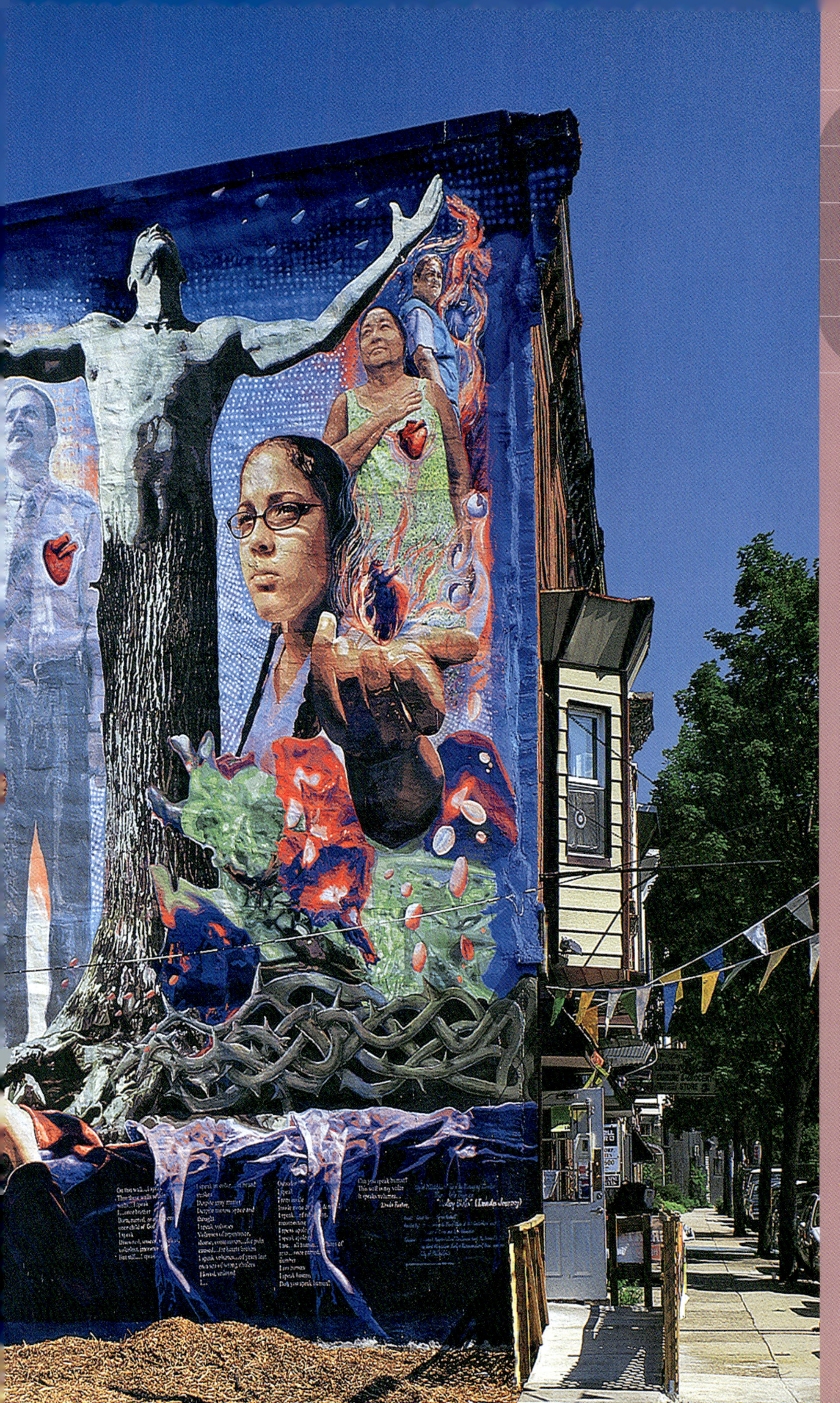

The Inmates' Journey, installed at its final location at 3049 Germantown Ave. Mural by César Viveros-Herrera, Parris Stancell, and the men of the mural program at SCI Graterford. *The Inmates' Journey* and the other Healing Walls murals have become symbols of positive transformation. They were made possible through the Ford Foundation, the Lindback Foundation, and the Suzanne F. Roberts Cultural Fund.

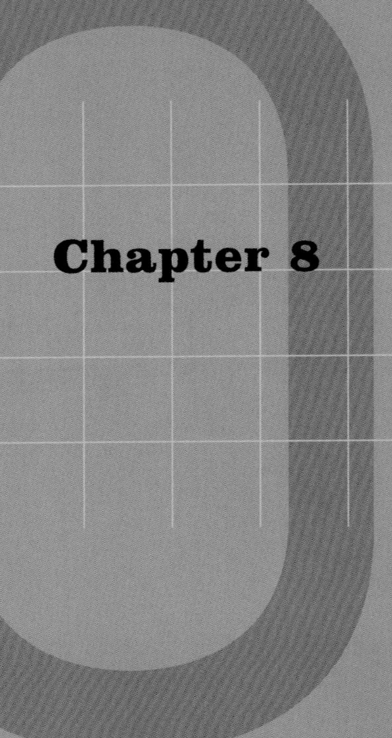

Chapter 8 Healing Walls

The fifteen-year-old had just walked through the prison door when Suave, one of the lifers, was in his face: "What's your name?" the heavy-set Latino man demanded. The slight boy opened his mouth. Suave didn't wait for an answer. Instead, he gestured to the paint-by-numbers canvas he was leaning over with the other inmates: "Here, pick up a brush. Come on. Come talk to me. What are you in for?"

"Armed robbery," the boy said, quietly, picking up a paint brush and sizing up the different shades of brown paint.

"Dang," Suave said, eyes moving between the boy and the canvas. "Who'd you rob?"

"Nobody," the boy replied.

There was laughter and knowing nods from the other adults. "Yeah, that's a good one, kid," Suave said.

And like that, they were talking—and painting—together.

Each month, groups of boys from St. Gabriel's Hall, a juvenile detention center, visit the men of the State Correctional Institution at Graterford—the sixth largest maximum security prison in the country. Here they work together on murals that will one day hang in the city of Philadelphia. They paint and talk, about life on the outside and life behind bars, and how one does not necessarily have to lead to the other. Sometimes, they forgo the painting altogether.

The Mural Arts Program first came to Graterford in 2002, offering the inmates a way to express themselves through art and a way to give back to the neighborhoods they'd once harmed.

But it quickly grew from a simple painting project into a potentially life-changing program for offenders young and old, victims and their advocates, and the community at large.

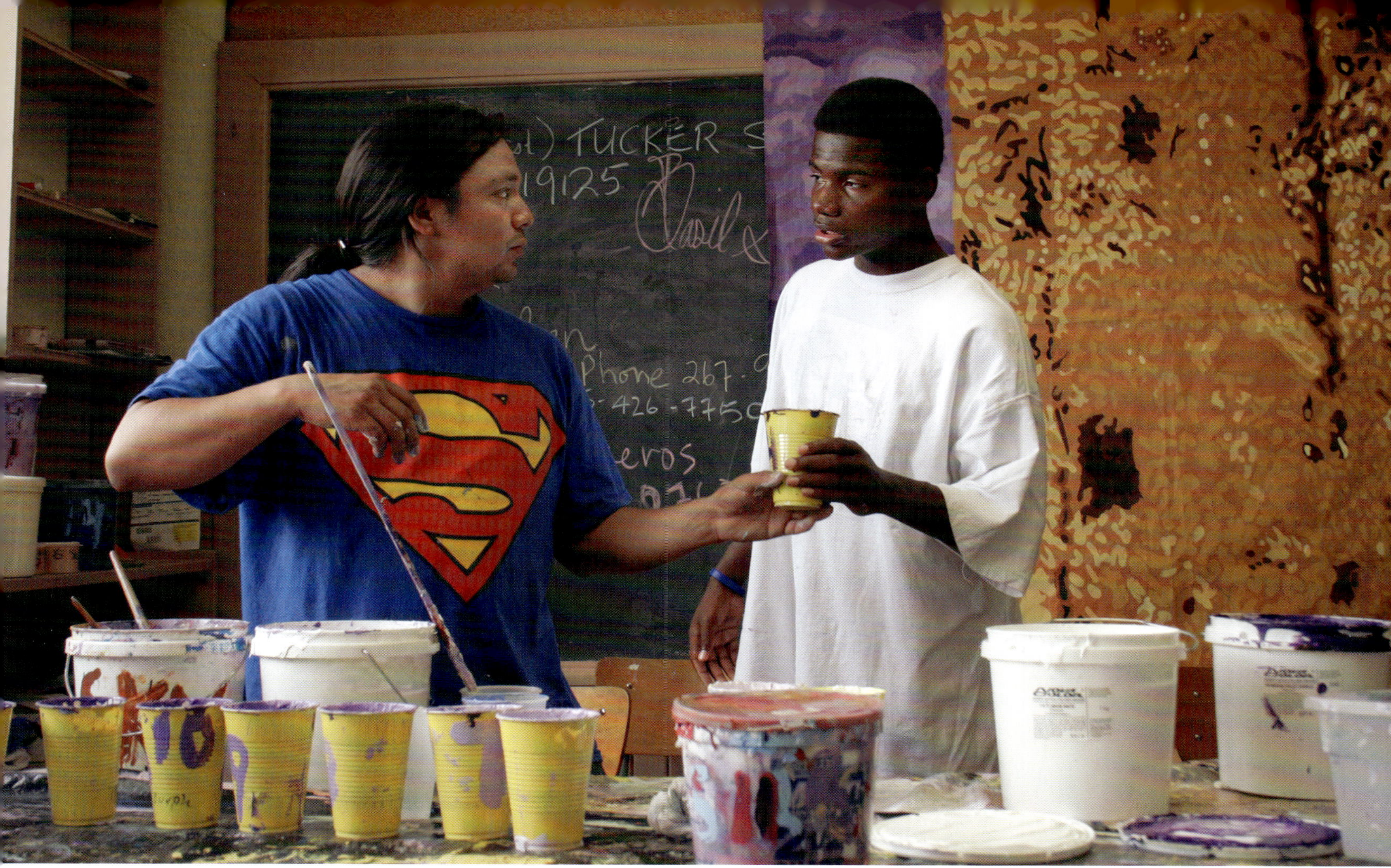

César Viveros-Herrera with Jamil Watson, Youth Works participant at St. Anne's School with the Balanced and Restorative Justice project.

The idea, originally, was for a Healing Wall, one mural worked on by each of these distinct groups, one project that would bring them together in the hopes of building understanding and compassion on all sides while creating a public work of art. It was an idea that was bold, complex—and, at some points, seemingly destined to fail.

Yet, before it was over, one mural would become three.

MAP had used planning and painting murals to bring together disparate groups before. In 1997, with racial tensions in the Grays Ferry neighborhood of Philadelphia overflowing, MAP Director Jane Golden decided the neighborhood needed a mural. She envisioned a project that would bring together people of all colors and allow them to beautify their community. But when she met with neighborhood leaders and asked for ideas, they all seemed to want different things.

But one image kept popping up over and over again during the community conversations: Hands. Joined together. United. The resulting mural at 29th and Wharton Streets is known as *The Peace Wall* (1998). It shows the arms and hands of neighborhood residents, eleven arms and hands that are white and shades of brown, coming together as if in a football huddle.

It was a sign, a symbol that this troubled neighborhood could survive. Murals, Golden found, could bring conflicting groups together.

Five years later, she was ready to try it again. MAP was already working at Graterford and was looking to expand the program so the inmates could work on murals that would hang outside the prison, painting on sections of parachute cloth that could then be affixed to the chosen walls. It would be a situation that benefited both parties: The inmates would have a new work program and a way to release artistic energy, and MAP would have a dedicated workforce that was paid fifty-one cents hourly.

Groups like the Pennsylvania Prison Society were eager to get the project off the ground: "Here was a creative way to bring victims and offenders together and talk about issues of accountability and healing," says Barb Toews, Manager of the Society's Restorative Justice Program. "People in prison find it really hard to find avenues to speak to the community about their care and concern and accountability and their desire for healing and all those human expressions."

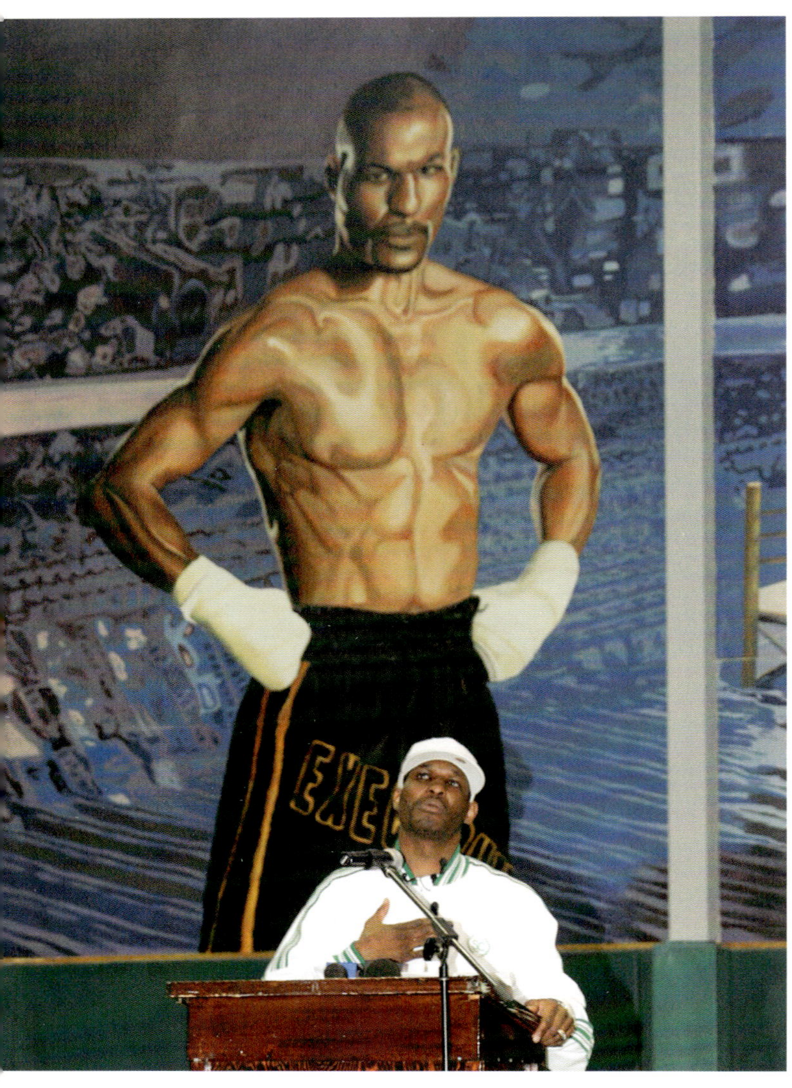

Art and life come together here at the State Correctional Institution at Graterford. Former Middleweight Champion Bernard Hopkins at the dedication of a mural of himself painted by Eric Okdeh and the men of the mural program at Graterford, now installed in SCI Graterford's gymnasium.

Golden also contacted organizations like the Pennsylvania Office of the Victim Advocate. Kathy Buckley, director of victims' services, says that she liked the idea of bringing together, through art, two groups that were usually kept apart. For victims, it would be another step in their healing journey, she says. "It's hard to see offenders, some of whom have committed heinous crimes, are also human beings," she says. "And for offenders, it's seeing, 'Oh. We're not totally hated by these people.'"

Despite everyone's willingness to come to the table, things did not start smoothly. The groups were polarized, Graterford Superintendent David DiGuglielmo recalls. "It was pretty contentious at times," DiGuglielmo says. "People were looking and reacting to each other from one dimension. During the evolution of the project, everyone learned that everyone was more complex than that."

The inmates wanted the mural to tell their story and to serve as a warning to neighborhood children. The victims and their advocates felt the emphasis should be on the victims and their pain. Some community members didn't want either group's story on a three-story wall, feeling that it was wrong to do anything to honor inmates and that images of victims would bring back bad memories.

"It was a wonderful experience, but also a really difficult one," Golden says of those meetings. "You go through times where nobody's listening and nobody's talking to each other and, at times, I just felt I was in way over my head."

The first design by artist César Viveros-Herrera, based on the conversations he'd heard, was too focused on the inmates for advocates like Buckley. She remembers that she and the others balked, saying, "This is the inmates' journey. This is nothing about the victims' pain. We thought this was a tribute to victims."

The solution? Two walls, two murals: One that focused on the cycle of violence from the perpetrators' points of view and another focused on the victims' journey to wellness.

After six months of debate and rancor, the design had finally been agreed on.

But, in some ways, that was the easy part.

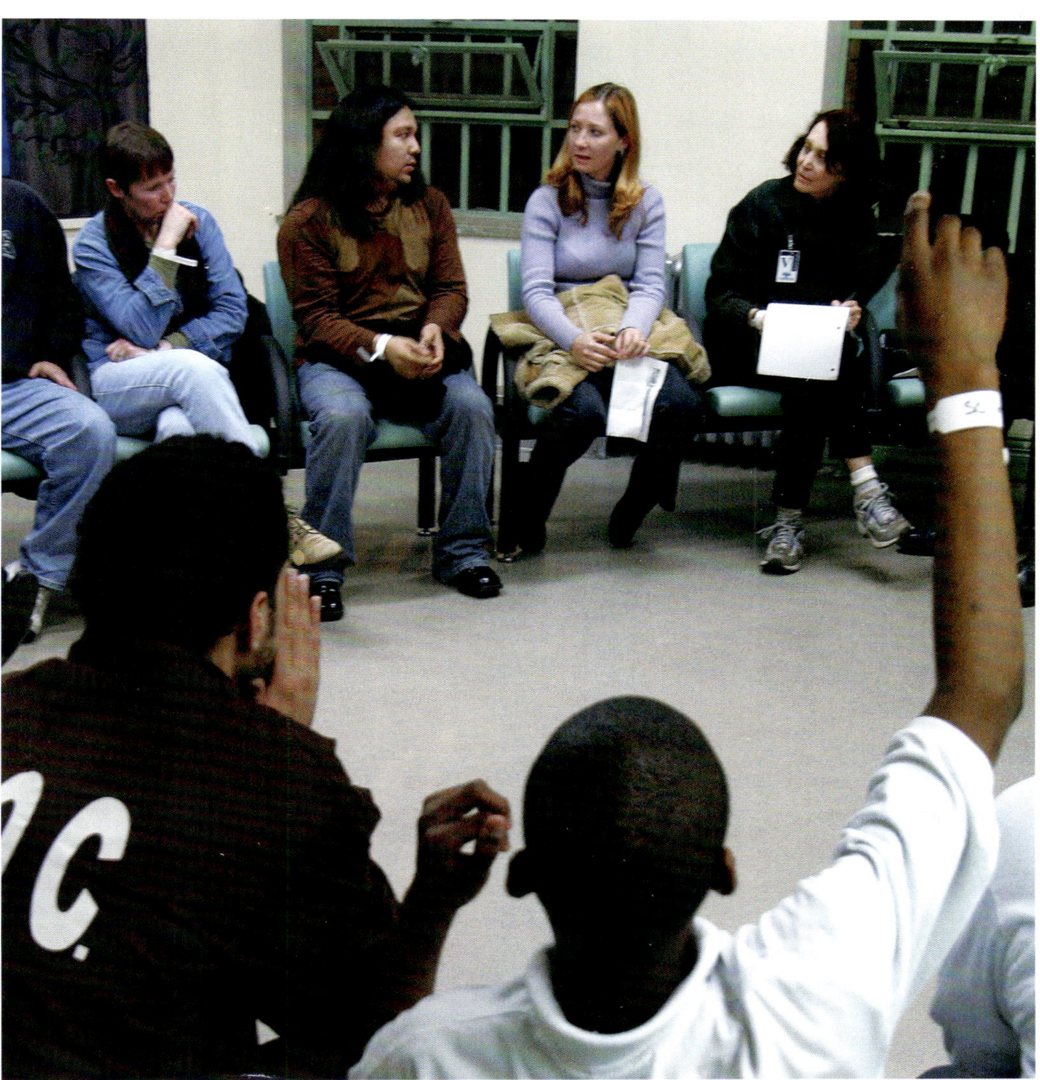

A community meeting is the very heart of a mural project—we see muralist César Viveros-Herrera and Mural Arts Director Jane Golden at a Balanced and Restorative Justice Community Meeting within SCI Graterford.

Artist Profile

César Viveros-Herrera

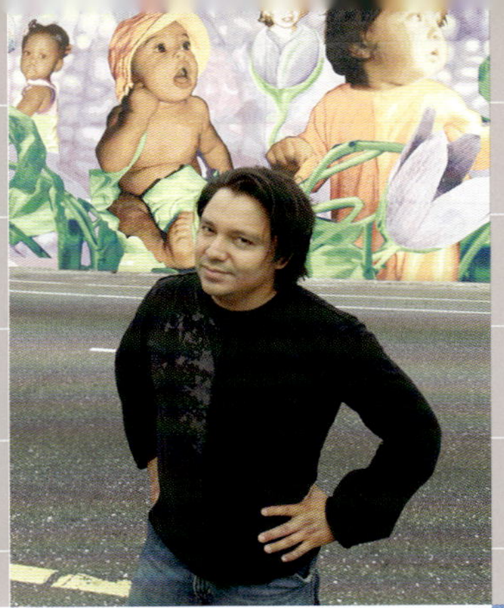

Philadelphia is one of the very few places in the world today where, with hard work and a little luck, aspiring muralists can learn the trade from the bottom up. César Viveros-Herrera, a young self-taught painter from Mexico, immediately recognized the significance of the ambitious murals that were being painted here. He was born in the Ciudad de Vera Cruz on the Gulf of Mexico, land of the Olmecs, and grew up with the heritage of twentieth-century Mexican muralism. An instinctive artist, young Viveros-Herrera dug up clay to make figurines of people and animals. "Other kids used to come and exchange their toys for the stuff that I made," he recalls.

He also made art in school; however, grown-up Viveros-Herrera became a deep sea diver, working on oil drilling platforms in the Gulf. He loved diving but hated lonely months sequestered on the platform. When weather temporarily halted diving, Viveros-Herrera found spots for small murals: dolphins in one area, underwater drillers in another. Soon he had commissions for portraits and other subjects. Painting was becoming his life.

At the age of twenty-five, Viveros-Herrera visited a friend in Philadelphia. One day they noticed Meg Saligman and her crew beginning work on the huge, eight-story *Common Threads* at a bustling Center City intersection (Broad and Spring Garden Streets, 1998).[1] "I said to my friend, 'If I ever have a chance to paint on a mural, it should be this one.'" Viveros-Herrera and his friend waited patiently for an opportunity to speak with Saligman.

"I told Meg, 'I love to paint and I paint in Mexico.' I said I would clean the brushes or whatever." Amazingly, considering the number of strangers who strike up conversations with muralists, Saligman, who has mentored several now-successful lead muralists, immediately accepted Viveros-Herrera as an unpaid volunteer. Showing up day after day, Viveros-Herrera soon proved his worth, as he quietly absorbed Saligman's knowledge.

Later, Saligman telephoned Viveros-Herrera in Mexico and hired him to assist her on another mural. In Shreveport, Louisiana, he helped on an enormous twenty-five-thousand-square-foot wall celebrating the millennium. "In Shreveport," Viveros-Herrera recalls, "I learned how to work with the community." In this case, the community was invited to paint the mural. Saligman and Viveros-Herrera transferred the design to sections of fabric and labeled areas so that untutored volunteers could fill them in—a kind of paint-by-number process. When complete the fabric panels were sealed to the wall with acrylic gel.

Recently, Viveros-Herrera used the same technique in a series of "Healing Walls," projects that grew out of the Mural Arts Program's work with inmates of the State Correctional Institution at Graterford, a maximum security prison. Prisoners, victims of crime, victims' advocates, and others determined the content of the *Victims' Journey* (3065 Germantown Avenue, 2004) and, nearby, the *Inmates' Journey* (3049 Germantown Avenue, 2004).

"Healing Walls" continues as the Balanced and Restorative Justice Mural Project. About twenty-five juvenile male offenders from the Mitchell Program at St. Gabriel's Hall Detention Center and inmates sentenced to life at SCI Graterford met and talked and shared hopes for change and ideas for the first mural. Viveros-Herrera says, "The idea was to connect this group of kids with inmates through murals." The topic was not so much "What will look nice on a wall?" but "What helps kids avoid the mistakes leading to crime?" A third group, residents of the community where this mural is located (East Lehigh Avenue between Tulip and Trenton Streets), also met for discussions and later painted parts of the mural at St. Anne's Church.

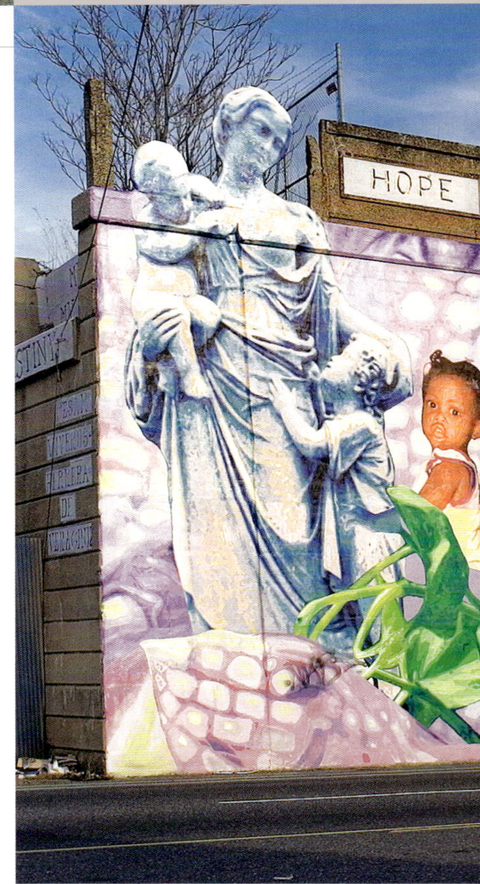

The three hundred by thirty-five–foot wall (a quarter of a mile) runs beside an unused railroad track in a neighborhood folks call "Port Fishington" because it joins Kensington, Port Richmond ,and Fishtown. Discussion was integral to the planning process. Using flyers, posters, and knocking on doors, MAP representatives and Viveros-Herrera met with residents.

The design Viveros-Herrera unveiled at a community meeting

Opposite
César poses in front of his Balanced and Restorative Justice mural, *My Life, My Path, My Destiny*, at 2157 E. Lehigh Ave.

Below
My Life, My Path, My Destiny—A Balanced and Restorative Justice mural project, in process, by César Viveros-Herrera, 2157 E. Lehigh Avenue. Over an eighth of a mile long, this mural depicts the journey, struggles, and triumphs of Philadelphia's youth, and was made possible by the Department of Human Services and the Samuel Fels Fund.

[1]For a detailed description of Meg Saligman's early work, the history of *Common Threads*, and a discussion of its iconography see Jane Golden et al., *Philadelphia Murals and The Stories They Tell* (Philadelphia: Temple University Press, 2002), 16–127.

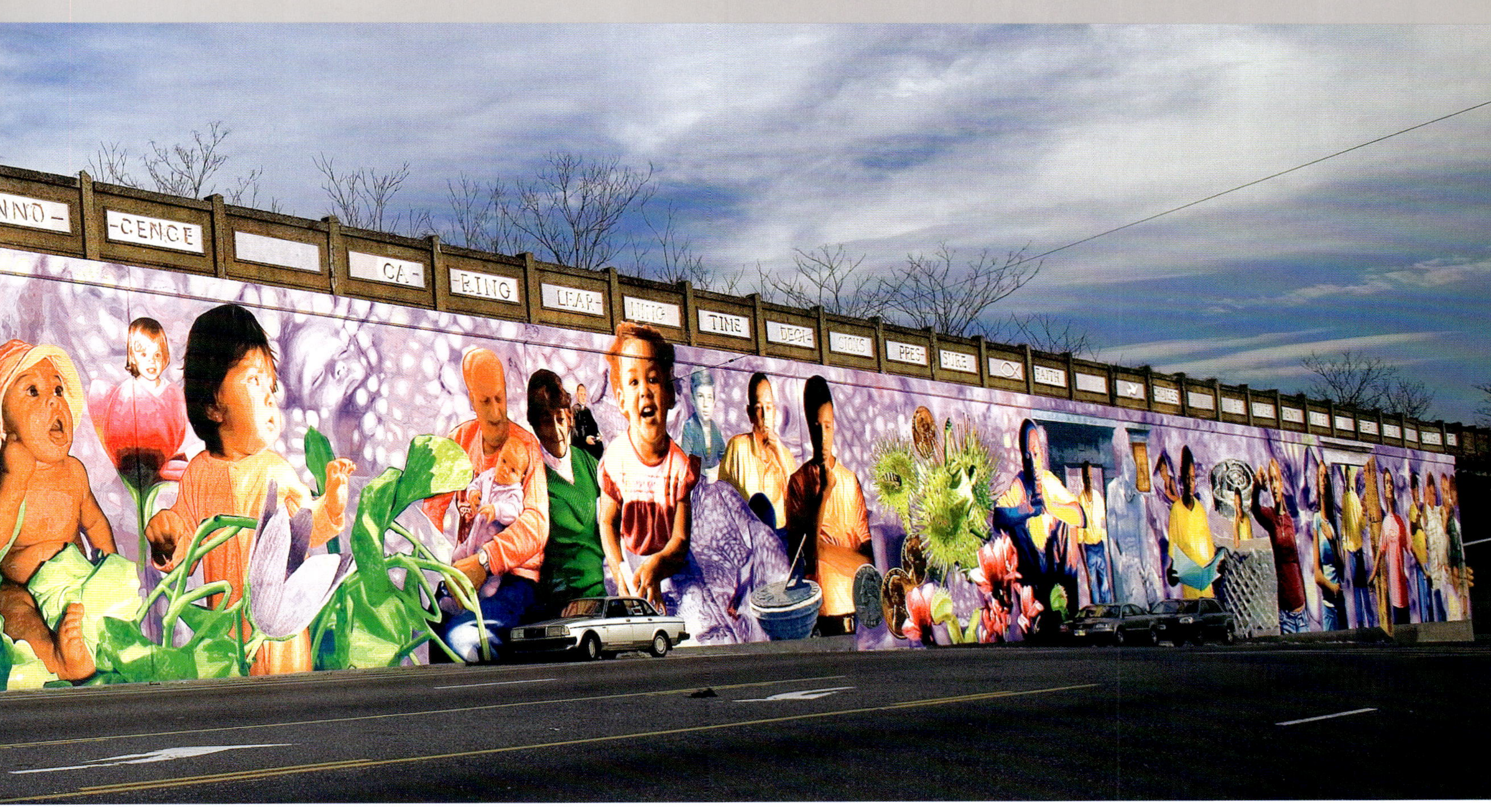

pleased most, but some felt that a predominance of African-American kids did not reflect the local community. "They were right," Viveros-Herrera says. "If you look at the neighborhood, there are just a few African Americans and a few Latinos." He reworked the design, changing models for some of the symbolic figures who illustrate decisive moments in growing up.

Groups of "Port Fishington" kids, students at St. Gabriel's, and inmates of SCI Graterford filled in 240 six by five–foot fabric panels traced by Viveros-Herrera. "I purposefully had *all* the groups paint on some panels just to make a symbolic physical connection between them."

Words running along the top of the completed horizontal wall describe the stages of life represented below, from infant "Innocence" to "Fulfillment" of adult dreams. After Viveros-Herrera had completed the painting, some neighborhood residents felt that the imagery in the central section, although mostly metaphorical, was too real, and the artist made more changes. As it now stands, the central section consists of: "Choices," in which a child is devoured by a huge Venus fly trap; "Pressure," which represents the lure of drugs and easy money; and "Facing Decisions," in which a closed door reminds us that some decisions are forever.

The elaborate panorama embodies a paradox. The allure of dangerous options is represented as glamorous, mirroring the real-life conflict between easy pleasures and lasting values. The consequences of bad decisions may be harsh, but Viveros-Herrera feels that although the elaborate panorama "shows the dark side which some deny, people are tired of waterfalls and flowers. They need something meaningful."

Victoria Greene's son, Emir, was twenty when he was killed in 1997. His was a drug-related murder and, to some people, that seemed to mean his death didn't matter, Greene says. That burned her: Her son was the man of his family, cherished by his four sisters and his mother, a father himself. As a youngster, he had taken part in a Mural Arts program, helping to paint a mural at Second and Callowhill Streets. He had been so proud of it. "My son was a person, whose life was valued, who was loved," Greene says. "There's no 'those people' and me. There's no separation. We have hard-working people whose children were murdered, whose children became involved in criminal activity, but they were their children."

She wanted to tell her story.

As part of the Healing Walls project, victims like Greene traveled to Graterford, thirty-one miles west of Philadelphia, to meet with men like Suave—lifers, many of them there for killing someone. The two sides were there to talk, to share, to find common ground, to accept the fact that they were intertwined—permanently, regrettably.

The meetings were often emotional, sometimes hostile, sometimes sorrow-filled: When one elderly man described living in fear after being mugged at gunpoint, an inmate asked if he could give the man a hug—and he did. One woman, whose brother was shot more than thirty years ago, was reconnected to him when an inmate revealed he had known and liked the dead man. Inmates described terrorizing neighborhoods without a care. Residents detailed suffering under the reign of lawlessness.

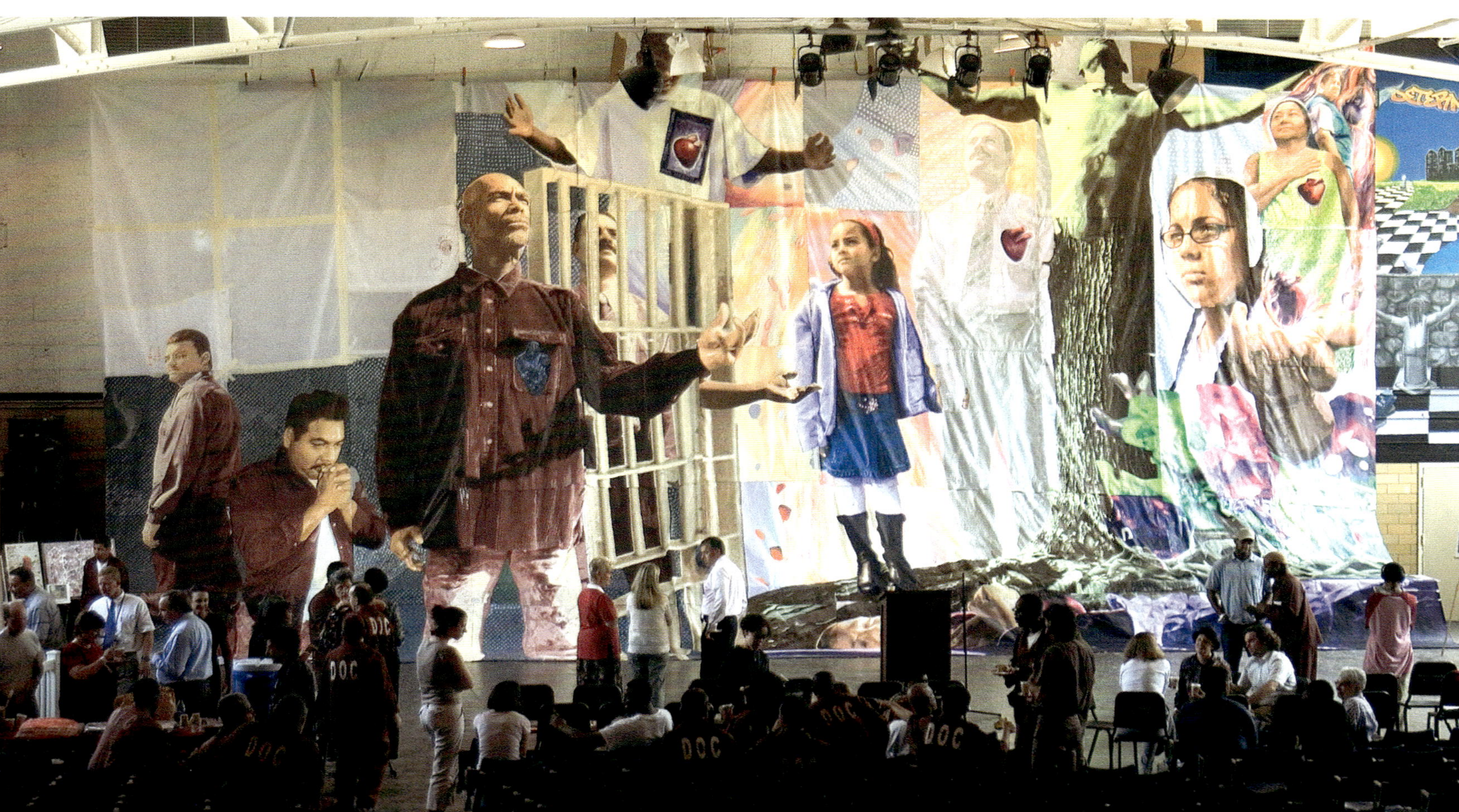

Seen here at the SCI Graterford dedication, the parachute cloth mural *The Inmates' Journey* could be painted behind the gates of SCI Graterford and installed later at 3049 Germantown Avenue. Created by César Viveros-Herrera, Parris Stancell, and the inmate muralists at Graterford.

Mary Catherine Lowery, program director for the St. Gabriel's Victims of Crime program, says she was apprehensive the first time she met with the inmates. She viewed the men as "those people out there that the people I deal with every day make the targets of their anger." She feared they would be hostile, too wrapped up in their own suffering and not see the pain of those she represents. She was afraid she would like them, and if she did, did that make her disloyal to the people she served?

Instead, she found most of the inmates at least tried to understand the victims' point of view. They were very articulate about their own feelings, perhaps because of the contemplative nature of their lives behind bars. The struggles they described further reminded her that "the world is not just made up of people in black and white hats. The world is every shade of gray experience," she says. "This brought me away from objectifying perpetrators and seeing them as real people."

Suave, thirty-six, grew up in the South Bronx, one of six kids. His paternal grandfather was the local barber, giving free haircuts to neighborhood kids, and Suave's hero. Suave was thirteen when his grandfather was shot twice while in the middle of a haircut. The shooter, a drug dealer, believed—mistakenly—that the barber was cooperating with police. Suave saw the murder and, in his own words, "I just started going crazy. . . . I wanted people to hurt like I was hurting."

The family moved to Philadelphia. Six months later, Suave, then sixteen, killed a man during a robbery. He has been behind bars ever since.

For a long time, Suave says, he considered cooperative prisoners "sellouts"—Until he became one. And he became one, in part, because of the Mural Arts program. He calls meeting Victoria Greene "the proudest moment of my life." Why? Because "she didn't come here to judge us. She came here as a mother, a victim and as a person who wanted to learn. And she accepted us. It felt like I was talking to my mother. That's what it felt like, like this is my mother here," he says.

Greene says her meetings with the prisoners were often profound. Many of them expressed remorse: One man said he saw his victim's face every night before he went to bed. Others were worried about their victims' families: One wanted to write to his victim's survivors but was afraid; another was worried about how his victim's mother was handling her loss.

"They surprised me," Greene says, "and they helped me. I was thinking, 'Maybe that's what my son's murderer does. Maybe he's worried about me. Maybe he has some remorse.' It was good for me."

The two groups talked, but they also worked. The twin murals—painted by community members, inmates, victims and their advocates—were affixed to two walls in the 3000 block

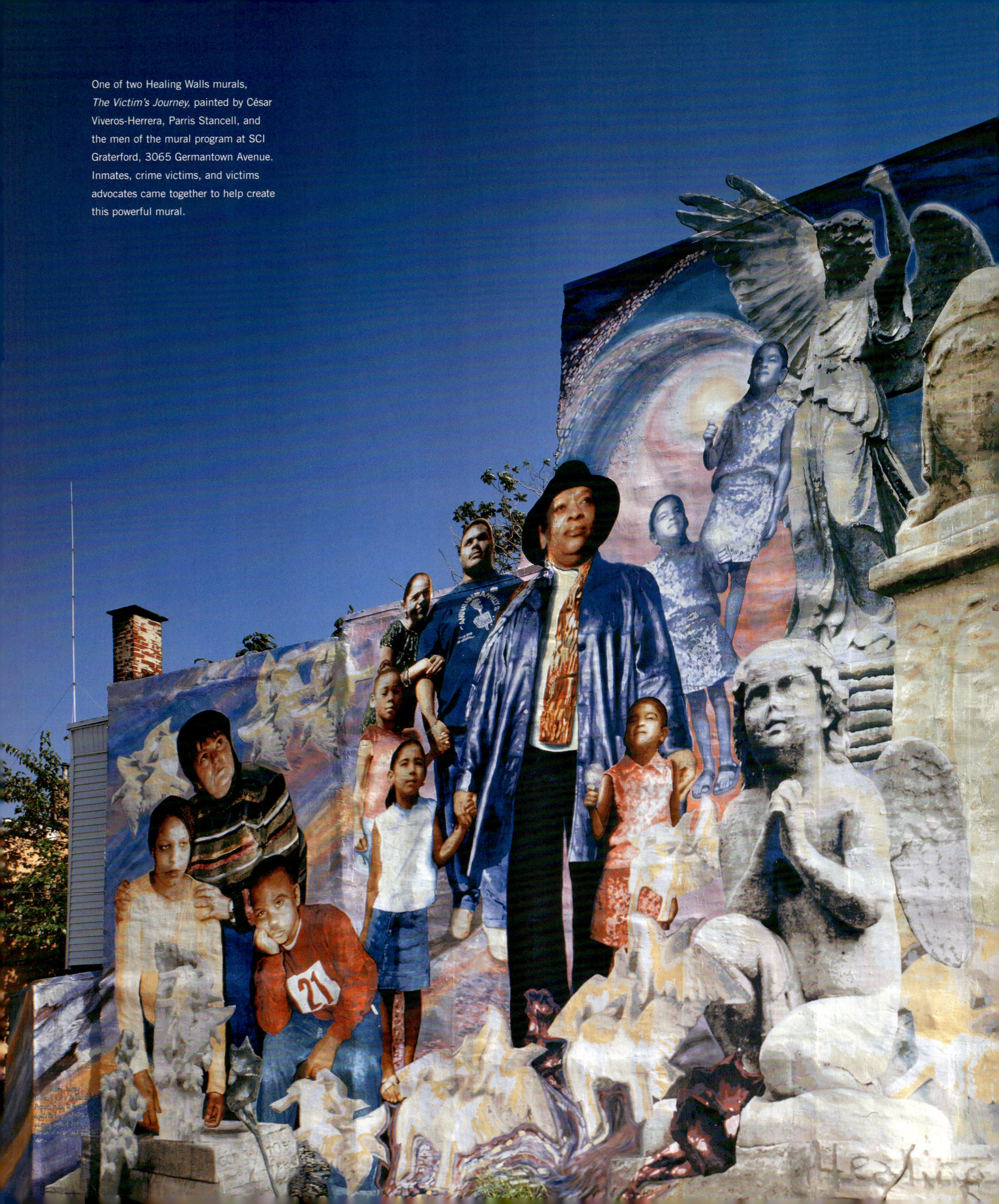

One of two Healing Walls murals, *The Victim's Journey,* painted by César Viveros-Herrera, Parris Stancell, and the men of the mural program at SCI Graterford, 3065 Germantown Avenue. Inmates, crime victims, and victims advocates came together to help create this powerful mural.

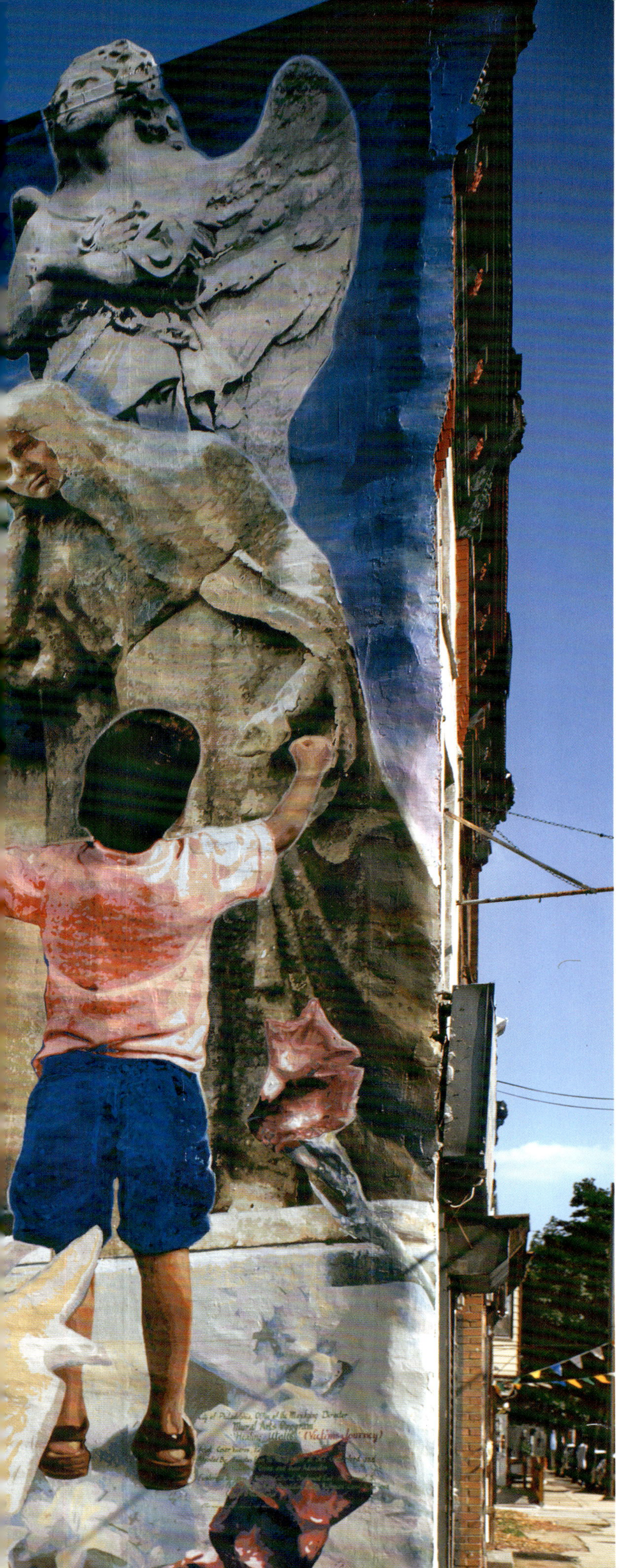

of Germantown Avenue in North Philadelphia during the summer of 2004 and formally dedicated at a ceremony in October of 2004. *The Inmates' Journey* (2004) shows, in part, a man reaching out from behind bars, another on his knees in prayer, another lifting his arms and head to the sky. *The Victims' Journey* (2004) has multiple depictions of angels carved as if for tombstones and different people touching—holding hands or arms or grasping shoulders.

Among those pictured are Victoria Greene, her daughter, and her six-year-old grandson—Emir, named after his father. "That was special. That was very special," Greene says. "It was so moving, so poetic. My son was an artist. He was so talented and involved in Mural Arts and seeing the end result, it was like a full circle thing. It all came back around."

Some people—perhaps most—would have stopped then, thrilled to have completed such a challenging project, content to take a break. Not Golden. She had another idea: Could she give teenagers from St. Gabriel's Hall the chance to paint murals as part of their redemption? What if she could bring those teens together with lifers at Graterford for lessons they could receive no where else?

DiGuglielmo, the Graterford Superintendent, decided to let her give it a try. He started his career as a psychologist and he says he's never quite sure if emotional experiences have a lasting or changing effect on people. There have been past programs where at-risk youth came to the prison to hear inmates speak about their lives, but he wondered how effective they were.

"I don't think sitting in a room and listening to a bunch of offenders talk does a lot of good, but this added a whole new dimension. The artwork is a medium to helping let down barriers," he says. "Art and creativity brings things out of people they may not be aware of."

The Balanced and Restorative Justice Project, another arm of Healing Walls, got underway in December 2004. The wall chosen for the mural was along East Lehigh Avenue in the Kensington/Port Richmond neighborhood. Mural Arts enlisted the help of the nearby church, St. Anne's, which hosted design meetings and painting days. Parishioners like Eileen Blair gave even more, donating time, effort, and emotion. Says Blair simply, "It changed my life. How could it not?"

When Blair was thirty, she was raped by an acquaintance who followed her home. She pressed charges and the man, who had twenty-two prior arrests for sex-related crimes, was found guilty of sexual assault and battery and sentenced to five years of psychiatric probation. Blair never spoke about the crime again.

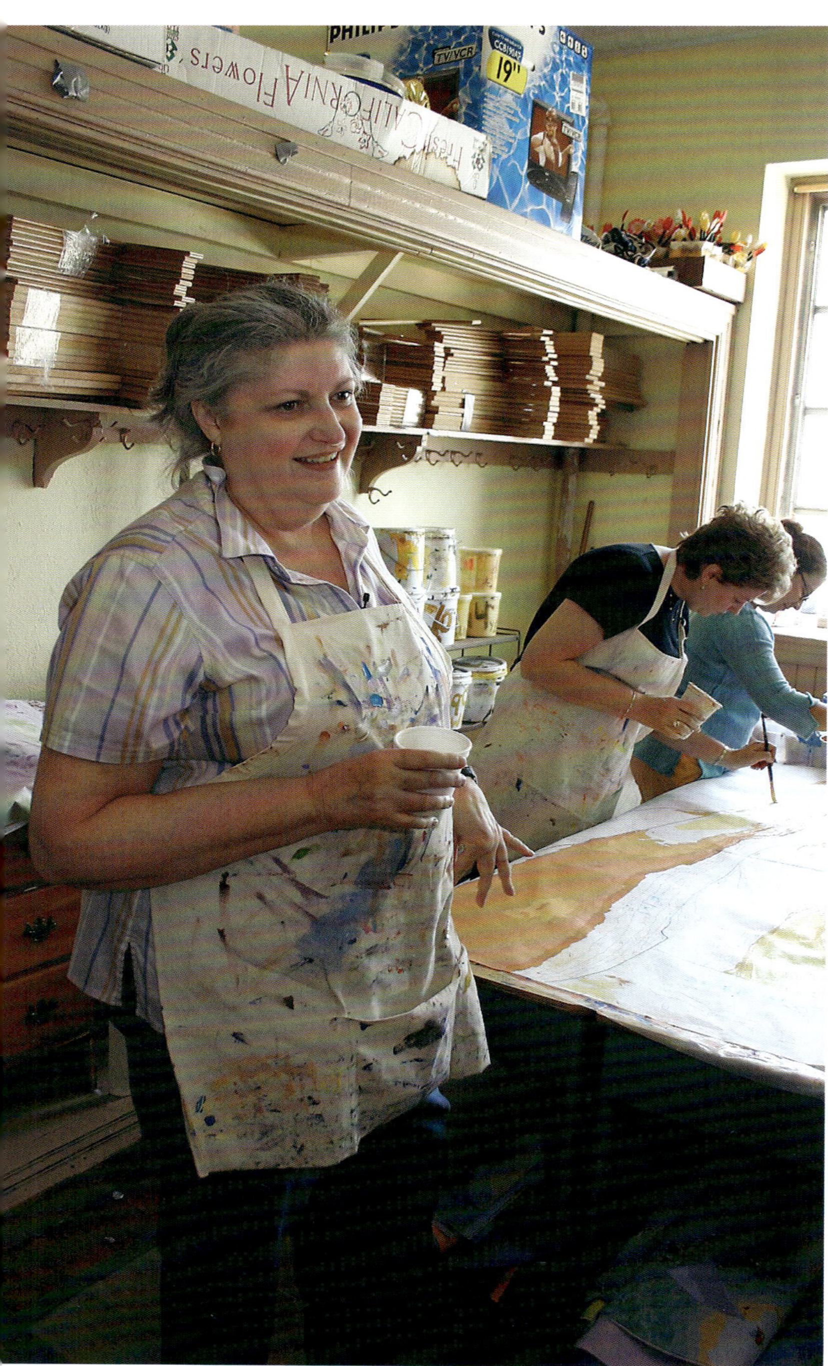

St. Anne's Church parishioner Eileen Blair restores balance and justice with dialogue, understanding, and a paint brush.

More than twenty years later, she found herself at Graterford, in a room with men incarcerated for horrible crimes that included rape and boys who were in danger of following in their footsteps. Someone asked her to tell her story. She did.

"I remember particularly talking to the boys, saying to them, 'This guy was probably like you at some point and nobody helped him and he just got worse and worse and worse. He kept falling through the cracks. Please take the opportunity to let these people help you," she says. "I looked them right in the eyes and they weren't afraid to look at me. It occurred to me then that rape is really a violent crime and all these guys had experienced terrible violence in their lives and that's why they were all looking at me with soft eyes."

Blair attended painting sessions at her church and at Graterford. But sometimes, the Graterford group chose to forgo painting in favor of talking.

Sitting in a sloppy circle, they would share whatever was on their minds. One night, one boy admitted he didn't know his multiplication tables. Another said his trips to Graterford had opened his eyes: "I know I'm not going to be in a place like this. I can't. I got too much to lose."

Then Julius, seventeen, began to speak. Nicknamed Shaq by the men because of his height, Julius has a sweet smile, a baby face, and a gentle air—and he was arrested for selling drugs. This night, he talked about what painting the mural and meeting the adult inmates had done for him. "When I first got (to St. Gabriel's), I was ready to snap. I didn't want to be there," he said. "Then this. And now, when I get older, I can show my kids, 'When I was in placement, I did this.'"

Julius began talking about his family. Like many of the men and boys there, he had grown up without a father. His mother, he said, "started nice," then started drinking, then couldn't pay the bills. "The only thing I could turn to was the streets. When we see that fast money, we run to it," he said.

I came here when I was sixteen. Twenty years. I got a life sentence. Half the people in this room, they're lifers. You've got to be really careful when you head back to the streets. You ain't got to be down. Being down ain't what's up.

The group was supportive, but silent. Julius continued: "My mom is about to die because I drove her to drinking because my father wasn't there. She's really skinny now. When she visited, the kids called her a crackhead," he said, choking back sobs and looking around the room with glassy eyes. "Since I've been coming here, since my second month here, I've been setting goals for myself. Suave told me to write my life story. I'm writing my life story and setting goals."

When Julius finished, he got loud, back-slapping hugs and hand slaps from the men. He was still teary-eyed when he left, but smiling that sweet smile again.

The night Suave met the fifteen-year-old was a painting night. As they dipped their brushes, Suave learned the boy's name was Tyree and he was from West Philadelphia. Suave told the boy he was lucky he'd been a juvenile when he was arrested. "You know how much this carries when you're eighteen?" Suave said. Tyree nodded, "Five to ten. I can't even take four months."

Suave grunted. "Someone gets hurt, killed, during that robbery, accidentally, that's a life sentence. You know what that means in this state? Until you die. Or until you get a new trial," he laughed at that, as did some of the other men around him. "So you better be careful out there, young boy. Watch your friends. You're even there, you get the same sentence. I came here when I was sixteen. Twenty years. I got a life sentence. Half the people in this room, they're lifers. You've got to be really careful when you head back to the streets. You ain't got to be down. Being down ain't what's up."

Zafir, another lifer doing time for murder, jumped in. "You become a number here. I'd rather see you become the Chief Justice."

Tyree told the men he'd gotten into six fights since going to St. Gabriel's, prompting Zafir to tell the story of a man he once knew who was sentenced to a year in prison on drug charges and ended up serving thirty because of misbehavior while behind bars.

"You know why you're here?" Suave asked the boy. "To learn not to come up here," was the answer.

Blair says one of the most powerful statements she ever heard during the sessions took place between an inmate named Spel—another lifer who knew Golden from his days as a graffiti artist—and a group of boys. They were all in a corner, joking around. "Spel said, 'I'm really happy to see you guys. We have so much fun when you're here. But I hope I never see you again. I hope you're never back here. You know all the laughing and joking we do while you're here? Well, then they take us back to our cells and we get locked in and we cry ourselves to sleep,'" Blair remembers. "To me, that was so courageous on his part. These guys can make a real contribution. They know what the kids are going to do before the kids know it. They can tell them how to get through and how to not come back."

The third mural in the Healing Walls project was formally unveiled in October 2005. Hundreds of people were there, including community members, city officials, the family members of inmates, and youth who had worked on the mural. Golden told the group that the project "was one of the more complicated ones we've ever done, but also one of the most satisfying."

She was referring, in part, to a controversy that had arisen once sections of the mural had gone up on the wall. Some neighbors were angry about the design. "The Journey of Youth" included images of an adult holding a baby to symbolize innocence, a Venus fly trap and a crack pipe and coins to symbolize pressure, a maze to show the choices youth have to make. The drug imagery made it seem like they were advertising drugs for sale in their community, the protestors said. The fact that one of the youths pictured had died of a drug overdose glorified narcotics, they said.

After a series of tense, public meetings—at one point, Golden said, she thought the whole wall would just be white-washed—she and Viveros-Herrera agreed to alter the already finished design. Viveros-Herrera got rid of the crack pipe, toned down the fly trap, and added, at the end of the mural, the image of a local police officer who had died in Iraq. That appeased most of the critics, some of whom attended the dedication ceremony on a cool Sunday.

"Do you know what we have achieved here?" Golden asked the crowd. "We have achieved a state of grace."

A choir sang "Let There Be Peace on Earth." DiGuglielmo spoke on behalf of the inmates, who couldn't be there, and others read letters the men had written. Julius, freshly released from St. Gabriel's, stood with boys who were still in the program, his bright clothing in marked contrast to their drab wear. "I couldn't really believe at first that I did it," he said, looking at the wall. "It makes me hurt inside that (the Graterford inmates) can't be able to see it."

Julius was back at home, taking classes and working with Mural Arts. His mom was still ill and struggling. His former friends were still pressuring him to join them on the streets. "I

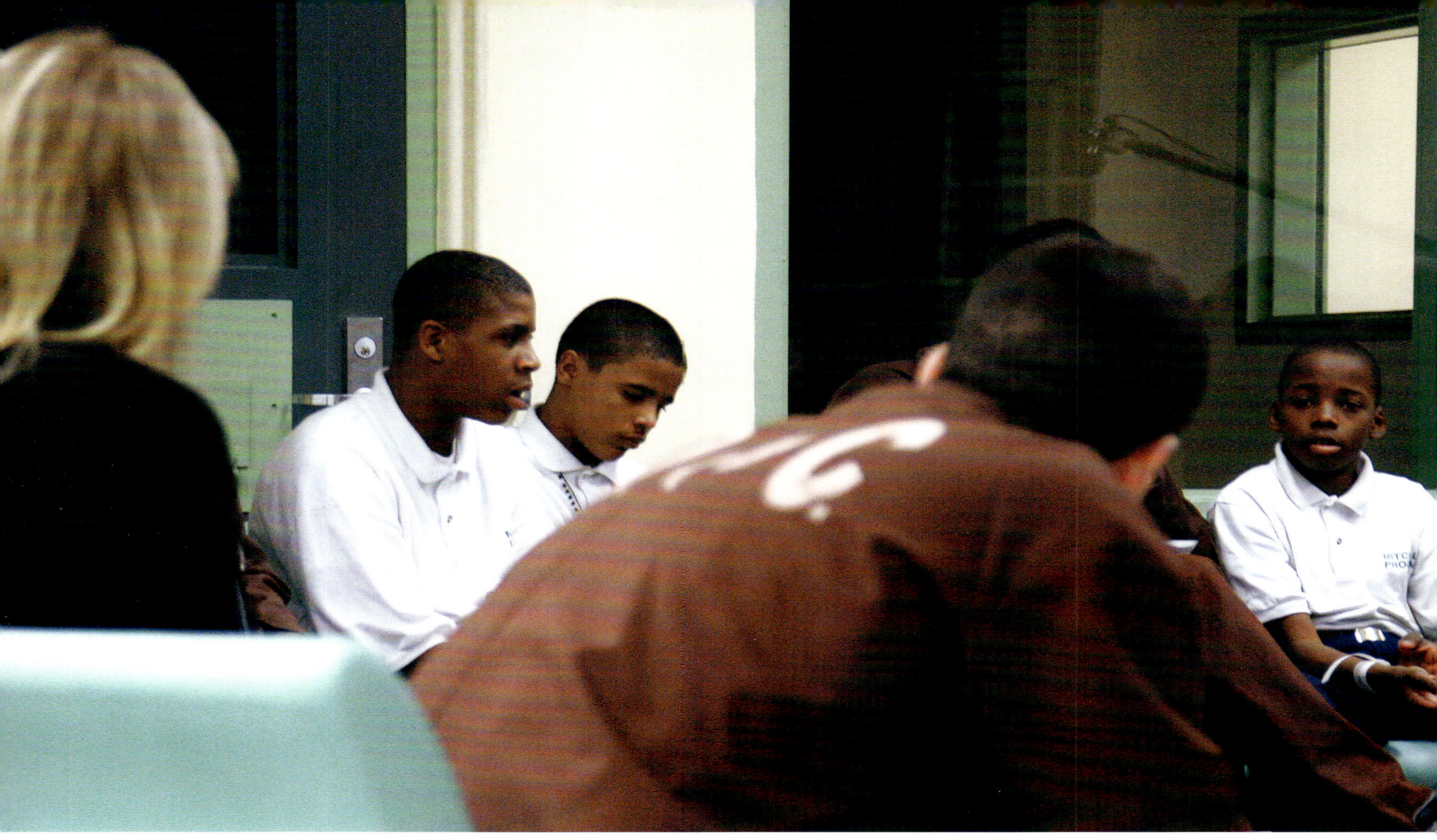

Translating an idea into paint—a Balanced and Restorative Justice community meeting at SCI Graterford.

know how to get past them now. I walk past them,' he said. "It feels so good to be out, but it's so hard to understand these boys."

A few weeks later, Golden visited the men at Graterford. She told them how the community had come to accept the mural, how beautiful the program was, how each of their names had been read aloud.

Julius had come to the ceremony and asked about them, she said. He was out, but struggling. Spel encouraged her to keep after the boy, just as she had once kept after him when he was a teenager defacing Philadelphia walls. "People give up on you. People have good intentions, but they've got to have follow through," he said. "They're not getting attention at home so they get it on the street."

Suave shook his head. Julius, he said, would have a hard time on the outside, because he was a nice kid. "He's the type of guy, when I was out, we looked for him," Suave said. "Because we could give him a little love and then use him."

The Graterford lifers then agreed that, although they would all like to see Julius again, they hoped they never would.

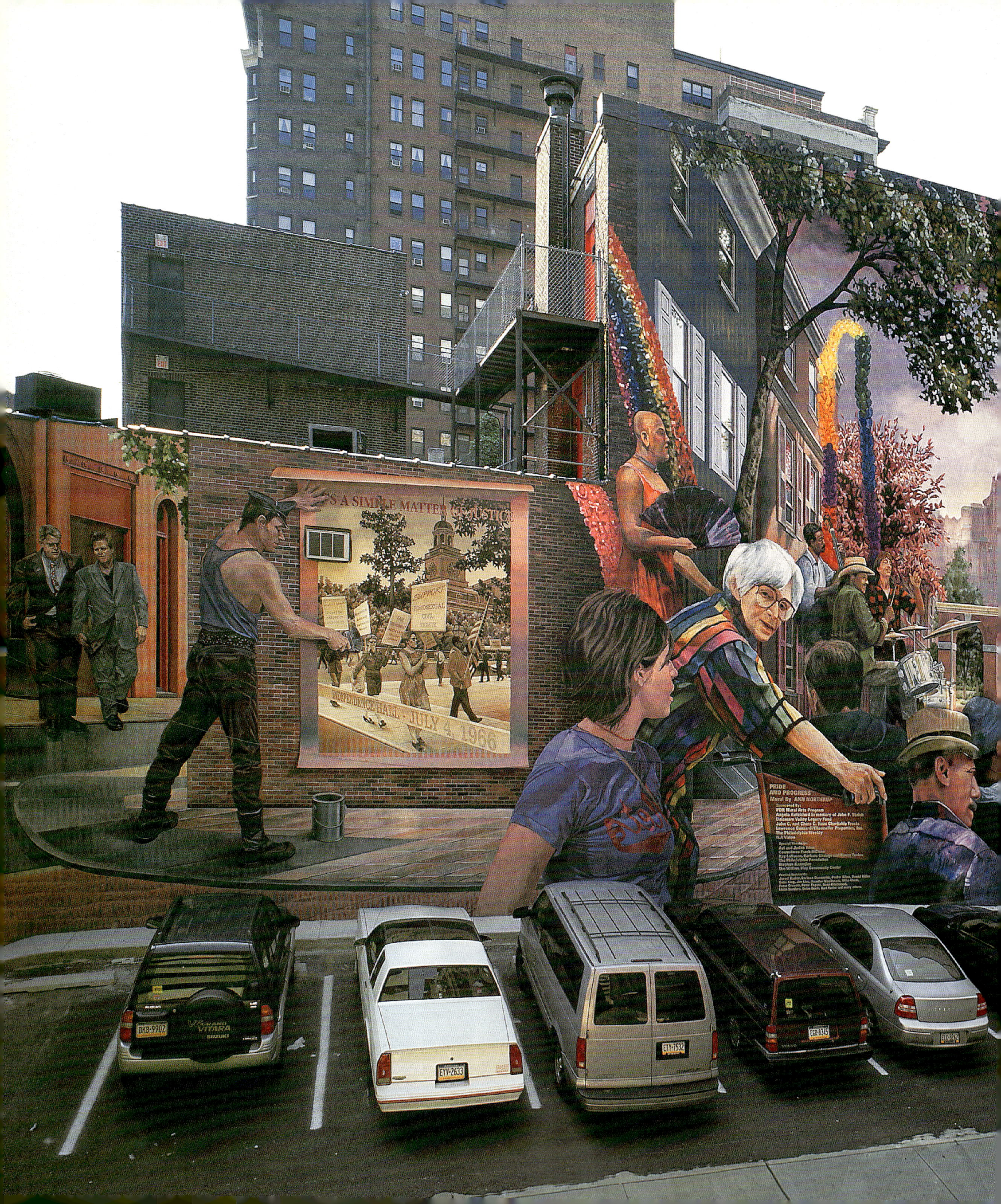
'S A SIMPLE MATTER OF JUSTICE
SUPPORT HOMOSEXUAL CIVIL RIGHTS
INDEPENDENCE HALL - JULY 4, 1966
PRIDE AND PROGRESS
Mural By ANN NORTHRUP
Sponsored By:
Delaware Valley Legacy Fund
The Philadelphia Weekly
TLA Video
The Philadelphia Foundation
The William Way Community Center

Chapter 9

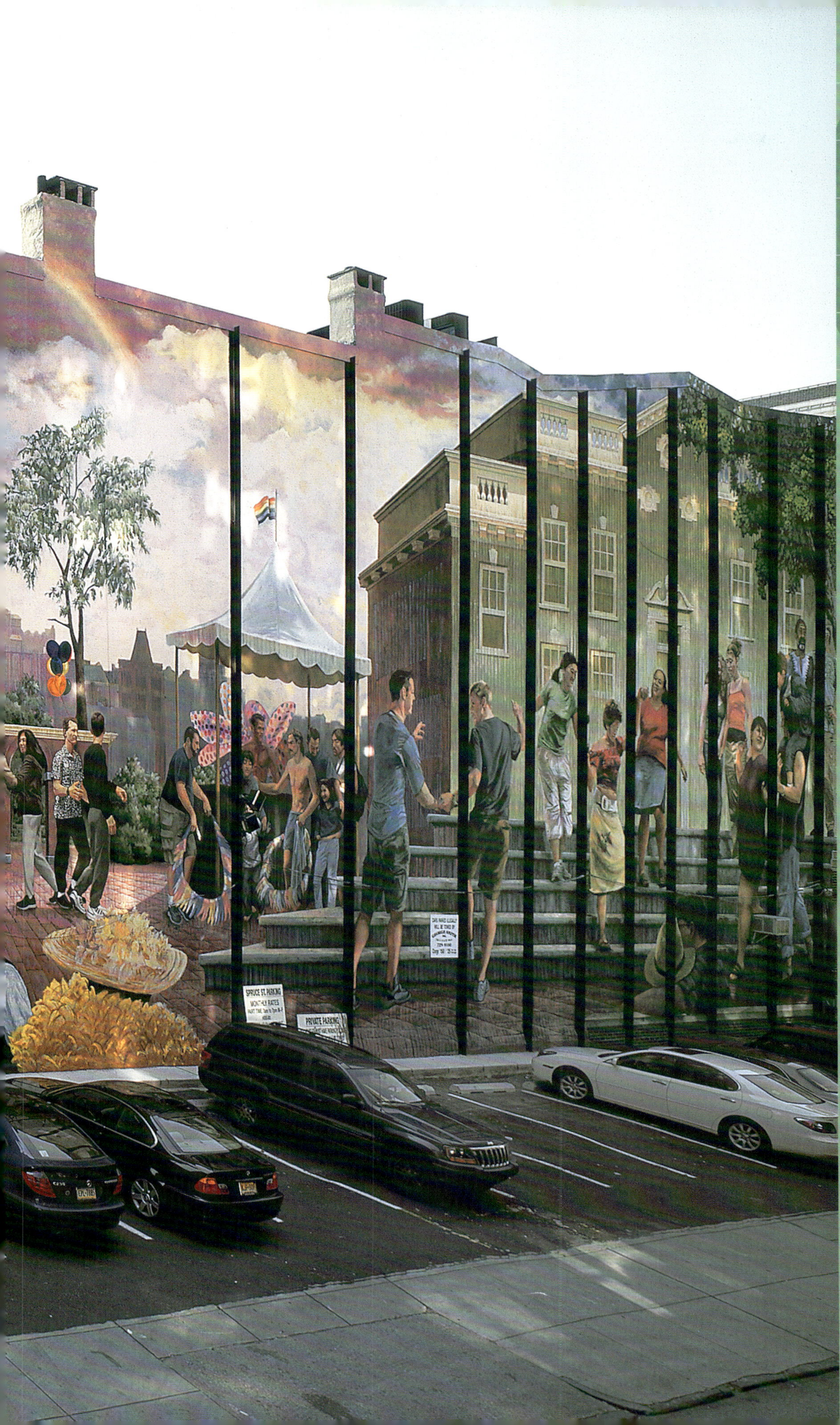

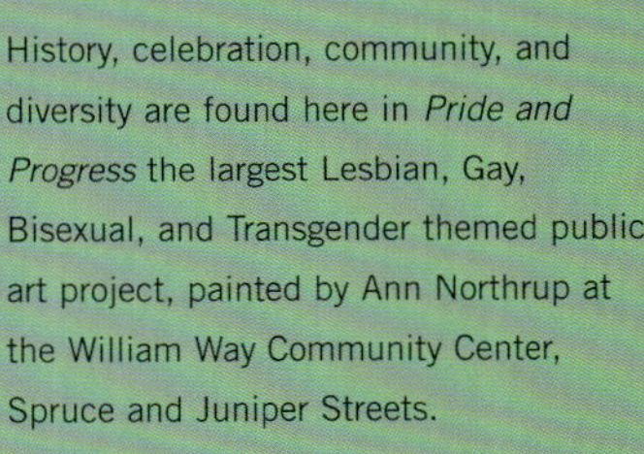

History, celebration, community, and diversity are found here in *Pride and Progress* the largest Lesbian, Gay, Bisexual, and Transgender themed public art project, painted by Ann Northrup at the William Way Community Center, Spruce and Juniper Streets.

Chapter 9

Philadelphia Stories

Patronage

If you want people to remember something, make it as big as you can and put it where everyone can see it. The rule holds true for images of monarchs, deities, and hamburgers. As Machiavelli notes in *The Prince,* " . . . men judge generally more by the eye than by the hand, because it belongs to everybody to see you, to few to come in touch with you" (translated by W. K. Marriott, 1908). The scale of an artwork is an index of power: political, spiritual, financial, or social. Murals today put this power within the grasp of the ordinary citizen—even disenfranchised members of the community.

Patronage, the record of who commissioned whom to make what, where and why, is a key area of study for art historians. The *where* is Philadelphia with its insatiable appetite for public art. It already has much and a percentage for art programs guarantees more. But most patrons of public art rely on "experts" to choose or approve it. The Mural Arts Program is not the only grassroots-oriented organization in the city, but it is unique in the way in which it reaches out to so many communities: neighborhoods throughout the city as well as groups sharing common nongeographic concerns.

MAP murals typically weave together several interests. The city is always a factor because MAP is a city program. Sometimes agencies like the city schools or the Department of Recreation suggest mural themes. Outside funding sources, which often pay much of the cost of a mural, are critical in determining the subjects of some murals. But no matter who pays for it, in residential areas, the majority of those who have a mural in their "living rooms" have the opportunity to respond to the design before it's painted. In bustling commercial areas, the design is aimed at a cross-section of the general public.

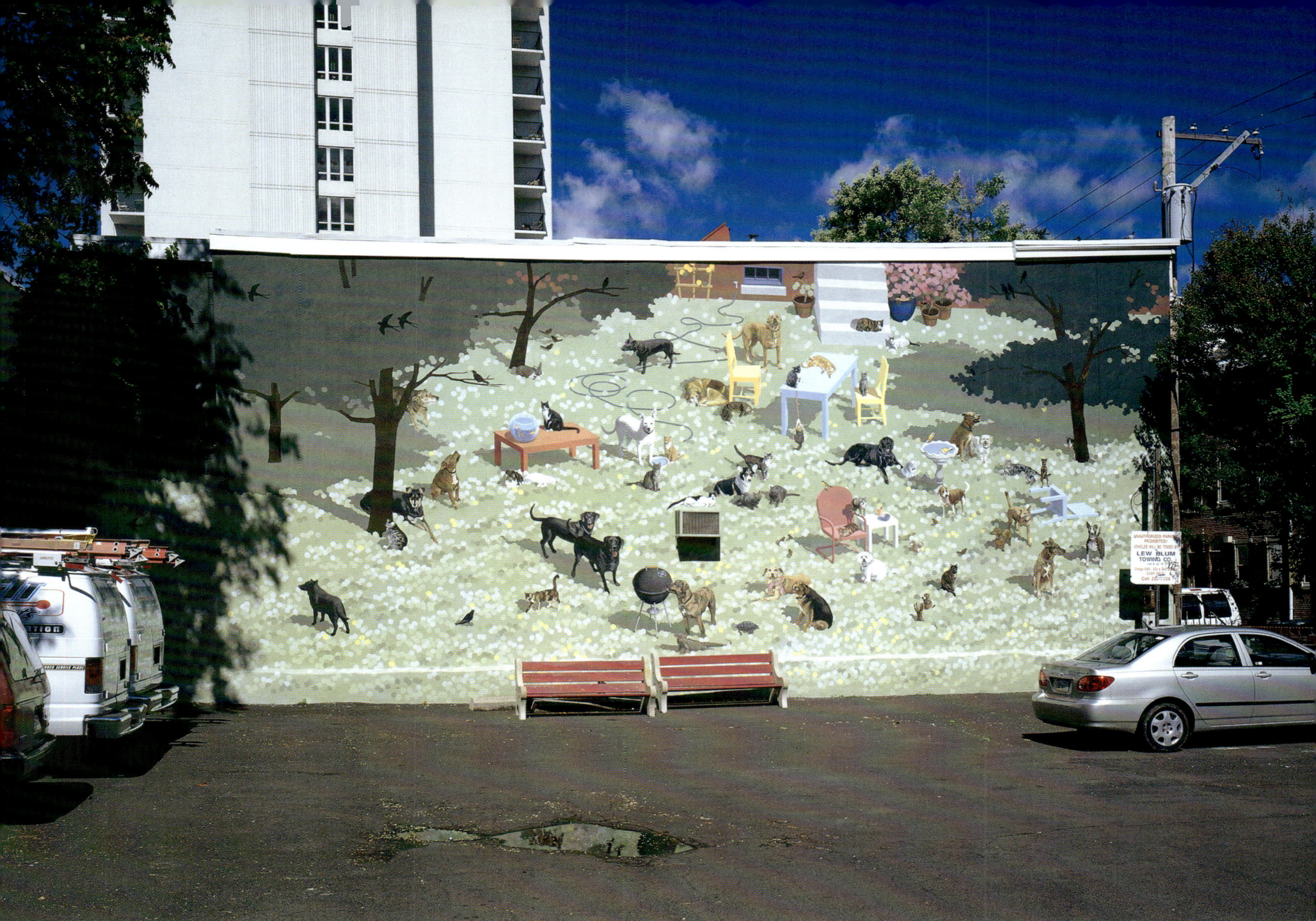

Lucky raffle winners found their pets immortalized in *Gimme Shelter*—painted by David Guinn, who grew up only a few blocks from the mural's location at 1236 Lombard Street.

A Mural's Best Friends

A mural with a serious purpose may have both substance and beauty, but few are as easy to enjoy as *Gimme Shelter*, a wall of the Morris Animal Refuge. David Guinn's landscape—crowded with pets and a handful of wild critters—makes no pretension to profundity, but it served an important cause. The subjects of the picture were determined by a raffle, the proceeds of which helped to provide funding for both the mural and the shelter. Purchasers of a winning $10 ticket could pick a pet whose portrait Guinn painted in the mural. The raffle was highly publicized and many tickets were sold. When the winning tickets were drawn, jubilant smiles mingled with tears of disappointment as participants realized not everyone's beloved pet would be immortalized.

In addition to the expected dogs and cats, Guinn added an iguana, a chameleon, birds, a turtle, a rabbit, and a goldfish. Exercising artistic license, Guinn also added his four cats as well as an assortment of wild animals to honor the broader spectrum of animal life.

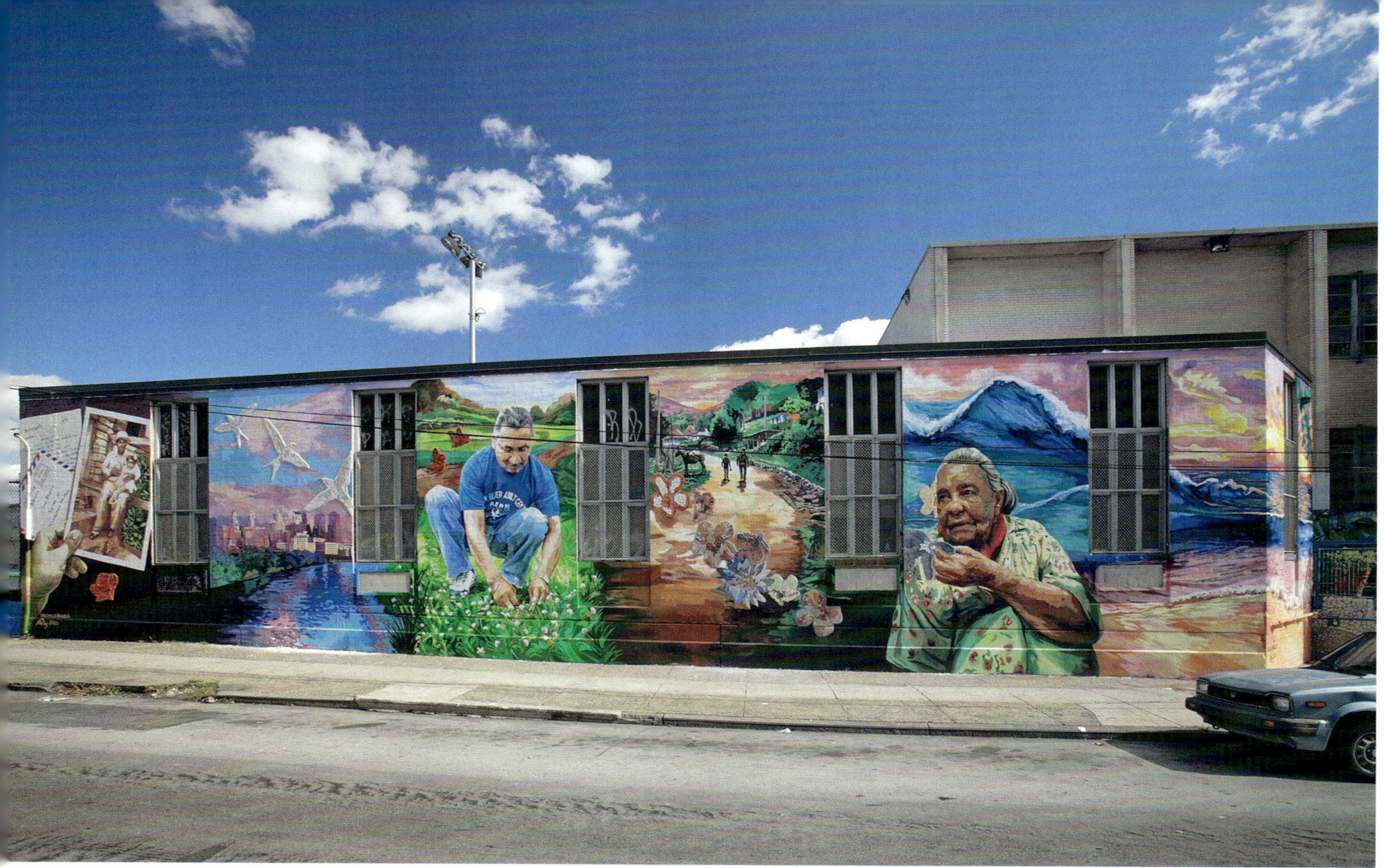

Life Reflects Nature: Memories of the Past, Traditions of the Present at the Mann Older Adult Center by Michelle Ortiz, 5th Street and Allegheny Avenue. Funded by the Knight Foundation, the Department of Aging, HACE and AARP, this mural is the first of many that pair ethnographers and muralists.

"Jane knew that I was an animal lover and I think that is why I was asked to do the mural," Guinn suggests. Most likely, another reason he was picked for the project was the fact that his other murals in Center City are consistently cited as among Philadelphia's most popular.

Guinn recalls, "It was an exciting project from the beginning. One of the things about mural painting that I like is meeting people. I contacted all the winners and asked for a picture of the pet. Some people brought the pet to me and I took a picture of it. I felt like the mural was fifty individual portraits of these pets and I took pains to be specific. I spent a lot of time on each pet and most of the owners came by while I was working to see if their pet was up there on the wall. Although I had always thought pet portraits were kind of corny, afterwards, I thought, 'I really like doing this—maybe I should take it on as a sideline.'"

But Guinn soon learned that there was a group who didn't have pets who also felt "ownership" of the mural. "Across the parking lot is a women's shelter, The Women of Hope. They kind of took me in and gave me lunch with the residents every day. They see the mural more than anyone else. Most are semipermanent residents with mental problems. Sweet people. I still see them on the street. They are very friendly and were very engaged in the whole thing. In one part of the mural, there is a cat looking at a [wild] bird. It really upset one of the ladies. She said, 'The cat wants to kill that bird.' And I said, 'You never know the bird might get away.'

"That was one of my favorite projects. The pet owners were so involved. It was working for a community, but it wasn't a geographical community."

Since *Gimme Shelter* was painted, animal lovers who did not have an opportunity to participate in the first wall have asked Morris to sponsor another mural and Guinn has agreed to paint it.

My North Philly

Ethnographer Zoia Cisneros listened to the people who frequent the Mann Older Adult Center. She spent hours with them, asked them questions about their lives and recorded their oral histories. She looked for common links between the group, most of whom were immigrants from Puerto Rico, Central America, and South America. They talked about flowers and working the fields, the respect they had had for their elders, how different the young people seemed today.

But the one thing they all had in common? "They loved to talk," Cisneros says. "They loved to talk about their lives. They were like, 'Yes, yes, let me tell you.' They were not shy at all."

Cisneros translated their stories from Spanish into English, and then MAP translated them into art.

Guillermo Sala and Juan Gutierrez (right) from Hispanic Association of Contractors & Enterprises, seen here at the *My North Philly* community meeting. Without the voice and direction of community leaders, projects such as this would rarely leave the ground.

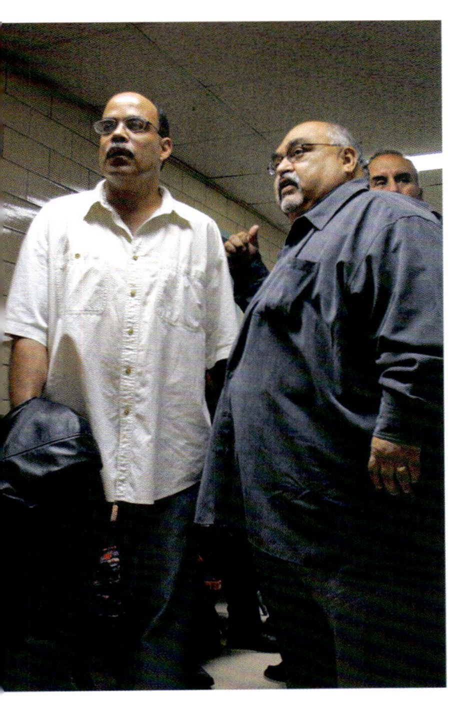

The resulting mural by artists Michelle Ortiz and Jose Ali Paz—*Life Reflects Nature: Memories of the past; traditions of the present/La Vida Refleja La Naturaleza: Memorias del pasado; tradiciones del presente*—is the first of about a dozen slated for the next three years as part of *My North Philly* Partnering with community organizations, MAP is collecting the oral histories of residents of this diverse area with the goal of creating a series of murals that illustrate their life stories. Much of the funding is provided by the John S. and James L. Knight Foundation's Community Partners in Arts Access Initiative.

"The goal is to give voice to the people in these communities in a way that has never been done before in a Mural Arts project," says Maria Moller, the project's lead ethnographer. "*My North Philly* is really based on the people's words. It's not just about their lives but also about their hopes, their histories. Each mural is going to be different because each neighborhood of people is different."

The original project proposal was four murals in four North Philadelphia neighborhoods, project manager Lindsey Rosenberg says. But once the first mural was underway, "the diversity and excitement of individuals in the area was so apparent that we expanded the proposal to capture more neighborhoods."

North Philadelphia is rich with different cultures: Hispanic, African-American, European, Asian. The first mural reached out to the Hispanic community. Moller is now interviewing residents of Kensington, a largely white, working-class neighborhood, for another. Other areas targeted for murals include Strawberry Mansion, a traditionally troubled area with a large African-American population, and Logan, a middle-class African-American neighborhood.

Another thing to consider about North Philadelphia is that, like most urban areas, it is constantly evolving, with new groups moving in and staking a claim, mixing with those who have lived there for generations. Poverty, caused by a loss of industry, is a problem here and one of the few things the area is rich in is closed factories and warehouses. Violence is another issue, and parts of the area are often viewed as tainted by outsiders.

Many residents feel that they're ignored by the local government, that their city services are subpar, that their voices are not heard. But that's changing as MAP works within the community, said Juan Gutierrez of Hispanic Association of Contractors & Enterprises (HACE). People who feel empowered to talk about the mural then want to talk about why their streets aren't clean and what they can do to change that, he said.

The Mann Older Adult Center, at 5th Street and Allegheny Avenue, is the type of place where members start lining up outside its doors fifteen minutes before its 8 A.M. opening. It serves a population sixty years of age or older, but also aims to be a resource center for caregivers and family members. The community around the center is changing—an area that was once mostly Puerto Rican is being infused by people from South and Central America. Taking part in *My North Philly*—meeting about the mural's design, telling stories, and creating tiles for the wall—allowed them to see they share more than a common language, said Center Director Ed Fagan.

"Everyone saw themselves as working together instead of from their own distinct backgrounds," Fagan says. "During one Community Day, people just talked. There was a lot of informal exchange of information, a sort of coming together. It was just a great day."

"Everyone saw themselves as working together instead of from their own distinct backgrounds," Fagan says. "During one Community Day, people just talked. There was a lot of informal exchanges of information, a sort of coming together. It was just a great day."

The finished work—completed with additional funding from HACE, the Philadelphia Department of Aging, and the AARP—contains orchids and palm trees, exotic birds and a burro, and various human figures, including Doña Nicolosa, a Mann Center member who is more than one hundred years old and who still loves to dance. The many different cultures are addressed in subtle ways: One man whose face is on the wall comes from Puerto Rico, another painting is based on a photograph taken in Ecuador, a third segment features an envelope with a postmarked stamp from Colombia.

"People had to stop and figure out what was going on and that captures their interest," Ortiz says. "It wasn't just the older generation that participated in the interview process but also the younger people walking by and coming over and asking, 'What's this? What's the story?'"

Center members like Maria Calvo, sixty-five, and Manuel Moya, sixty-four, shared their tale: The married couple came to the United States from Costa Rica twenty-five years ago to work in the North Philadelphia factories and build on the American dream. They came without papers, without a car. They left their children behind until they had enough money to bring them over.

But they were determined to make their mark, and they did—buying a home, sending their children to city schools. When the mural artists came to the Mann Center, they also had a chance to leave a physical mark on the wall. Moya is also an artist—although he is too modest to say so—working with ceramic tile. He asked if he could incorporate some of his work into the mural. The artists agreed, and let other members contribute painted tiles as well.

"The mural is beautiful as a physical entity, but it has also built a sense of ownership and pride in the membership and the immediate community," Fagan says. While it was being painted, he said, two other homeowners on the block spruced up their brick facades with new coats of paint.

Calvo and Moya echo Fagan's sentiment. They bring their grandchildren to the mural. They point out the tiles Moya crafted. Looking at the wall, Calvo says, she is "orgullosa." Proud.

Her husband, listening in, nods: "Ay, si," he says.

Pride and Progress

It was a project that was so high profile, so socially complex, and so politically loaded that the first artist backed out: a seventy-five-hundred-square-foot mural that would become the first Lesbian, Gay, Bisexual, and Transgender public art project in the country.

But not muralist Ann Northrup. When she heard that MAP needed someone to take on the unprecedented *Pride and Progress* mural, she stepped up. The results of her efforts now cover a wall of the classical Federalist building housing the William Way Lesbian, Gay, Bisexual, and Transgender Community Center (1315 Spruce Street; see page 122).

After extensive discussions with the William Way board, she began painting in August 2002; but, although she had so many assistants, both paid and volunteer, that "we covered the scaffolding with people," work continued deep into the fall and winter. Breaking off for the holidays, painting began again in the spring and the mural was dedicated in May 2003, between two significant LGBT celebrations, Equality Forum, and June's Gay Pride Month.

The mural wall is divided by steel girders that break up the panorama and make it impossible to see the whole mural from some points of view. Northrup overcame this problem by representing a carnival-like gay pride street festival in perspective. The figures appear to move through space behind dark verticals, functioning dividers between friezelike panels. "I hope that as you move past the mural you get the feeling almost of watching a moving picture," Northrup says. In response to the William Way board's request, she orchestrated the mostly

Muralist Ann Northrup at *Pride and Progress,* Spruce and Juniper Streets. The artist worked into a particularly cold fall and winter in order to complete the mural on time.

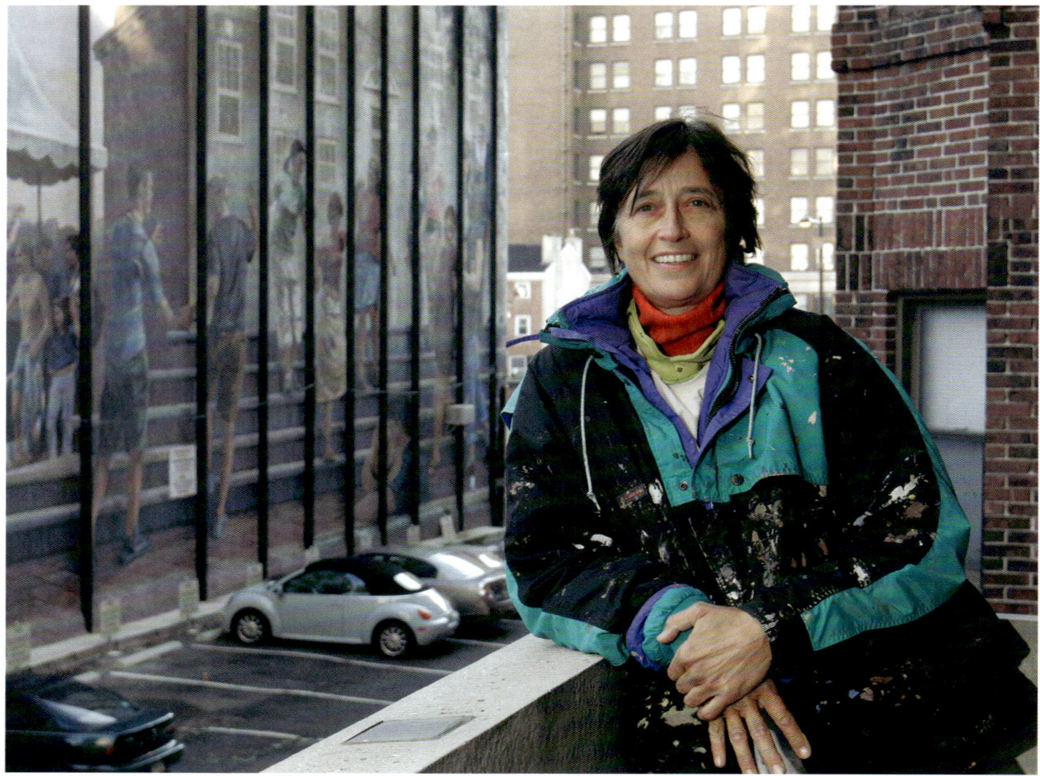

life-size figures—the tallest is about twenty feet—to express "a positive life-affirming acceptance of people and their love. The board wanted to represent everybody: every racial and every gender group and every age and different kinds of abilities. "It's the idea represented by the rainbow symbol seen throughout LGBT culture and pictured subtly in the sky above Northrup's idealized cityscape. "Anytime you get into people, you have to think about diversity. I like the challenge it pushes me to be creative," Northrup says.

The William Way group, "a very diverse creative bunch of nonconformists," Northrup says admiringly, had asked her not to depict specific individuals. However, an exception was made for Barbara Gittings (b. 1932), often called "the Grandmother of Gay Liberation," and her partner, journalist Kay Lahusen. In the 1960s Gittings, an author, helped organize the first gay rights demonstrations at the White House, the Pentagon, and Philadelphia's Independence Hall. In the 1970s, she was instrumental in persuading the American Psychiatric Association to change its position that homosexuality was a mental illness. Two brothers and local real estate developers, the Guzzardis, paid for the section of the mural in which Gittings and Lahusen are represented, so, with everyone's agreement, Northrup made portraits of the siblings at one side of the mural, like donor portraits in Renaissance art.

At the mural dedication, the community celebrated in dance and song. The last act was a drag cabaret singer. She tottered out on spike heels and quipped, "This mural leaves someone out! And that someone is . . . the bitter old queen." Northrup laughs ruefully, "She did not get in but she could have if we had known sooner."

One day as Northrup was working on the mural, a tour trolley pulled up. The guide jumped out and said, "The tourists want to speak to the artist. Will you come in the trolley car and speak to them?" With some trepidation, Northrup climbed in and explained that the mural was about gay pride and celebrating. Inwardly she fretted, "'Oh, these people are wearing hats and dressed like church people; They will disapprove.' But when I finished," she smiles, "they stood up and applauded!"

In her short documentary film, *The Story of Pride and Progress,* Olivia Antsis interviews passersby on the street near the mural. The comments are mostly favorable. One young man says approvingly, "They don't really bash you over the head with the fact that they're gay people." A young woman named Ebony thinks, "It's pretty idealized," while an older man in a suit who identifies himself as Chairman of the Pennsylvania Council on the Arts in the 1970s says, "There wasn't anything like this [then]. I think it's wonderful!"

Waterview Island

Even a small mural can make a lot of little folks very happy. Originally there was a swimming pool next to the stately, templelike Waterview Recreation Park building in East Germantown, but pools are expensive to maintain and the city has been unable to keep all of them open every summer. Recently the city decided to fill in some pools and turn them into spray parks where young children can play in jets of water without a lifeguard on duty. They chose Waterview as one of five pilot projects.

When Diane Pieri first visited the park to plan a mural for the fountain play area, she took photographs, especially of the wall she would paint. It had been decorated years earlier with

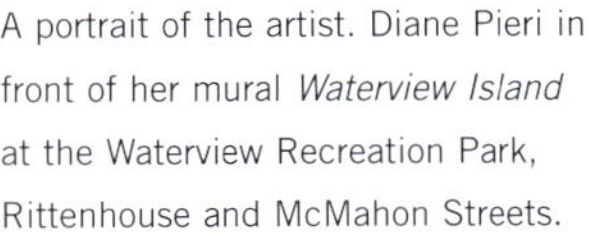

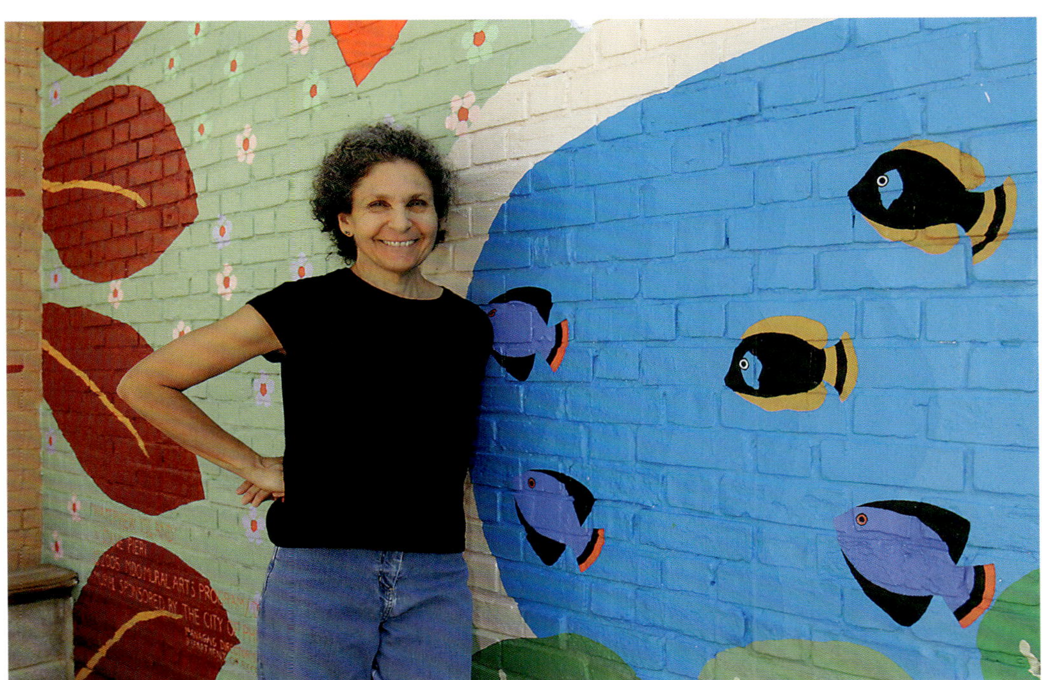

A portrait of the artist. Diane Pieri in front of her mural *Waterview Island* at the Waterview Recreation Park, Rittenhouse and McMahon Streets.

now-faded "huge blocks of sad-looking color," she recalls. The spray fountains were not yet installed but she was able to see pictures of them on the website of the manufacturer: playful rainbows, palm trees, and abstract shapes, one like a giant question mark. Two that are called cannons send out pulsing jets of water.

Pieri made a small preliminary painting with landscape imagery scaled to the wall. "I like to work flat, matte." The soft, organic colors were inspired by a recent trip to Japan. MAP's Amy Johnston made color copies that were distributed throughout the neighborhood with a notice of a meeting to discuss the design. At the meeting, residents explained that they hoped the new spray park would be a focal point for neighborhood revitalization "to heal the community of crime and violence." They wanted it to attract kids who would remember, "I went to Waterview every summer."

"As soon as I started painting, people would come over and give positive feedback. One woman who lived across the street came every day. I felt I was giving the community exactly what they wanted."

The people at the meeting liked Pieri's idea but not the colors. They told her, "We have a lot of Caribbean people living here. We need *red."* Pieri got the message: "So, that's when I went home and got out my authentic Caribbean stuff and reworked the mural." Luckily, her daughter lives in St. John and Pieri has visited there. She had plenty of photographs and also pressed leaves and flowers from the island. "I just brought them home because they were beautiful and I thought I could use them sometime." Indeed, they inspired new images, as did photographs of fish which her daughter sent her. The now tropical wall included pools containing multi-colored fish, red flowers, and blue "sky medallions" with clouds.

When Pieri showed her new vision to others at the rec center and to community leaders, they said, "Great!" She recalls, "As soon as I started painting, people would come over and give positive feedback. One woman who lived across the street came every day. I felt I was giving the community exactly what they wanted. The water fixtures were dedicated about half-way through the mural. The water didn't reach me where I was painting but the kids were scampering around and playing. They loved the mural. They would come up and say, 'Ooh, look at the fish!' I would say, 'Does it make you feel like you're on an island?' They would say, 'Oh, it does. Look at those flowers!'"

Black Cowboys: A Tribute to Urban Horsemen

It's a thrill to see Philadelphia's African-American horsemen ride by. Philadelphia is one of the few Eastern cities to consistently pay homage to the black cowboys and the black Buffalo Soldiers, true legends of the old West. In recent years, many urban stables have been torn down to make room for more lucrative business. Janice Cook, President of the Cowboys and Cowgirls Association of Philadelphia, says riders struggle to find stabling for their mounts inside the city. Fletcher Street stables, one of the few that remains, is threatened with closure. Cook and members of the association were active in promoting a major mural for the Strawberry Mansion neighborhood. "We're trying to fight for Fletcher Street," she says. "The horses help keep the kids out of trouble."

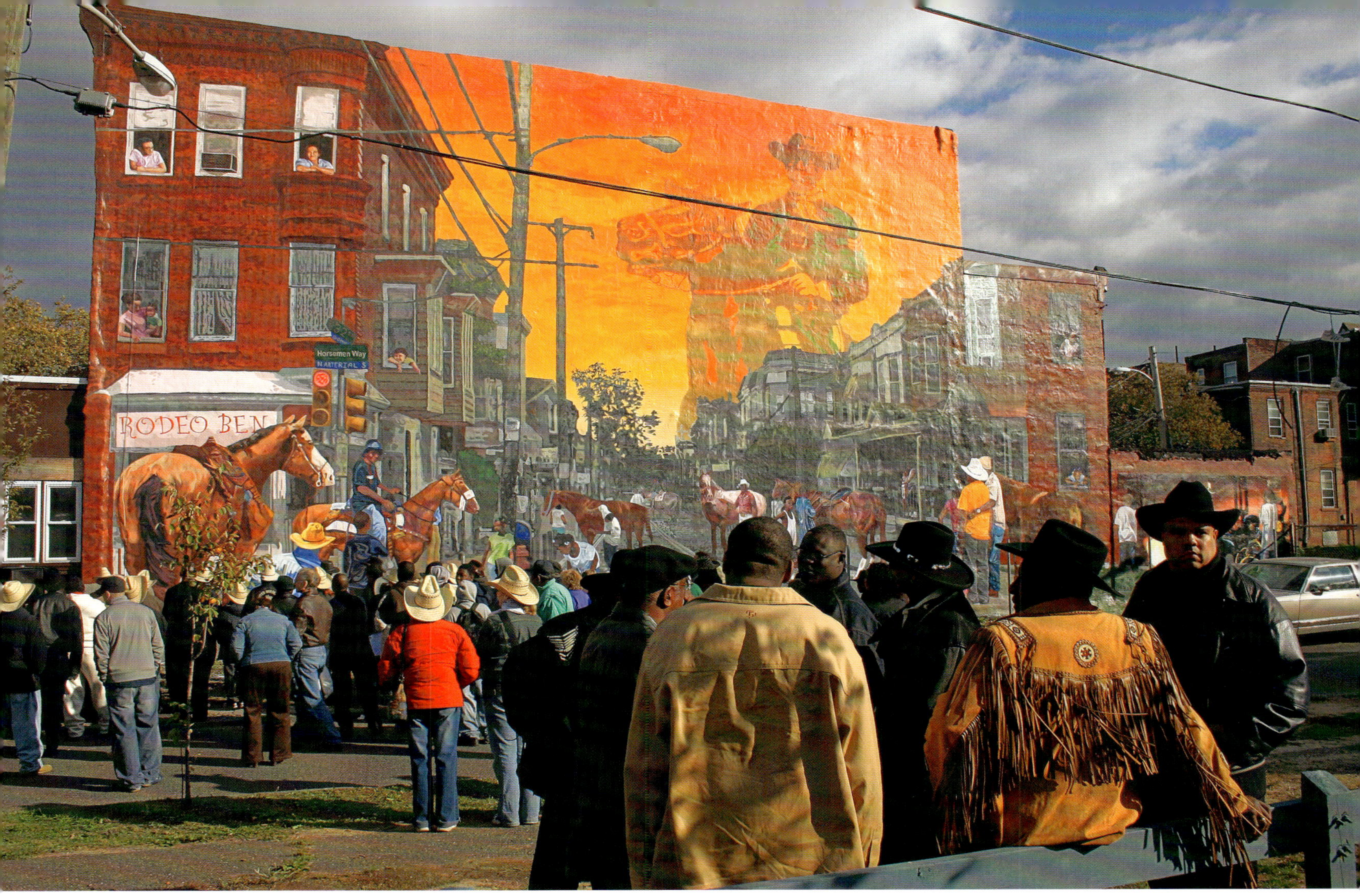

Big Sky country at 3222 W. Montgomery Avenue, *Urban Horsemen* by Jason Slowik and participants in the ARTscape Program.

Her husband Ervin "Baker" Cook reinforces the point. He says that members of the "young generation who can't afford a horse" volunteer to feed and water and "pamper the horses and help exercise them. They come to the stable every day like clockwork."

Baker Cook recalls "I got into riding through my father. He had a couple of horses. My kids ride and my grandkids ride." He laughs, "When I was riding as a kid, I always used to stop when I saw a bakery and get off and buy a dozen of doughnuts and that name, 'Baker,' stuck with me."

Cook owns a thoroughbred called Big Red. Other riders mostly have thoroughbreds or quarter horses. They enjoy riding the trails together in Fairmount Park, the nation's largest city park. "You're going through the brush and you've got on chaps and your hat and your boots. You're brushing against thorns. Sometimes you have to get off and pull a rock out of your horse's foot. We carry sandwiches and we might stop and sit down for a bit," Cook says. Fairmount Park is threatening to close some of its trails to horses and restrict them to riders of mountain bikes, but Cook doesn't see a real conflict between horses and bicycles.

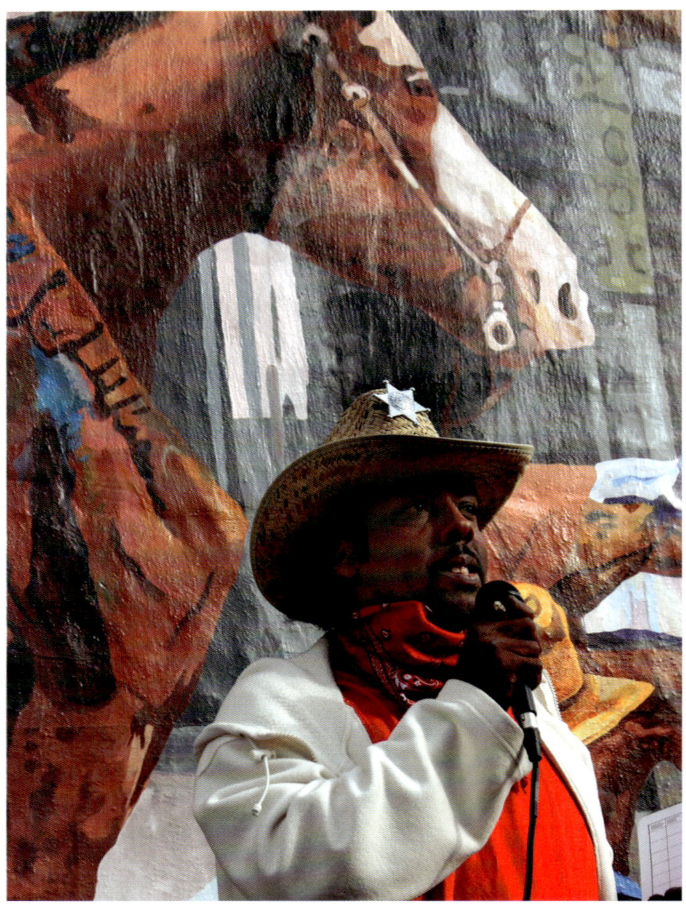

Local horseman John Coleman speaks at the *Urban Horsemen* dedication during Mural Arts Month, October 2005.

The Cowboys and Cowgirls Association shared a collection of old photographs with the painters of *A Tribute to Urban Horsemen* (3222 W. Montgomery Avenue, 2005). Artists Jason Slowik, Brad Carney, Charles Barbin, and Strawberry Mansion resident Keir Johnston all contributed to the mural, which unites elements of today's reality with the glory of the past in a single street scene. Near the painted intersection of "Horsemen Way" (a real street in the neighborhood) and 32nd Street, contemporary children look down from *trompe l'oeil* windows, while others play in the old-fashioned cobblestone street that is lined with tracks for the old horse-drawn trolleys from the 1930s. One child writes the phrase "We remember."

Horses and riders of today move through the old Philadelphia streets and above this compressed urban history—a mythic horse and rider, a Buffalo Soldier from the old West—gallop through the sky, haloed in a golden sunset.

"We are part of the history of the black cowboy, but sometimes we just call ourselves 'horsemen' because we don't work the cow," Cook explains. "Some of us are related and some are not, but we are all family, whether white or black or Hispanic or Jamaican. There were a couple of Chinese people in the group a while back. Horsemen have everything in general. We all pal around." Everyone who worked on the *Black Cowboys* mural hopes it will begin a discussion about the need for creating permanent stable space for Philadelphia's horsemen.

Stories in Words and Pictures

It's five thousand square feet of colors, figures, and words along a wall on the Schuylkill Expressway, one of the main thoroughfares into Philadelphia. There's no mistaking the centerpiece of the *Passing Through* project for anything but what it is: a glorious mural.

The other works in the project are harder to label and to find. Some are little more than signs; others are small and seemingly random. Some are just words. Muralist Meg Saligman, who led the project, says she wanted it, "to challenge what murals typically are. We know murals can have a big, powerful voice, but I was very interested in altering that, speaking in a different volume and having them scattered around the city, like surprises."

To celebrate twenty years of MAP, the *Passing Through* team created twenty text-based murals throughout the city. The only clear link between them? The project logo, a small rendering of an interstate highway sign. *Passing Through,* after all, is about signs—the ones you read, obey or disregard, and the ones that are seen as omens or indicators of events past or future.

"It's about paying attention to the signs," says Sue Spolan, the project's text director. "There's the idea that someone will pass a sign fifty times and then say, 'Wait a minute. That's not what that's supposed to say.'" With some murals, the mystery is gone after a few viewings and they become, Spolan says, "just wallpaper, tantamount to a blank wall." The ambiguities and complexities of the spectacular, larger-than-life mural on the Schuylkill—as well as the entire *Passing Through* series—means people will keep looking and keep questioning.

Passing Through may be one of the most modern and unusual projects MAP has endorsed. Jane Golden said it's important to use a wide range of techniques that appeal to art lovers of all sorts. The completed works, she says, are "beautiful works of art that are challenging and evocative in their own way."

Spolan wandered the city for months, listening and recording the conversations of strangers-first with a tape recorder, then with just a notebook. Part of her job, she says, "was distilling out the profundity from the simplicity of every day speech." She and Saligman said they were

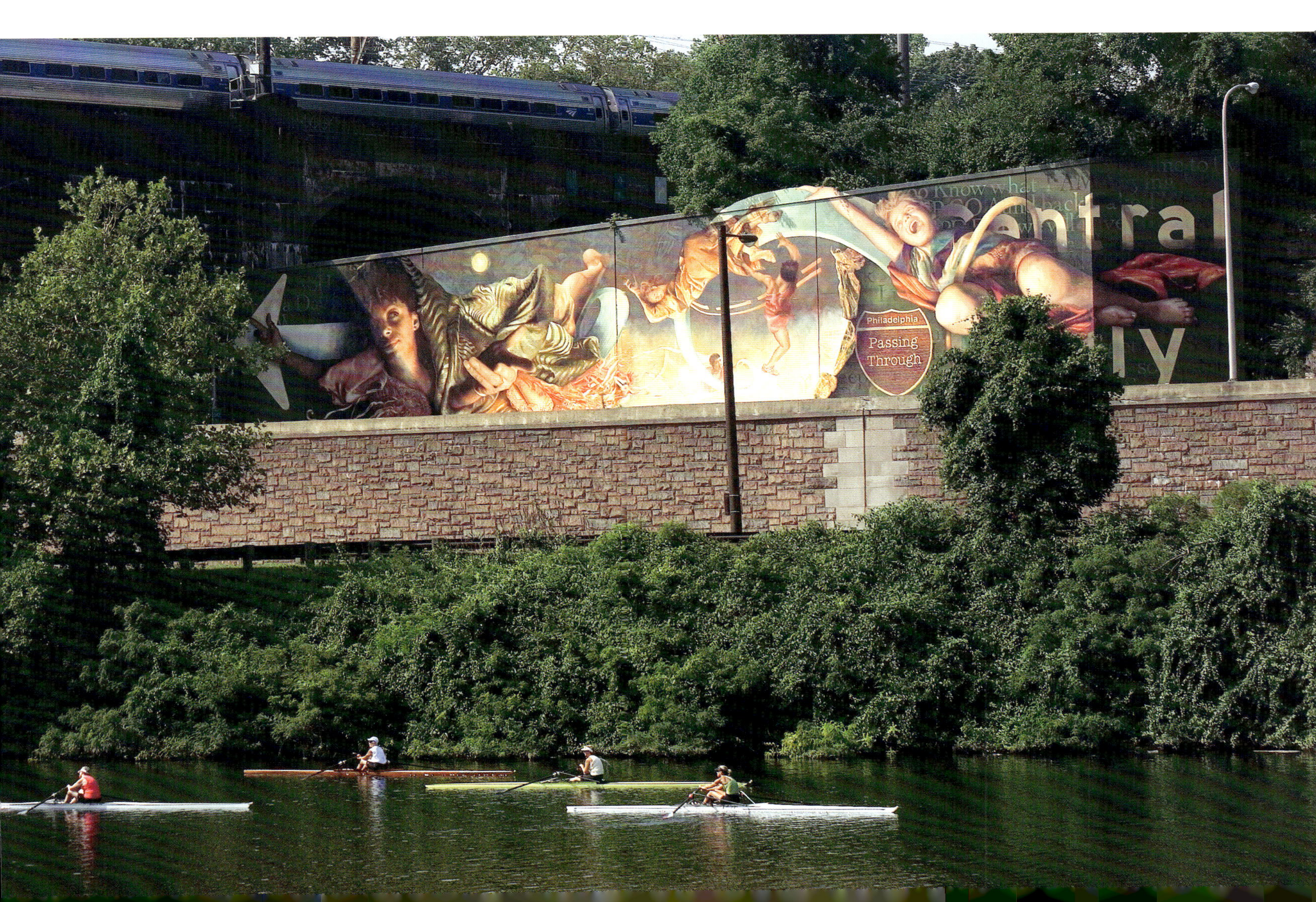

Philadelphia landmarks: The Schuykill River with rowers, Fairmount Park, and the new *Passing Through* mural by Meg Saligman, located on I-76 near Girard Avenue. Made possible by the Independence Foundation.

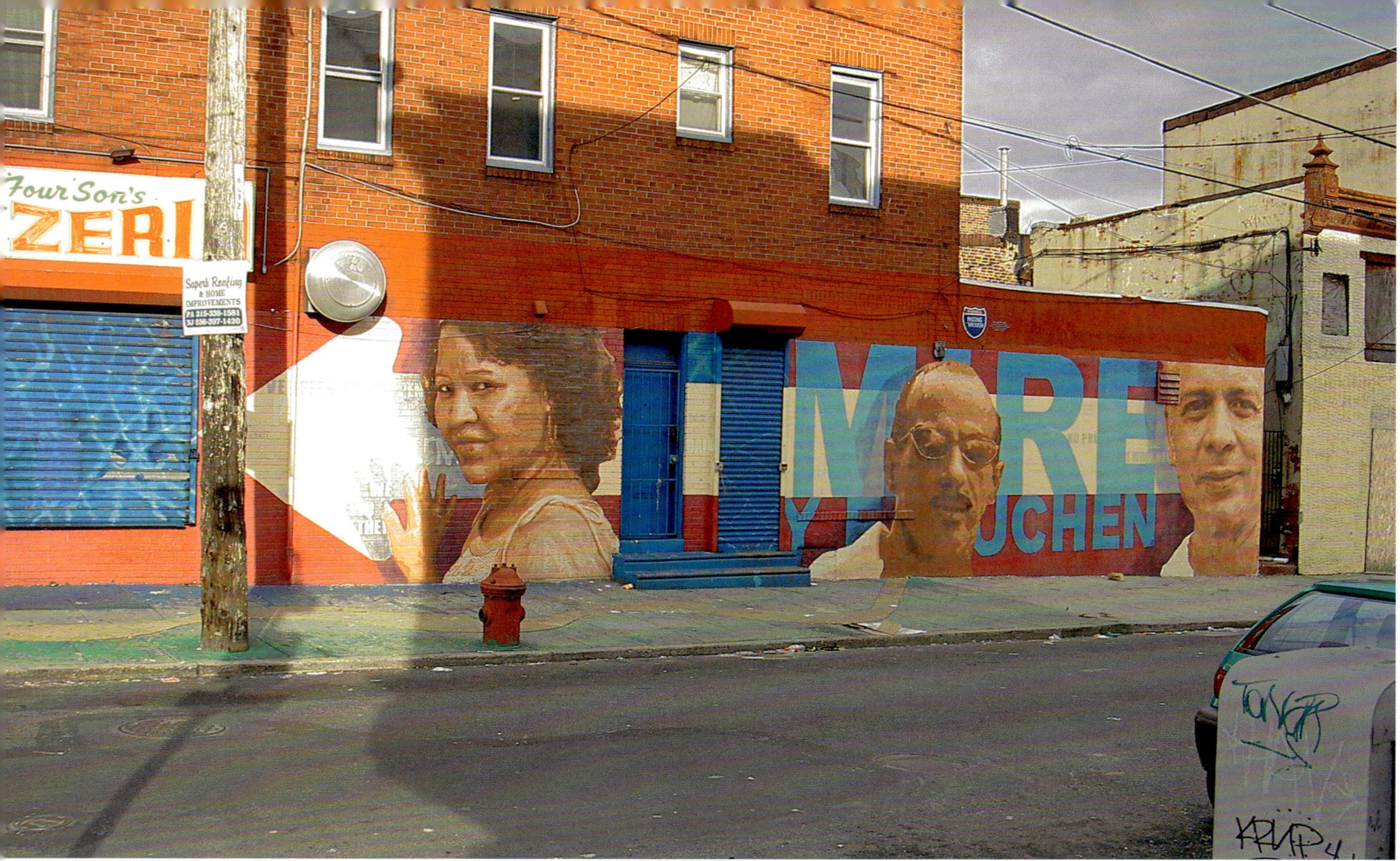

Faces and overheard sayings make the substance of *Look/Listen* by James Burns, 5th and Cambria Streets, one of the many *Passing Through* murals.

amazed at the things people would say out in public. "You hear very private things," Saligman says. "You hear a lot of planning. People were always planning where they where going to go."

During one stroll from Center City's Rittenhouse Square to the Kimmel Center, Spolan noticed that most of the conversations involved medical terms. Those phrases became part of a mural that adorns a parking lot door in that area. In North Philadelphia one day, she heard lots of talk about money. In fact, the three most commonly overheard words, in all parts of the city, were "Mom, cash, home." That became a mural all its own at 3rd and Spring Garden Streets. Saligman says the most commonly heard phrase was "Let's go." That appears three times in a mural on Aramingo Avenue in Fishtown.

Because the project's name implies movement, the team chose to put murals on buildings that refer to cars, like auto repair shops and gas stations. Because it was about words, a print shop and a paper manufacturing plant became mural sites. The plant, in the Port Richmond neighborhood, once ran three shifts around the clock. Now it is a ghost structure, "with one or two guys who work in this massive building and a boss who presides over it all from the top floor," Spolan says. The paintings on the building reflect its glory days—with shout-outs to each shift and the three generations of family who have run the plant—and honor the owner, a World War II veteran who said he sometimes felt his sacrifice, like his building, had been forgotten. "We will never forget you" and "You turn around and you come back" reads some of the text along the building's top edge.

Some murals in the series are easily identifiable as public art works, like the yellow and orange one in North Philadelphia that, besides words about cars often heard at the shop there, includes depictions of the roosters often heard crowing in that neighborhood. Others may appear to be signs, not murals at all. Along with an advertisement that the pork is tender and juicy, new signage adorning an abandoned sandwich shack reads, "Beats me" and "Nobody is watching the children."

Two of the pieces of *Passing Through* are already out of commission: A delivery truck that carried images and words seen and overheard in the Italian Market section of the city is no longer running. (The phrases on it, "She's better than Bruce Lee. Better than Rambo. Better than Rocky," came from an overheard conversation about actress Lucy Liu.) Two gas pumps decorated with words and phrases pulled from fliers left in the abandoned station they occupied have been taken down.

But that's what happens, Saligman says. Nothing is permanent. "Things pass through," she says. "These murals will pass through the community. People pass through the city."

Many of those who pass through travel via Interstate 76, the Schuylkill Expressway. They can't help but notice the main *Passing Through* mural there, a work so layered that even daily commuters, speeding by at sixty miles per hour, will need years to take it all in. At first, they may notice the flying people, then the cityscape and the country scene, then the words pulled from the other text-based murals and the authentic looking road signs, including the one of the artists' design: "If you can read this, you're stuck in traffic."

One of the flying figures is Jonathan Kirby, an eighteen-year-old who assisted with the project. Sick with a terminal brain tumor, Kirby still managed to work almost every day, the first one in and the last to leave. The hand/eye coordination required for painting seemed to ease his physiological decline, but he died a few months after the project was completed. "In the mural, he's soaring off into the sky," Saligman said. "It really is a passing through. It is a metaphor for life."

Each mural records its patrons' lives: their memories, their faces, their favorite colors, their heroes—even the touch of their hands in contributing to the wall. Together, it all adds up to a history of the city. From the mystic ghost rider of *Urban Horsemen* to the multifaceted magic realism of the Mann Older Adult Center mural to the direct colorful island design for the children's water park, murals speak many languages, and almost always we understand them.

Artist Profile

Michelle Ortiz

"When people see me painting murals—me being a young Latina woman, and my assistants are older men they think that *I'm* the assistant. People say, 'Aren't you married? You don't have kids? You finished college?'"

Michelle Ortiz exemplifies today's young artists whose multifaceted approach to muralism emphasizes process. She received a summa cum laude Bachelor of Fine Arts degree from Moore College of Art and Design in 2000 and has worked steadily as a studio painter, mosaicist, and muralist since then. Nevertheless, Ortiz made a subtle change of direction in her next level of study, earning a Master's degree in the Science of Arts and Cultural Management from Rosemont College in 2002. Among her primary goals are "teaching cultural diversity and global understanding through the arts, battling stereotypes, and breaking down barriers."

To this end, she works with young people, mostly middle school or high school age. But she also leads organizations, serving on the Mural Arts Program's Board of Directors, and acting as co-director for the nonprofit Multicultural Youth eXchange (MYX), a community service program of workshops and art activities that supports Philadelphia's only gallery dedicated to showcasing youth art work. She's also worked with the Taller Puertorriqueño, the Congreso de Latinos Unidos, and numerous other nonprofit organizations. Ortiz has made collaborative murals in Ecuador and recently led a small group of high school students in a project in Costa Rica.

Ortiz's interest in introducing young people to cultures outside the United States grows out of her own experience. Although she's still a resident of South Philadelphia, where she was born, she vividly remembers her first visit to her mother's home country of Colombia when she was seven. "In Colombia, I had to wash my clothes by hand for the first time. I had pets like birds and armadillos," says Ortiz.

Like many people who have thoroughly experienced the "identity, surroundings, and upbringing" of more than one culture from the inside, Ortiz sees herself as both insider and perpetual outsider. She has a sense "of not belonging here or there. When I would go to my mother's homeland or my father's homeland (Puerto Rico), I would be viewed as a gringa, a North American girl. Here, it's the opposite."

Ortiz worked with a group of fifteen kids with truancy problems referred by ArtWORKS!, a MAP program, and Congresso de Latinos Unidos to make *The Doors of Destiny Are in Your Hands* . The site, 125 feet long by 25 feet high, is large, but the biggest challenge it presented was the three garage doors that interrupt the wall. "The students came up with the theme," Ortiz says. "The whole idea about the doorways is that they represent past, present, and future. I didn't want happy-go-lucky imagery. I wanted anybody who sees that mural to get a hint that the decisions you make will affect your life. In a lot of our conversations, we were talking about, 'What do you want to close the door on? Violence and drugs? What do you want to open the door to? Happiness? Success?'

"But another question was, 'When have you felt that the door was closed to you?' A lot of them are African American or Latino. A lot felt that college was a privilege not a right. A lot of them felt that you have to have money. I just used myself as an example. It was interesting to see how they responded."

The students painted images on the doors and Ortiz painted the heroic-scale figures—their faces are about six feet high—who present the panels to the viewer. Students volunteered to model for these allegorical figures of Past, Present, and Future.

The first door, with its design of a little girl and a duck and a little soldier, represents childhood innocence. The figure of "Past," represented by a girl named Eugenia, "is remembering being a child. A lot of these girls have had to grow up very quickly," Ortiz says.

The second door depicts a group of young people and a view of Philadelphia. A circular pattern suggests music, "a way of communicating. Today the music's messages are more explicit." Ortiz notes that the figure of "Present," a boy named Luis, looks out at the viewer. "In my work, when anybody has eye contact with the audience, that person represents the present time."

Representing the "Future" was Guilberto, "a special case in the project," Ortiz says. "He came every day and was very involved in the process. For the painting on that door, the kids designed a picture of people, protesting with signs, going onto a bridge and fighting to get across. The idea is that they are fighting for peace and equal rights."

Ortiz finds working with young people satisfying. "In my classroom, I'm very strict. There's no cursing. It's one person in the bathroom at a time. But we also goof around and have a good time. I'm telling them that they have to *use* this experience. When you see the development of the kids, that's a good feeling."

Below
Muralist Michelle Ortiz at the Mann Older Adult Center, 5th Street and Allegheny Avenue.

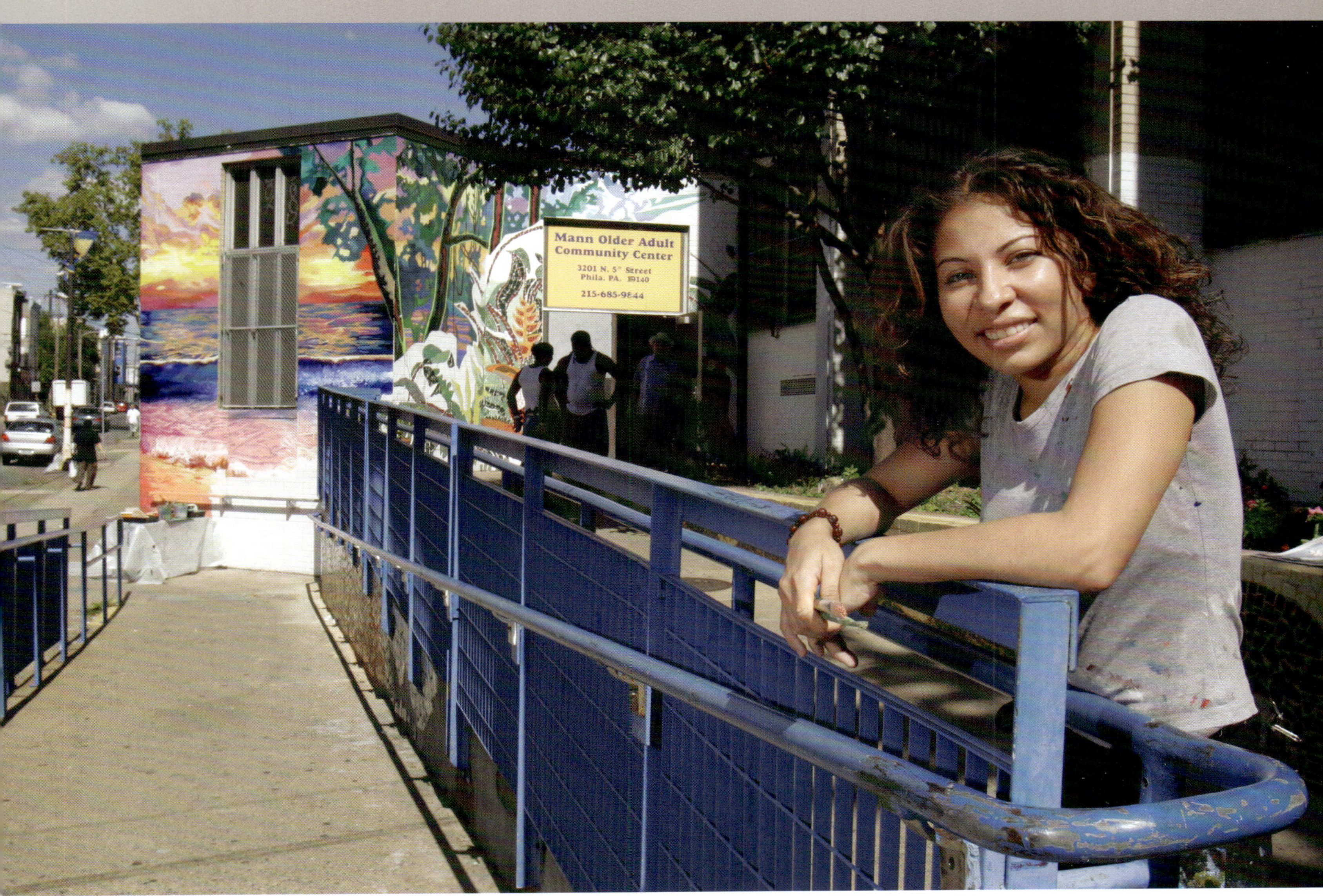

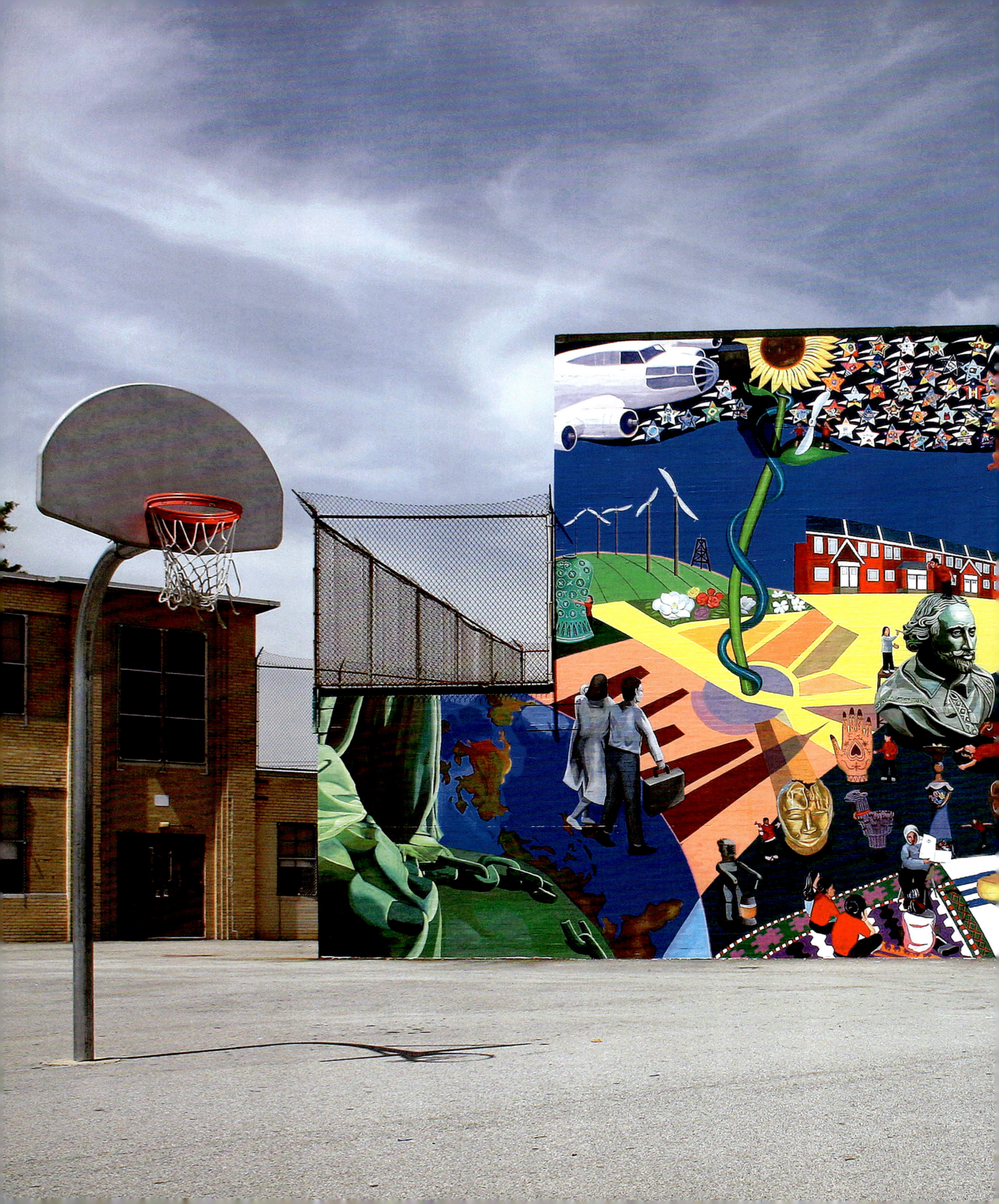

Chapter 10

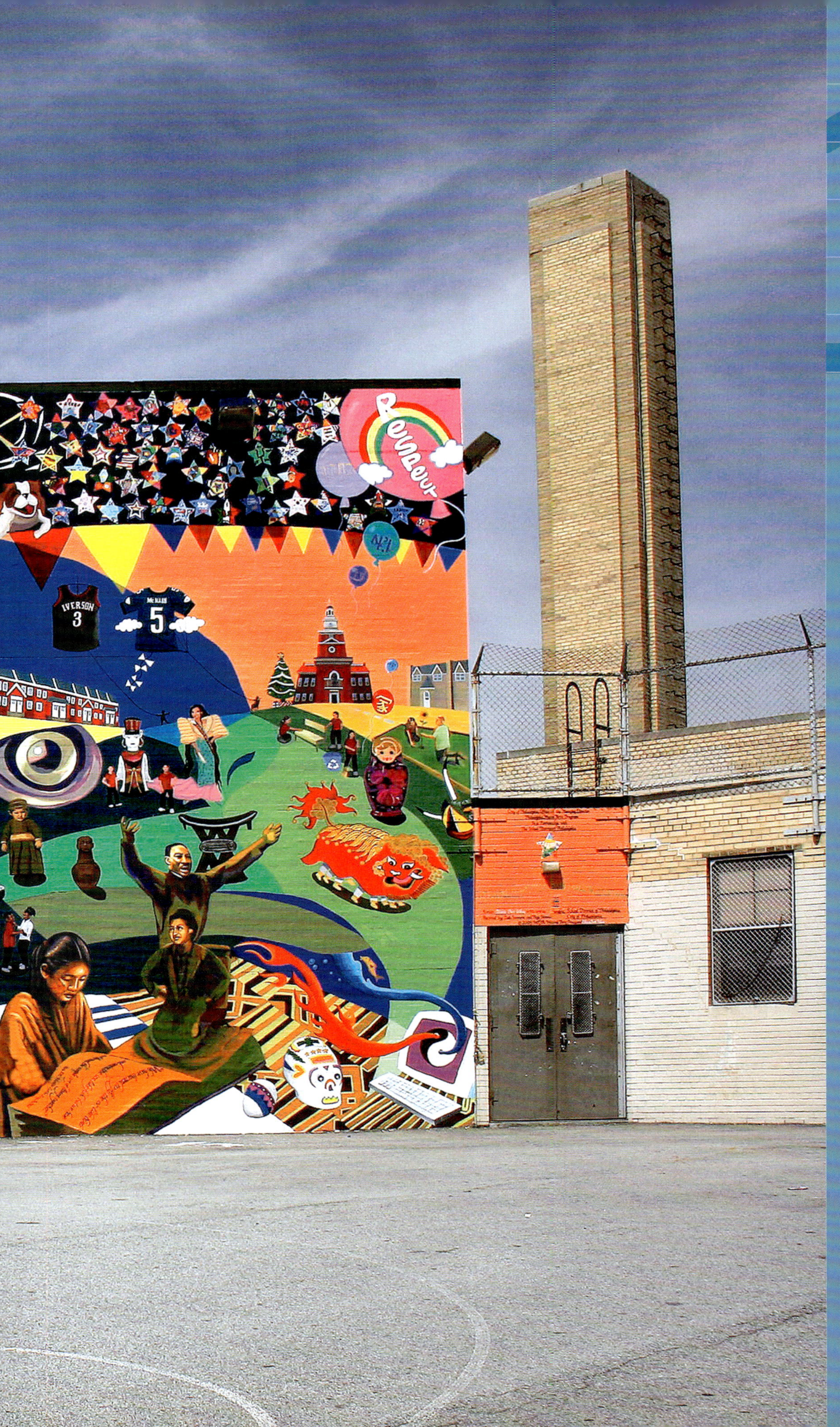

Coming to America and Making it Stronger, by Eliseo Silva at the Gilbert Spruance School, 6401 Horrocks Street.

Chapter 10 A World of Murals

One conclusion that emerged from the 2004 National Mural Conference held in Philadelphia is that the mural movement must continue to evolve in response to the needs of the community. Protest walls and other politically motivated murals in Los Angeles, San Francisco, Chicago, Boston, and even Belfast, Northern Ireland, often have short lives. These unnaturally truncated spans suggest that mural messages are regarded as sufficiently powerful or threatening. Being effective is good news for murals, but the loss of these murals isn't good news for mural lovers.

Like graffiti, controversial murals tend to survive primarily in the form of photo documentation. Many cities, including North Hollywood and Pomona, California, have passed ordinances that limit the kinds of murals that are painted even on private property. Such walls can be overpainted without a formal evaluation or an opportunity to appeal. Philadelphia has seen relatively few hard-hitting privately or publicly funded murals. Steve Powers's *Stop the Bull* (c. 1990), a protest parodying a television advertisement for malt liquor (a cheap form of alcohol marketed to poor urban neighborhoods), was commissioned by a church and was not disturbed.

In Chicago, the nonpermission *Anti-Police Brutality* (1998) mural painted by Rob Moriarty with assistant Lee Wells and others suffered the typical fate of protest murals. It remained in situ for only a few months. The mural is well documented in photographs and in an interview with the artist on the Chicago Public Art Group Web site. Its message lives on, but only for those who know where to look for it—not for the general public.

Few painters make a career practice of focusing on a single, narrow-issue subject. One exception is the muralist who goes by the name of Wyland and bills himself as "the premier ocean artist." In recent years, Wyland has made easel paintings and sculptures, but his chief claim to fame is eighty-four whale murals painted in seven countries. Generally well sited and simple and similar in palette and design, these murals by "the whale guy," whose name is even

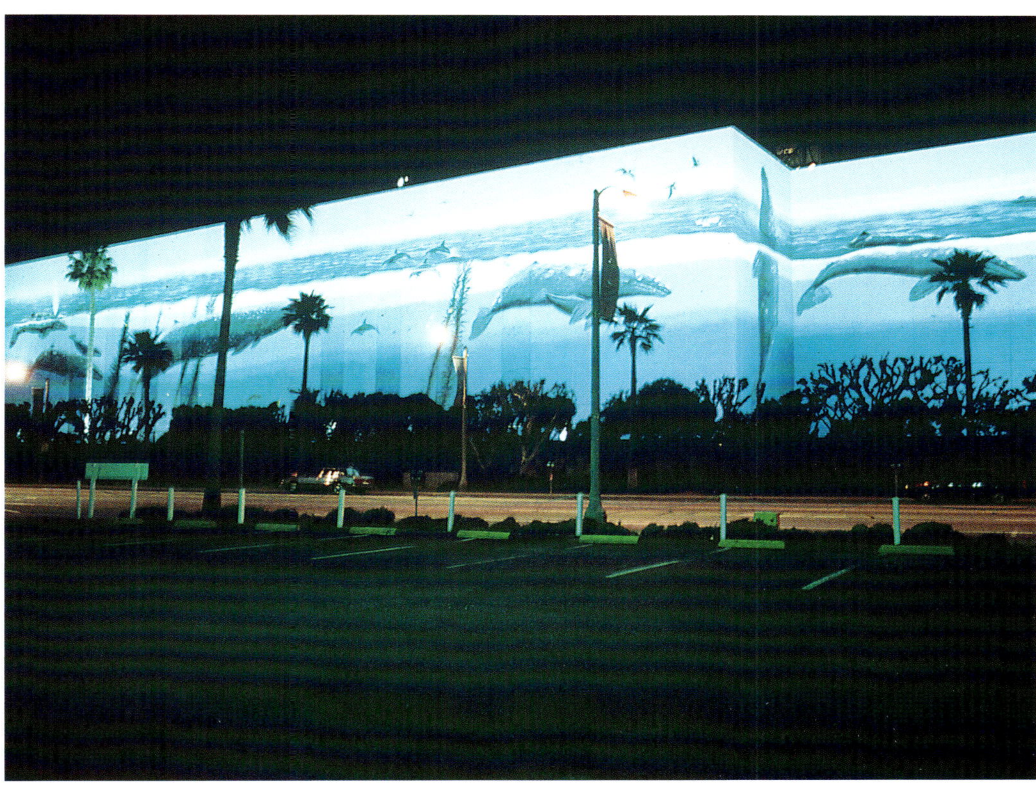

Wyland, *Grey Whale Migration.* Redondo Beach, California, 1991. This is just one of the dozens of whale murals Wyland has painted in seven countries.

pronounced like "whale," are clearly beloved by the public as numerous restorations and several successful legal battles to save endangered whale walls demonstrate.

Judy Baca is another muralist who has worked the same territory for decades, but even Baca widened her focus from Chicano history and women's politics to embrace world peace. Baca effectively built on her thirty-four years as "the Mural Lady"—she says she didn't mind being a mural *person* but being a "lady" was a problem—by developing a worldwide mural project with thematic roots in her *Great Wall of Los Angeles.*

By shifting her cause to a global community, Baca is determined that her work will be more than "a Band-aid on a cancer." Her *World Wall: A Vision of the Future without Fear* consists of seven "two-sided"–ten by thirty–foot portable mural panels on canvas. It will travel to several countries and each host country adds a new section. Russian artists worked on the wall in 1990. In Finland, artists for nuclear disarmament contributed.

Technology

Using a computer, Baca is able to design mosaic murals that are executed by others for sites that she knows best through photographs. Josh Sarantitis's sophisticated *Tilepile* program makes digital mural design even easier. The practical reality of remote digital techniques will increasingly impact future mural-making. It is now practical for successful artists to execute commissions in geographically scattered locations, perhaps visiting the site only to prepare for or see the final installation—or perhaps never visiting at all.

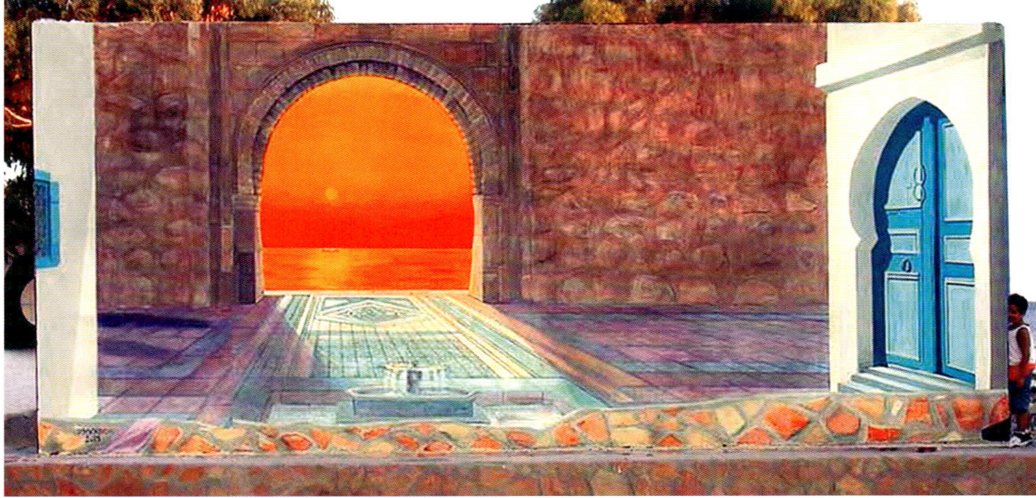

D. S. Gordon, *Strangers Visit Abraham.* Mahares, Tunisia, 2003. Gordon painted this mural for the Sixteenth International Festival of the Arts in Mahares.

Increasingly, muralists are itinerant celebrity workers, making their marks in locations around the world. Similar conditions have applied to top artists for centuries. Peter Paul Rubens, perhaps the biggest international success in history, made cycles of interior murals and simultaneously worked as a diplomat in Italy, France, England, Spain, and France. American artist Frederic Church traveled around the world to research his mural-size paintings and then sent the paintings on tour. From Philadelphia, Meg Saligman and Paul Santoleri are among a growing number of artists who regularly make murals throughout the states and outside the country.

Technical advances allow smaller or poorer communities to have great murals for less money, but it would be unfortunate if these developments limited opportunities for younger regional muralists because they are passed over in favor of big names. Jon Pounds, executive director of the Chicago Public Art Group, is keen on identifying and encouraging younger artists as a way of uplifting the entire mural community. He says, "Old dogs learn new tricks better with new dogs around." With its broad system of art classes for young people at every level, The Mural Arts Program fosters skills that encourage many students to work in computer graphics, architecture, and related fields. Traditional apprenticeships and direct mentoring, whether through formal programs like MAP's or more informal arrangements, remain the most effective training for aspiring muralists.

The Physical Context

Global interest in muralism has grown in recent years. Not surprisingly, few murals are painted in well-preserved historical areas because there are no suitable walls. More are painted in recently built-up or badly decayed urban areas. Throughout the United States and Canada, recent murals can be found in large and small communities, especially in educational settings. Tucson has an active mural scene and Portland Metro Murals is widely respected. From Winnipeg, Manitoba, Canada, which has hundreds of well-documented murals, to Boston and Atlanta, cities define themselves partly through murals and visitors are eager to visit and photograph them.

Australian murals are still often executed in historic *fresco secco,* a technique in which the pigment penetrates and bonds with the medium of the wall itself. When sealed, *fresco secco* is stable and weather-resistant. One must have experience with this technique to use it effectively because pigments change color when they penetrate the lime-infused underlayer. Experienced artists memorize what final color will result from a particular combination. Bowen, sometimes called the "Mural Capital of Australia," has twenty-four such murals executed over a period of years on both historic and contemporary subjects.

Communities that lack the funding to initiate mural programs still elect to paint just one or two. Often, an individual artist or group has an idea, locates an available wall, and simply gets permission from the owner. Antonio Puri, who makes large paintings on unstretched canvas using staining and other accidental effects, was inspired to paint *Cascade* by its specific site, a long, stained horizontal wall above a store in Haddon Township, New Jersey. Puri's studio is nearby and for some time he had studied rust patterns forming on the upper level of the building. They seemed reminiscent of his own work.

"The wall originally looked like a cascade of rust. I'd pull over to admire it every time I drove by. I thought, 'Can't we work that with a mural?'" He asked the building owner for permission to paint. Puri's mostly blue drips layered with red and yellow circles echo the rust, but Puri respects and even encourages this organic process. He places nails in locations where he hopes the rust will flow. But he's also sealed his painting with spar boat varnish so rust can't eat up the entire mural. It's a work in progress, he says: "I'm collaborating with nature. It'll be a tension between the rust and the varnish."

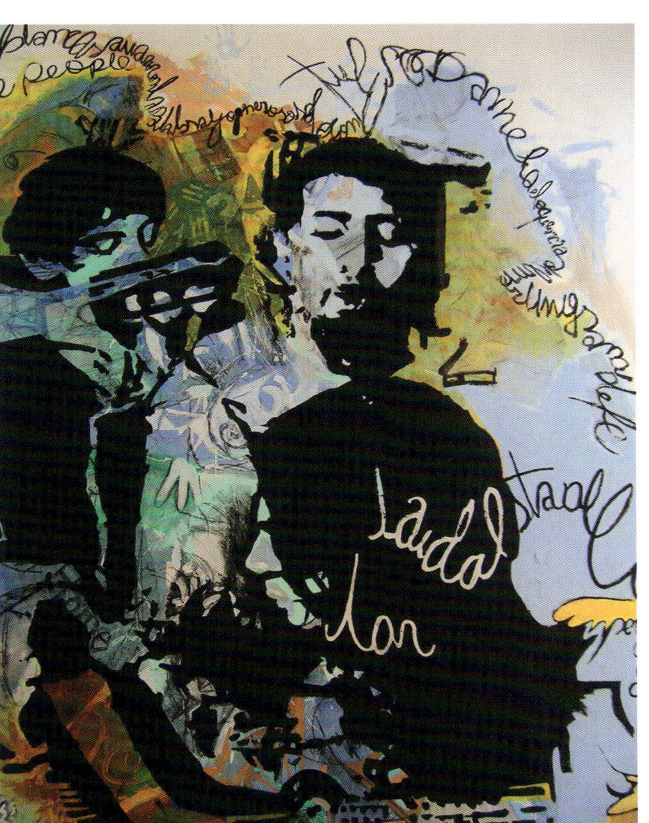

Collaboration led by Betsy Casañas, detail, *Una fusion de las artes (A Fusion of the Arts).* San Alehandro esquela de artes plasticas (St. Alexander School of Fine Arts), Havana, Cuba, 2005.

Although Puri's mural has symbolic meaning relating to cycles of creation and destruction and relative scales, few equally abstract murals are commissioned. It's baffling, really, and ironic to recall that the "inventors" of abstract painting, like Wassily Kandinsky, imagined abstraction would become a universal and spiritual language.

Since the dissolution of the Soviet Union, few community murals are painted in parts of Europe where socialist realism flourished; however, the illusionistic style of representation favored by socialist realists is much in demand in the land of the free.

Northern Ireland has been a fertile center of mural painting as political expression. Political and paramilitary walls, documented by Bill Rolston in *Drawing Support: Murals in the North of Ireland* (1992), are often extraordinarily powerful,

Artist Profile

Michael Webb

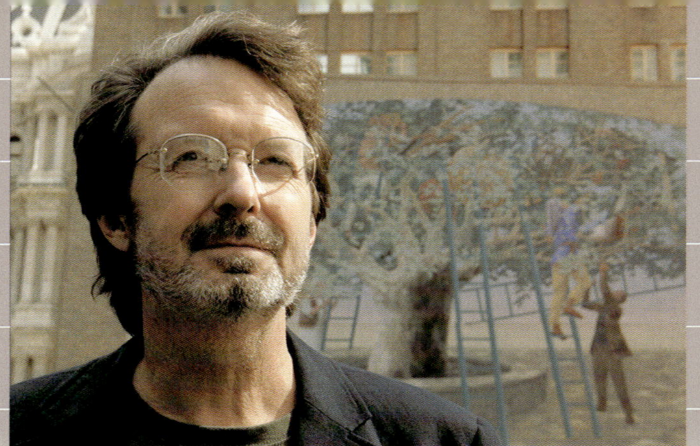

"Painting murals is a pretty grand enterprise emotionally, mentally, and physically. It has a feeling of operatic bigness." Michael Webb should know; he has painted many murals since his first *trompe l'oeil* details on the façade of a house in Bryn Mawr in 1979. Webb sees himself as "halfway between an artist and a designer" and chooses projects scrupulously. "Sometimes the best design solution is not to do a mural. My idea is the right mural in the right location for the right reason.

"Murals must feel as much a part of the architecture as possible. I don't like a mural that screams out at you; I want to draw you in. The scale of the image, the amount of detail, and size of the mural and objects represented need to feel in proper proportion to the environment," says Webb, who averages one or two commissions for the Mural Arts Program annually.

Relating to Center City architecture, which includes Philadelphia's imposing City Hall heavily ornamented with oversize sculpture, was one of the "stimulating not limiting" problems Webb encountered in painting *The Tree of Knowledge* (1301 Market Street, 2003). The commission came from the Eisenhower Fellowships. Named for President Dwight D. Eisenhower, the program offers international travel and study opportunities to emerging leaders in every nation, often in the fields of science and education; Jane Golden traveled to Northern Ireland on an Eisenhower Fellowship in 2003.

Like the MacArthur Foundation, the Eisenhower Fellowships does not accept applications. Webb's mural was commissioned to commemorate the organization's fiftieth anniversary conference which was held in Philadelphia. Webb worked directly with a committee from the foundation. They explained the ideals of the organization. For Webb, it was an intriguing assignment. "It's hard to come up with a broad metaphor in one image about empathy and communication among cultures of the world." After several discussions with the committee, he returned to a thought he had originally dismissed: "a tree of knowledge full of objects to represent human endeavor."

Webb typically has concentrated on representational images. Even the fanciful "Masquerade Ball" Rococo figures he painted on the stairway in the posh Rittenhouse Hotel (private commission, 1990), are naturalistic; however, he had just completed a series of children's murals for Saint Christopher's Hospital (2nd Street and Erie Avenue). "They were a bridge to new ways of thinking about making images from the imagination. When I did the Eisenhower wall I was at a point where I was comfortable with using more decorative color and painting in a less photographic way."

The mural is set into its architectural surrounding inside an arched niche of painted bricks, which perfectly match the adjacent bricks and avoid "the billboard look" Webb hates. Through this arch, we see people working around and on a tree. Some of the color, like teal ladders, is decorative and unexpected, though not jarring. Even the fact that interesting objects—a French horn, an abacus, a satellite, a one-person boat (representing personal journeys), and scales of justice—are scattered among the trees branches seems subtly understated. The distracted passer-by will probably not wonder, "Why is a person with a sextant sitting at the top of the tree and looking at the sky?"

"I wanted them to be hidden enough so that people would have to stop and search out what is going on, to become engaged." Are the figures in the mural coming or going? Are they bringing things to the tree or taking things away from it? "It's up to the viewer to make an explanation. I don't want to spoon feed," says Webb. He feels that this request for thoughtfulness on the part of observers is "close to the spirit and goals of the Fellowships."

But, he adds, "All my murals have this ambiguity that stimulates the imagination. No ambiguity is terrible. Too much is dangerous or nothing."

Webb thinks of a muralist as a problem solver. He is the "designer and coordinator of all the resources that I have, human and otherwise. This is not solitary tortured van Gogh painting. I take suggestions. I have had brilliant ideas from people just walking down the street."

He painted one of his favorite murals in the rotunda of the American College of Physicians (6th and Race Streets, 1991). It is a metaphorical landscape that radiates out from the rotunda and includes the legendary tree on the island of Cos under which, according to legend, Hippocrates first administered his famous oath to his students. A distant valley represents time; a circular reflecting pool represents the art of medicine; and small distant islands represent knowledge and its application in medicine."

"I've always wanted art to be like life," Webb muses. In his own life, he is committed to growth and change. "I think there are other ideas about murals yet to come and I hope to be there to usher them into reality."

Opposite

Master of *trompe l'oeil* Michael Webb in front of his *Tree of Knowledge.*

Below

Tree of Knowledge. 1301 Market Street, 2003. Sponsored by the Eisenhower Fellowships. Through carefully chosen color, details, and imagery, Webb subtly integrates his murals with their surroundings.

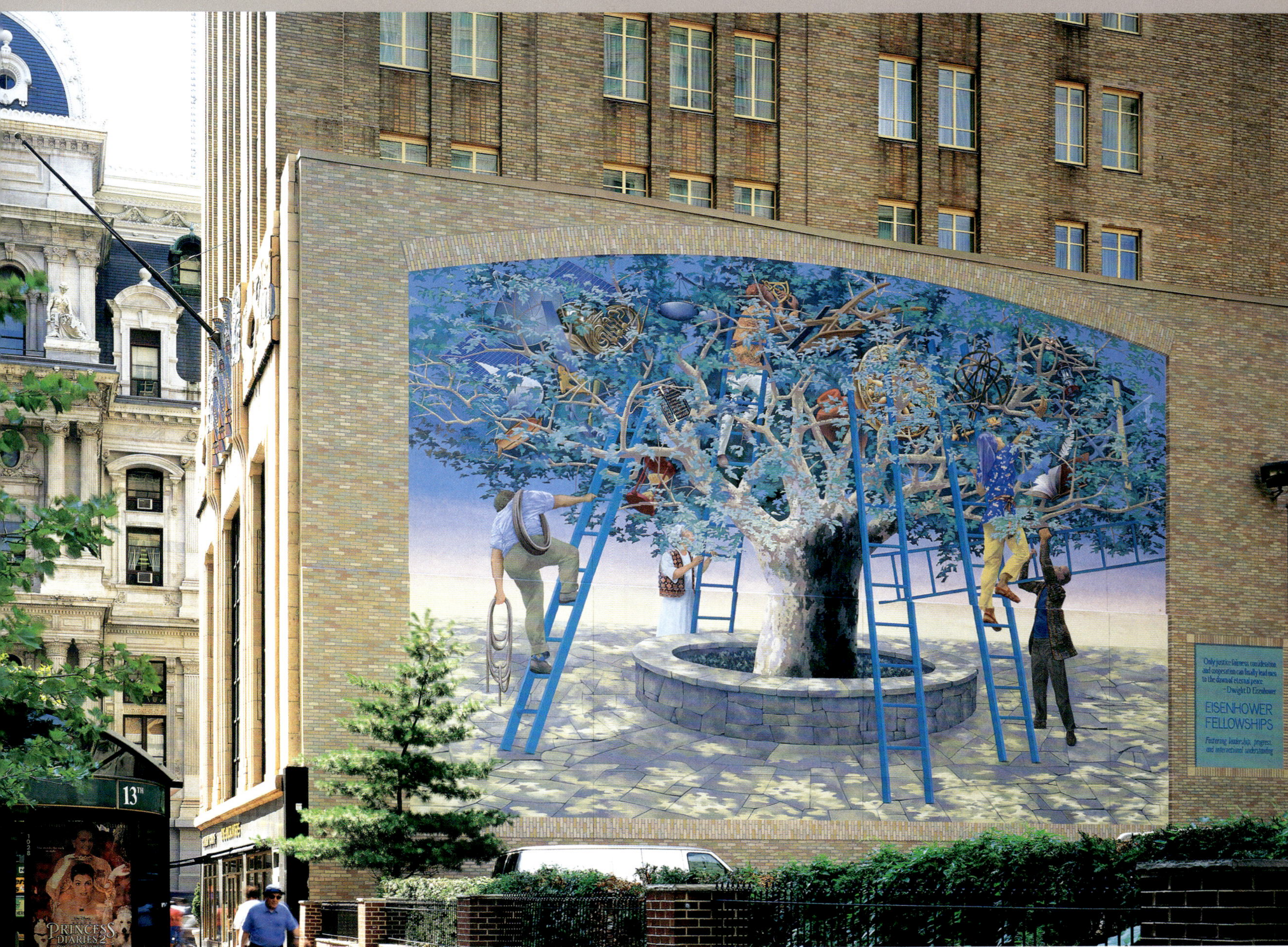

Anonymous Loyalist mural, *For As Long as 100 of Us Remain . . .* East Belfast, Northern Ireland.

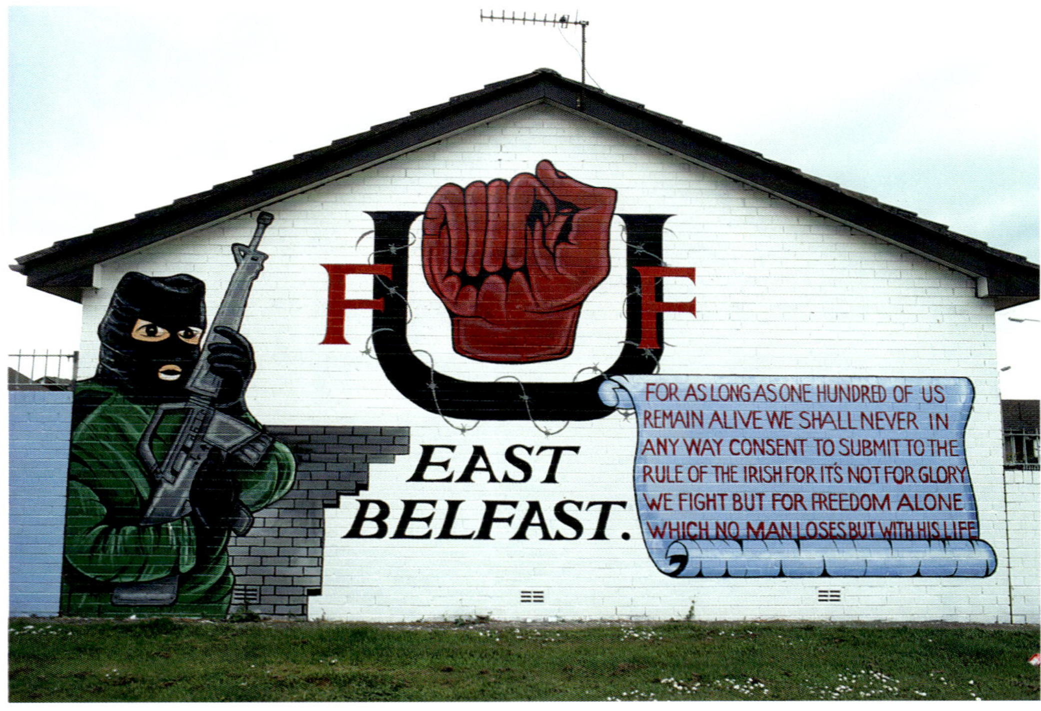

though the subject matter is disturbing. Rolston says, "Political prisoners on both sides have taught themselves to paint in prison." Although several muralists—especially some from Philadelphia including Jane Golden, Betsy Casañas, David McShane, and Don Gensler—have completed productive residencies in Northern Ireland, Rolston has little optimism about successfully importing the Philadelphia mural process, which has so often helped to resolve social tensions here. He says, "The solutions in the U.S. don't translate to our society. In Northern Ireland most people live in neighborhoods with shared politics and religion. It's very segregated. There are some people who would say that the surest sign of healing in our community would be no more murals." Interestingly, the majority of recent murals that do not, as Rolston says, "express hate" are on benign topics such as education and are visually dull compared to the stark political murals with pungent slogans.

"There are some people who would say that the surest sign of healing in our community would be no more murals."

By contrast, Casañas, Golden, and other Philadelphia muralists who have worked with young people in Northern Ireland report excellent rapport with classes and strong interest and commitment among their Northern Irish students. They believe in the potential of contemporary Northern Irish muralism.

Preservation

We know outdoor murals were painted in Renaissance Florence, but none survive today. In Los Angeles, the *Great Wall* is still being restored and preserved and it reminds us that the content as well as the physical substance of murals ages and fades from fashion. The big challenges for mural programs today are: which murals should be preserved? And can we estimate what will be meaningful to the next generation—or the one after that?

Judy Baca and many other experts plead for the preservation of murals. "In the U.S., we have a failure to remember who preceded you," Baca has said. Murals communicate ideas in non-verbal, visceral ways—one of the values of art which endures beyond its original period of creation. Our understanding of the past is inevitably flawed, but compared to other art forms, murals seem to open a bigger, more vivid, more personal window onto a temporal context. This is one excellent reason for restoring these community works, even some of which seem to have outlived their original inspirations and patrons.

In terms of a historical record, it's important to remember that mural "patrons," those who chose a particular artist and design or took the initiative as individuals to paint, were often not elites. Throughout recorded history, the artistic expressions of the wealthy and politically powerful have tended to survive because these people have the ability and will to make and preserve art for future generations. Murals, by contrast, record the vision and experience of ordinary, even marginalized, people. They are fragile records.

Collaboration led by Michelle Ortiz, *Bienvenidos a La Isla de Chira.* Isla de Chira, Costa Rica, 2005. Ortiz worked with fifteen students from Philadelphia and Costa Rica on this project sponsored by the Multicultural Youth eXchange (MYX).

It's fitting that Chicago, home of the lost 1967 *Wall of Respect,* now strives to preserve its mural heritage, which includes murals dating to the beginning of the twentieth century. In fact, Chicago seems to be doing more to restore old murals than to paint new ones. William Walker, one of the original painters of the *Wall of Respect,* was recently honored by the

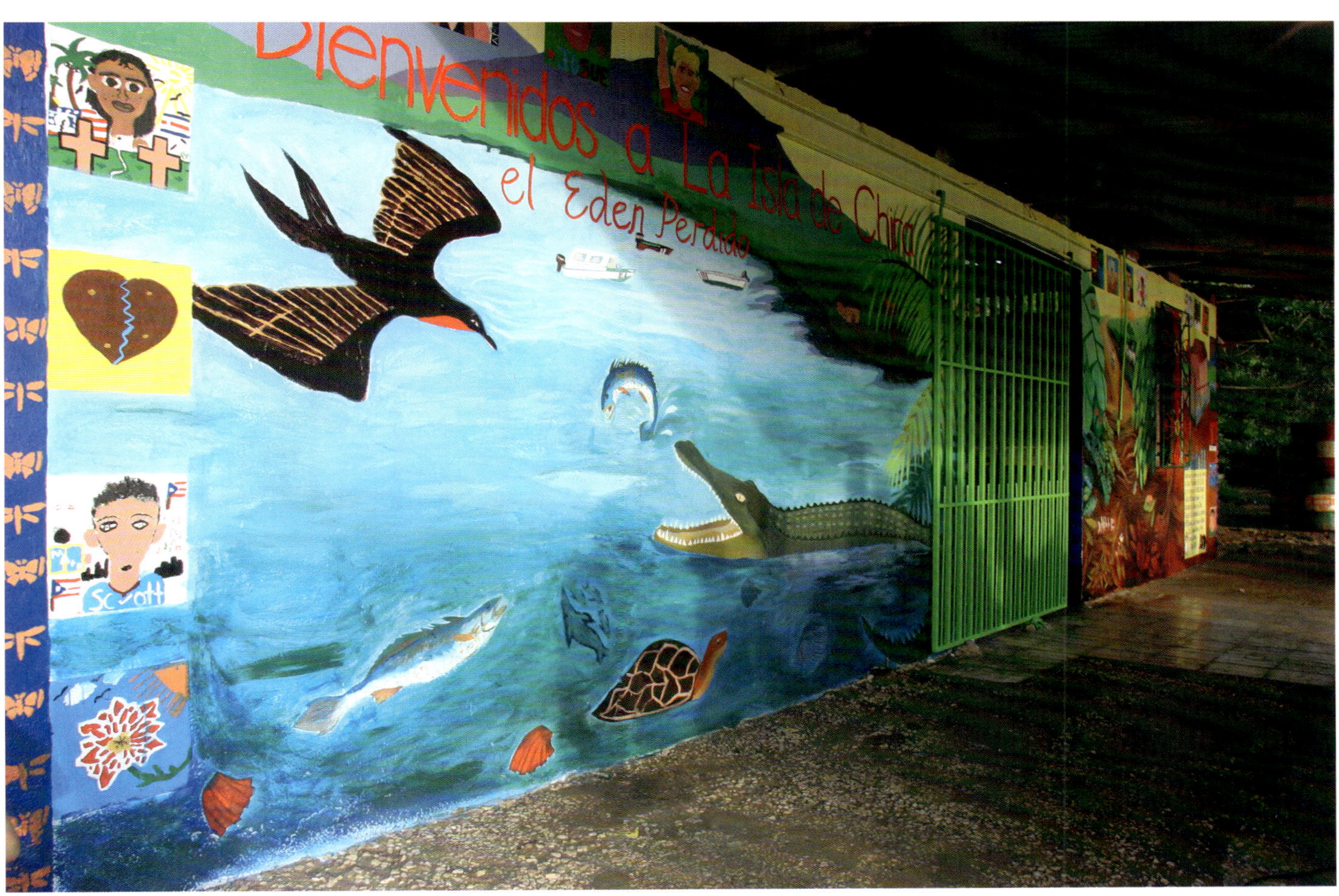

Chicago Public Art Group, a multicultural cooperative that Walker cofounded with fellow muralist John Weber in 1970. Weber's 1971 *Unidos Para Triunfar (Together We Overcome)* was restored in 2005.

Because they are directly connected with nonelite makers, some community murals, such as those in San Francisco's Balmy Alley, have been recognized as especially rich material for historians. Portland is also serious about preserving and painting new murals.

Change is Inevitable

Everyone in Philadelphia eventually crosses the Spring Garden Street Bridge and the history of the murals along its sides parallels the development and strategies of MAP, especially because the first two murals painted by the Philadelphia Anti-Graffiti Network (predecessor of MAP) were here. It was a rush job improvised to cover decades of grime, inept graffiti tags, and weird anomalies in the wall itself. Golden led a group of high school students who painted a series of urban vignettes along both sides of the six-hundred-foot span. The subject, Philadelphia street scenes, unselfconsciously dwelt on things young men notice such as automobiles and women with enormous breasts. The paint was low-quality, chalky beige latex, which Golden tinted as best she could to make other colors. It had one virtue: It was free.

In 1984, Jane Golden (pictured) and kids from Mantua painted the first murals on the Spring Garden Street Bridge for the Anti-Graffiti Network.

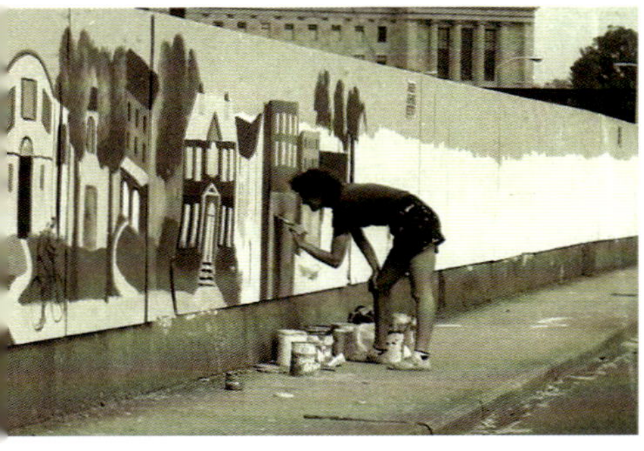

A rippled metal surface and cheap house painters' brushes made the execution, in the words of muralist Shira Walinsky, "basically like painting with bricks." But, from the perspective of local residents, the improvement was incalculable. Drivers paused on the well-traveled bridge to thank and praise the artists at work.

The residents of Mantua, a struggling West Philadelphia neighborhood (see Chapter 4 for more on Mantua's murals), regard this bridge as the gateway to their neighborhood. It is the westward channel for traffic traveling past the heroic fountains of Eakins Oval and the famed "Rocky steps" of the templelike Philadelphia Museum of Art. Unfortunately, a photograph of Golden's sign on the bridge, "Welcome to Manchua," appeared in the *Philadelphia Inquirer* with the remark that the painter certainly was not a native of the city. "I've never been much of a speller," Golden admits.

As the years passed, sections of the bridge panorama were repainted, but criticism of the obviously amateur effort grew. In the late 1990s, one local art critic named it the "Worst Mural in Philadelphia." However, around 2002, when Golden proposed a change, citizens of Mantua and neighboring Powelton Village objected, even though the old bridge was at that time slated to be replaced in less than a year with a dazzling new glass-covered structure.

Golden says, "We assumed that everybody wanted it repainted, but I remember getting many calls from people saying, 'When we go over that bridge, we know we're almost home.' I learned that when *I* feel that a mural is not that good, I can't assume that everybody wants to see it replaced." Even Shira Walinsky, who eventually made the replacement murals, was a little ambivalent. Her studio is nearby and she uses the bridge regularly. She was fond of the quirky old mural's "strange, ad hoc" vision of the city.

In July 2002, Golden asked Walinsky to make a proposal at a meeting sponsored by Spiral Q, a community organization which leads workshops in puppet-making, music, writing, and performance. Walinsky was told the mural would be torn down in six months to make way for the new glass bridge. She presented two ideas. She could see the murals as a quilt—just a design with no people—in which different patterns and fabrics come together as a metaphor for the lively complexity of Mantua and Powelton Village. Or she could use the quilt patterns to frame portraits of people living in the neighborhoods. The second idea won hands down. "They said, 'We need people,'" Walinsky remembers.

In August she began taking head shots using an odd automatic Minolta that she'd found. "It took these slightly exaggerated pictures with exaggerated light and shadow and a sort of gold color."

Almost immediately, a problem arose. Tony Wrice, the son of neighborhood activist Herman Wrice, had worked on the first murals as a youngster and he had not heard about the new plan. He wasn't sure he wanted to see the old paintings covered over. "We stopped the mural for two weeks," Walinsky recalls. She talked with Wrice for a couple of hours and Golden met with him. As he learned about the new design and the way it would reflect local residents,

Shira Walinsky, detail, *Mantua Stars*. Spring Garden Street Bridge, 2002. Originally intended to be temporary, these portraits of local residents alternate with quilt patterns on both sides of the bridge.

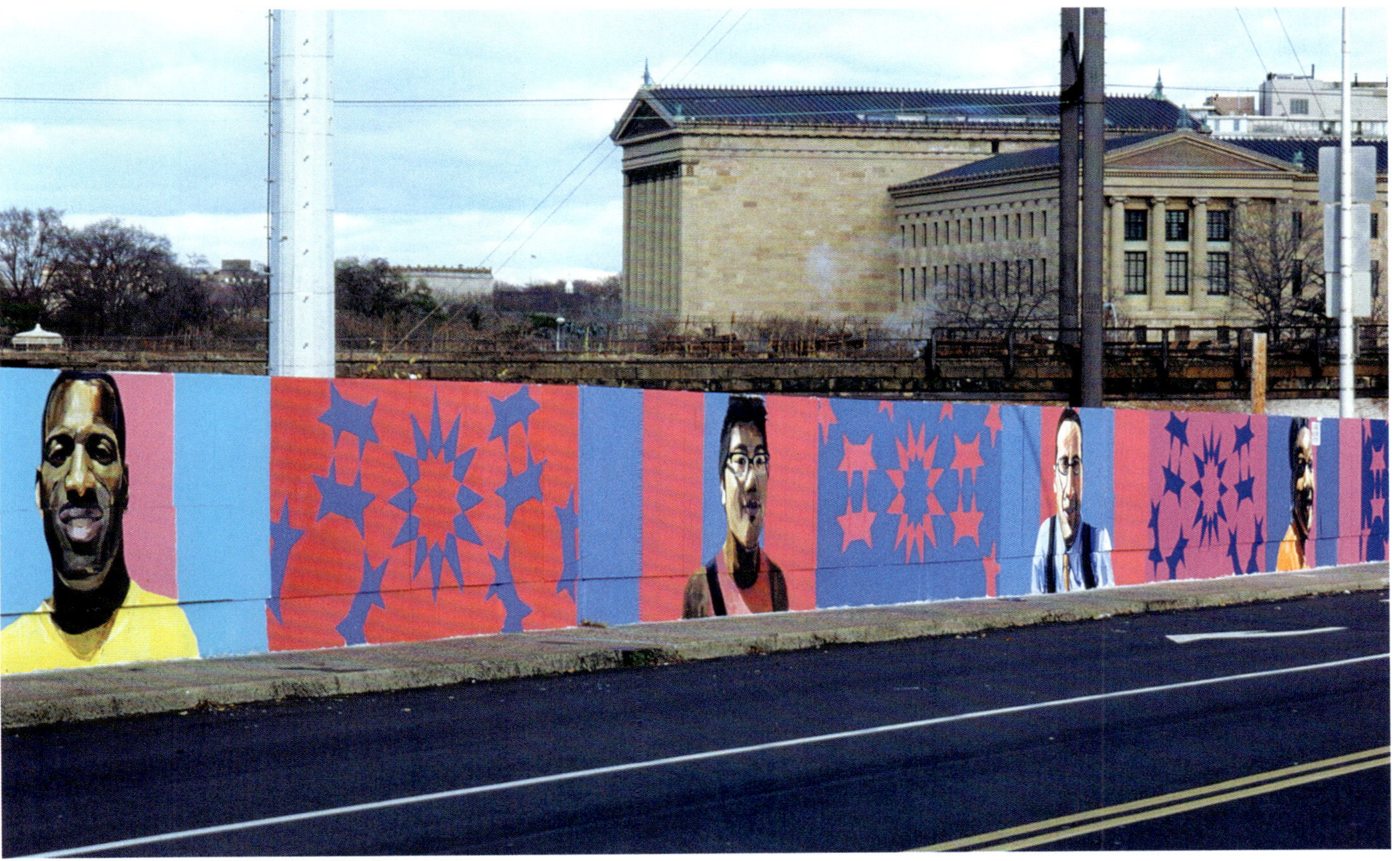

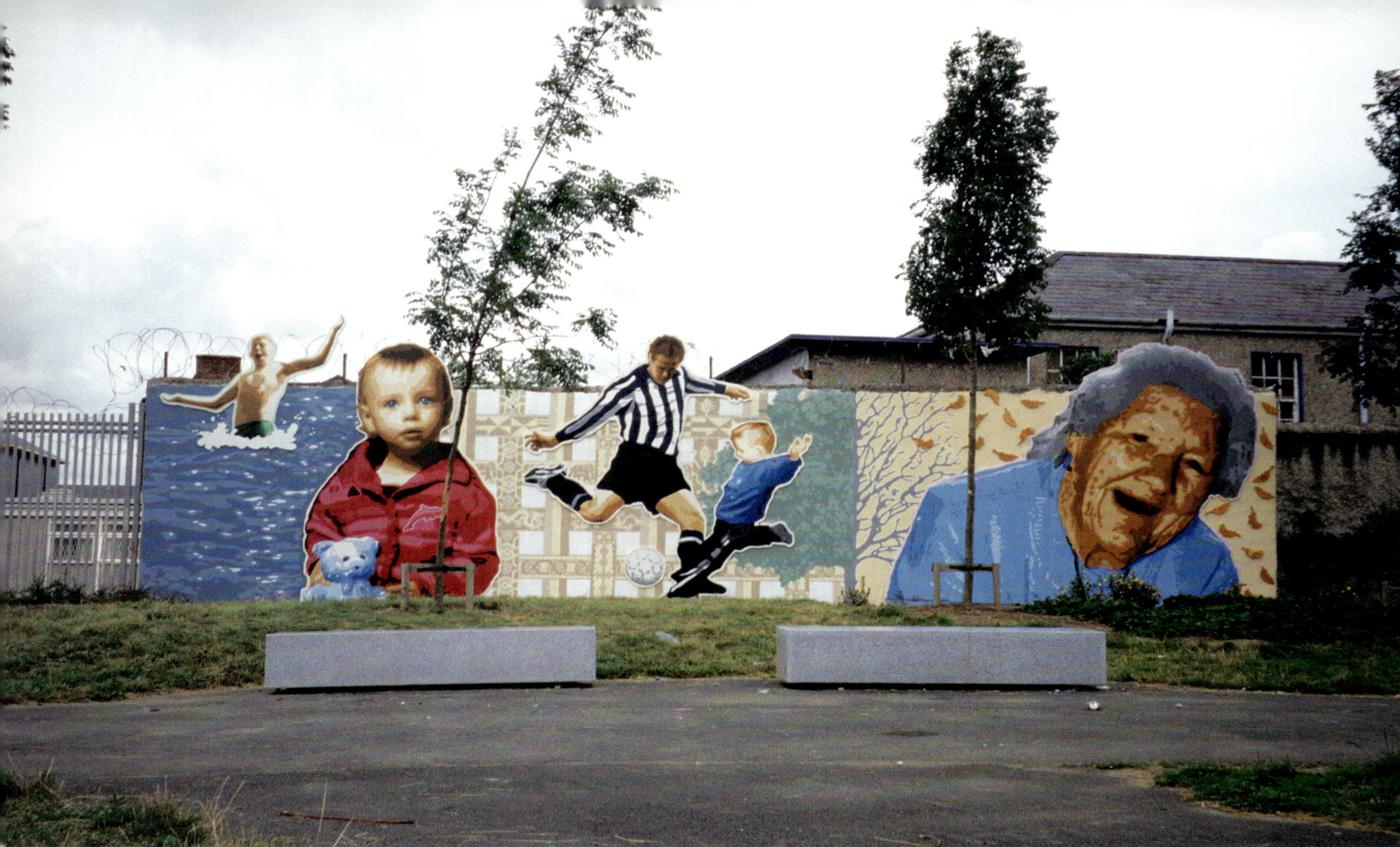

David McShane, with young people from the Rialto Youth Project led by Fiona Whelan. Dublin, Ireland, 2005. The Rialto Youth Project/Common Ground sponsored this cheerful family-oriented mural.

he became intrigued and, finally, convinced. Ultimately, Wrice's grandmother, who lives two blocks from the bridge, was one of many residents Walinsky photographed and painted.

It took Walinsky through December 2002 to paint both sides of the bridge—twelve hundred feet. "It was a really cool project because it could evolve and change. People would stop by and suggest new faces for the mural." She went to some people's homes; others came to a community center where, at specified times, she photographed whomever turned up. Working on the bridge exposed her to "different sources of input. I got to see so much and to know so many people that I [still] recognize around town." She especially appreciated the patrons of a "drop-in day center for homeless guys. They were just great. One guy told me that he lived under the bridge—these really difficult lives. There's a whole world of Philadelphia that you might not know about."

While she was painting, Walinsky chuckles, "People from Powelton would drive by and say, 'This is a great mural. Too bad it's going to be replaced.'" She would have been satisfied if the murals were in public view for just three months, but years later the murals still stand and greet travelers to Mantua and Powleton Village, with no immediate plans for a new glass Spring Garden Street Bridge. And Walinsky, who sees it daily, faithfully touches up the colors and covers graffiti tags, keeping her Mantua/Powelton portrait gallery intact.

MAP's growing sophistication, both technically and in terms of community interaction, is illustrated by these two bridge murals painted decades apart. Both served the community well. Although effective strategies for gaining community input and approval have become institutionalized, MAP still has the sensitivity to respond to a single individual who is concerned about the content of a mural. The true public muralist is a facilitator of communication, not just visually but through the offering of nonjudgmental fellowship. Today, MAP is responsible for many loved and aging murals. It does its best to find resources to restore and maintain as many as possible, often through the generosity of artists such as Shira Walinsky.

With no program or official umbrella to protect them, the loss of "old style" graffiti murals is enormous because graffiti walls were, and are, with rare exceptions, illegal, and generally mandated for destruction as soon as possible. Luckily, in many parts of the country including Philadelphia, "old style" graf artists are now occasionally commissioned to make legitimate murals, preserving elements of graffiti style.

Today, new graffiti in the United States, Europe, and other parts of the world often takes the form of stenciling—simple advertising-inspired designs sometimes called "logos"—and silk-screen, wheat-paste posters. It is global, visually sophisticated, and media-savvy. The well-traveled British artist using the pseudonym Banksy is probably the most famous practitioner because he also sneaks his own art onto the walls of major museums around the world. The mass-produced—although low tech—nature of stencil logos ensures that some original versions of them will survive in private hands, but although public, these aren't really murals; the individual pieces are often smaller than television-marketed "Starving Artists" factory-fashioned "sofa-sized paintings."

The sense of global culture which pervades the mural community is evident in The Tile Project, a 2004–2006 project with "1 goal: to unite the world." It's the work of the artists' group TransCultural Exchange. These artists have exhibited in cities which including Paris, Tokyo, Seoul, London, New York, and Ho Chi Minh City. The Tile Project involves twenty-two sites around the world and the installations of tiles by many artists.

Challenges for the Future

At Philadelphia's mural conference, Jon Pounds, executive director of the CPAG, expressed a common perception when he said that the "bureaucratization of art" distinguishes the mural environment of today from that of twenty years ago. Back then, he said, "people worked organically with the community. We're more likely [now] to have a complex infrastructure.... Twenty years ago we had less draconian legislation, fewer kids incarcerated, less severe laws against immigrants." Pounds believes that quality of life issues are more pressing today than ever. "Artists should be able to express both personal and community values. It's very important for people to express their ideas." We need to be increasingly innovative in communicating "what we know in our hearts is great."

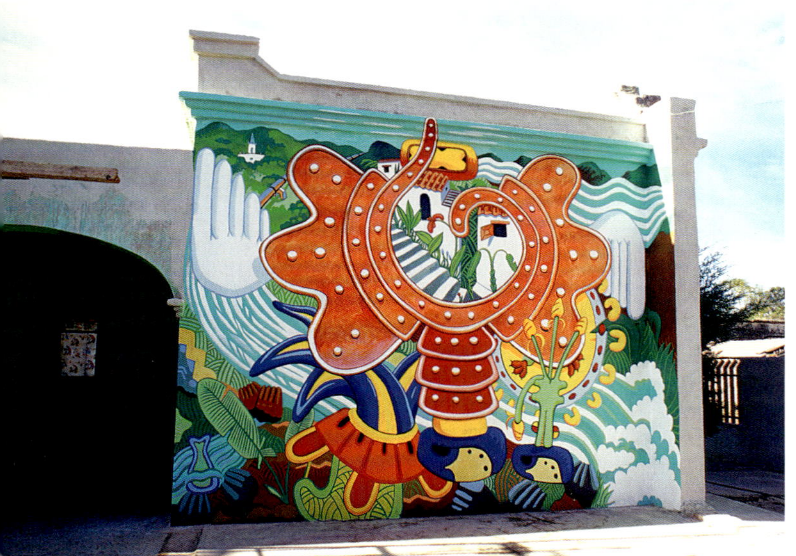

Paul Santoleri, with the help of children at the Benito Juarez elementary school, *Aire de Zapotec.* St. Augustine, Etla, Oaxaca, Mexico, 2001. This wall and two related ones were painted in about four days.

But mural artists know that sometimes the things people feel most deeply are not acceptable to governments. Philadelphia painter Ernel Martinez has experienced the complexities of dealing with religion in a public context. Although there are a number of murals that celebrate religious themes and leaders in the city, MAP is restrained when approaching these topics.

At the Philadelphia mural conference, Judy Baca mentioned the official suppression of religious subject matter as an example the bureaucratic controls that affect murals today. In Los Angeles, she says, there is a law against using public money for religious murals, but, she points out, many images of the Virgin of Guadalupe are still painted and protected.

The goal for mural artists is to take the vision and energy of the 1970s and 1980s and make it meaningful and vital today. MAP's success shows how murals can ride the wave of dynamic community evolution by responding to neighborhoods' needs and by creating environments which nurture the abilities of young muralists. "The future of muralism depends on thinking about how murals can be relevant in new ways," says Golden. She is currently planning a citywide nonviolence project that will involve groups of adults and children working in many media including charcoal drawings, printmaking, and quilt-making. Muralist Don Gensler will take a mobile studio to different neighborhoods to lead workshops. A mural incorporating images and text will result from this series of interactions.

As part of its education program, MAP will soon open the Lincoln Financial Mural Arts Center in the building adjacent to its current residence at the Thomas Eakins house.

Another initiative involves the long corridor of Girard Avenue, which travels through the city from the Delaware River to the zoo. It passes through neighborhoods of different ethnicities and concerns: working class, industrial, commercial, even artistic. Many artists and activities, including mosaics, will enhance and highlight this important thoroughfare. Robert Phillips and Cheryl Levin are celebrating the transformation with *Metamorphosis,* a series of large-scale butterfly and dragonfly sculptures, to be sited at 31st and Girard.

"Embrace murals as a form of public art that can be beautiful, captivating, and augment the growth of a city."

Golden says, "It's a challenge to maximize our impact and see how public art can influence a space. Neighborhoods shift. There's always a question of how to have change that embraces beauty and art and simultaneously reinforces the integrity of a neighborhood. The future of murals can play a vital role by helping a neighborhood hold onto its identity and past."

Golden is committed to working in concert with social services including public health, the Department of Human Services, and prisons. She sees muralism as an educational tool. One route muralism has taken in Philadelphia is to return to its roots, almost its grassroots, by seeking renewed relevance to individual lives, like the murals growing out of the "My North Philly" project. "Art can be a mirror," she says. "Embrace murals as a form of public art that can be beautiful, captivating, and augment the growth of a city."

Long ago, Golden decided that mural quality was more important than quantity even if the future means that more time is devoted to the processes of communication and education than to the actual painting of walls. Some of the most meaningful murals of the past grew organically from gradually recognized community perception. "The challenge for all of us," Golden says, "is to ask ourselves, 'What do we believe in?' and act on that. The potential is limitless."

Murals, not walls, make good neighbors.

Paul Santoleri, *Sphere Music.* WXPN World Café Live! 3025 Walnut Street, 2004. Mural sponsored by WXPN-FM. *Sphere Music* is at the top of a staircase and visually relates to a mural on a lower level, *Tower of Babble.*

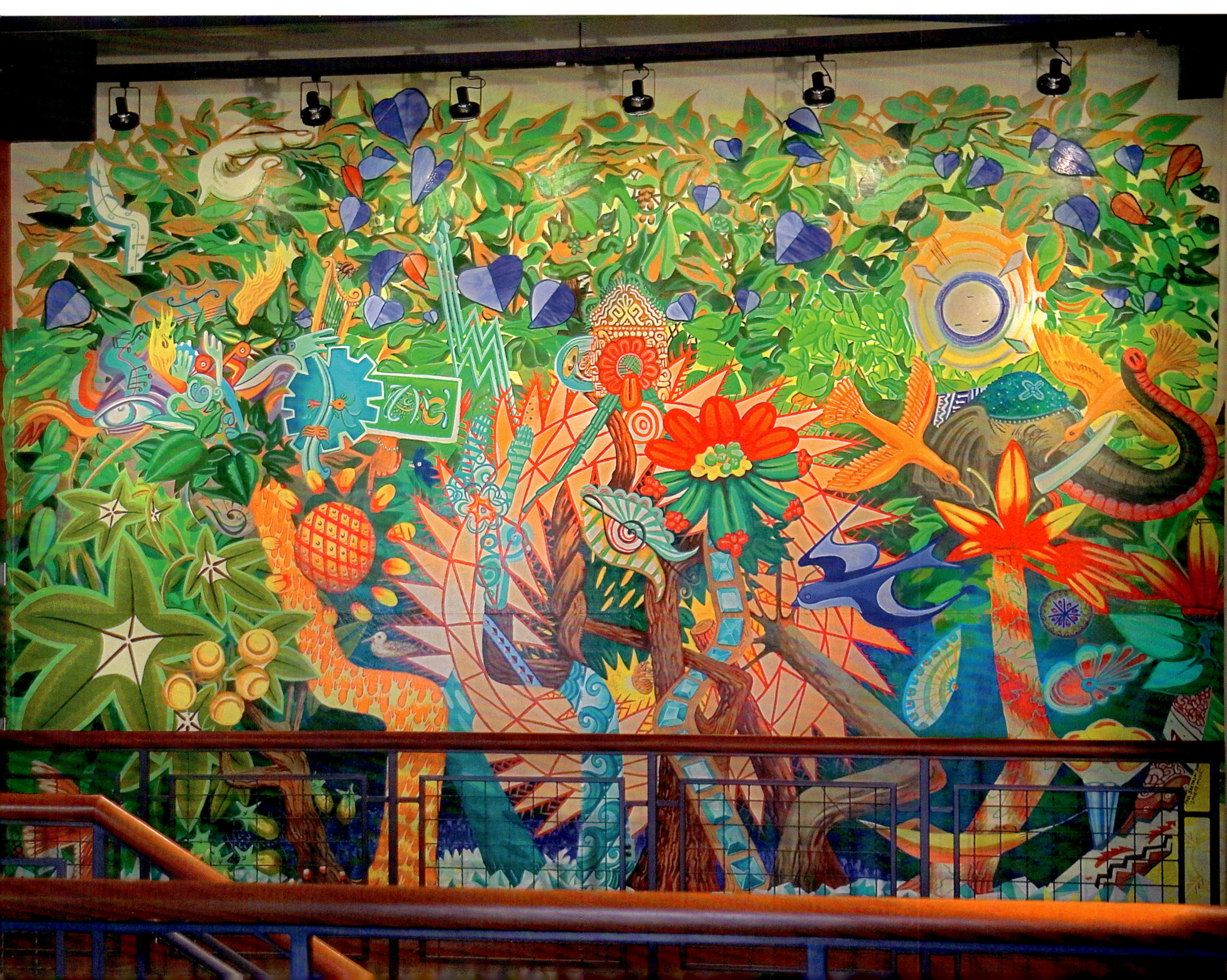

Mural Map

1 *Bomba y Plena* by Betsy Casañas, 2740 Mascher Street, 2003.

2 *Butterflies of the Caribbean* by Salvador Gonzalez, 163 W. Susquehanna Avenue, 2000.

3 *The Doors of Destiny Are in Your Hands* by Michelle Ortiz, American and Somerset Streets, 2004.

4 *A Family Garden* by Donald Gensler, 801 N. 40th Street, 2004.

5 *Four Seasons* by Mike Smash and Harvey Weinreich, Hawthorne Cultural Center, 1200 Carpenter Street, 2005.

6 *Higher Aspirations and Striving Higher* by César Viveros-Herrera, Parris Stancell, and men in the mural program at SCI Graterford, Edward Gideon School, 2817 W. Glenwood Avenue, 2004.

7 *Gimme Shelter* by David Guinn, Morris Animal Refuge, 1236-42 Lombard Street, 2004.

8 *Growing Up in Germantown* by Ann Northrup, 110 W. Rittenhouse Street, 2004.

9 *Heads to the Sky* by Cavin Jones, 22nd Street and Lehigh Avenue, 2004.

10 *Holding Grandmother's Quilt* by Donald Gensler, 3912-22 Aspen Street, 2004.

11 *I Too Have a Dream* by Cavin Jones, 2203 W. Somerset Street, 2004.

12 Healing Walls: *The Inmates' Journey* and *The Victims' Journey* by César Viveros-Herrera, Parris Stancell, and men in the mural program at SCI Graterford, 3049 (*Inmates'*) and 3065 (*Victims'*) Germantown Avenue, 2004.

13 *Life Reflects Nature: Memories of the past; traditions of the present* by Michelle Ortiz and Jose Ali Paz, Mann Older Adult Center, 3201 N. 5th Street, 2005.

14 *Lifespan* by David McShane, Wilson Park, 25th and Jackson Streets, 2004.

15 *The Lighthouse* by César Viveros-Herrera, 152 W. Lehigh Avenue, 2003.

16 *Lincoln Legacy* by Josh Sarantitis, 707 Chestnut Street, 2006.

17 *The Magic Wall* by Ana Uribe, 1230 S. 47th Street, 2005.

18 *Malcolm X* by Ernel Martinez, 3211 Ridge Avenue, 2005.

19 *McKinley School Project* by Shira Walinsky and Jennie Shanker, 2101 N. Orkney Street, 2003.

20 *A Message to the Child . . . the Hero Can Be Found* by John Lewis, 3403 N. 17th Street, 2004.

21 *Metamorphosis* by Josh Sarantitis, Ridge Avenue Shelter, 1360 Ridge Avenue, 2001.

22 *Moving Toward Your Dreams* by Donald Gensler, 700 Pattison Avenue, 2003.

23 *My Life, My Path, My Destiny* by César Viveros-Herrera, 2157 E. Lehigh Avenue, 2005.

24 *One World, Many Cultures* by Mike Smash and Jonny Buss, Norris S. Barratt Middle School, 1599 Wharton Street, 2005.

25 *On the Block* by James Burns, 3956 Pennsgrove Street, 2005.

26 *Passing Through* by Meg Saligman, I-76 near Girard Avenue (main mural), 2004.

27 *Patti LaBelle* by Peter Pagast, 3402 Mantua Avenue, 2004.

28 *Potter-Thomas School* by Ana Uribe, 3001 N. 6th Street, 2005.

29 *Pride and Progress* by Ann Northrup, William Way Community Center, 1315 Spruce Street, 2003.

30 *Reaching for Your Star* by Donald Gensler, 629 N. 37th Street, 2003.

31 *Songs of Hope* by Donald Gensler, 3413 Haverford Avenue, 2002.

32 *South Philly Musicians* by Peter Pagast, 1235 E. Passyunk Avenue, 2005.

33 *Symbols of Change* by Donald Gensler, 2110 Market Street, 2004.

34 *Thank You, Mr. Blackwell!* by Peter Pagast, 4203 Haverford Avenue, 2003.

35 *Tribute to Frank Guarrera* by Peter Pagast, 1532 S. Broad Street, 2003.

36 *A Tribute to Herman Wrice* by David McShane, 3335 Spring Garden Street, 2000.

37 *Urban Horsemen* by Jason Slowik, 3222 W. Montgomery Avenue, 2005.

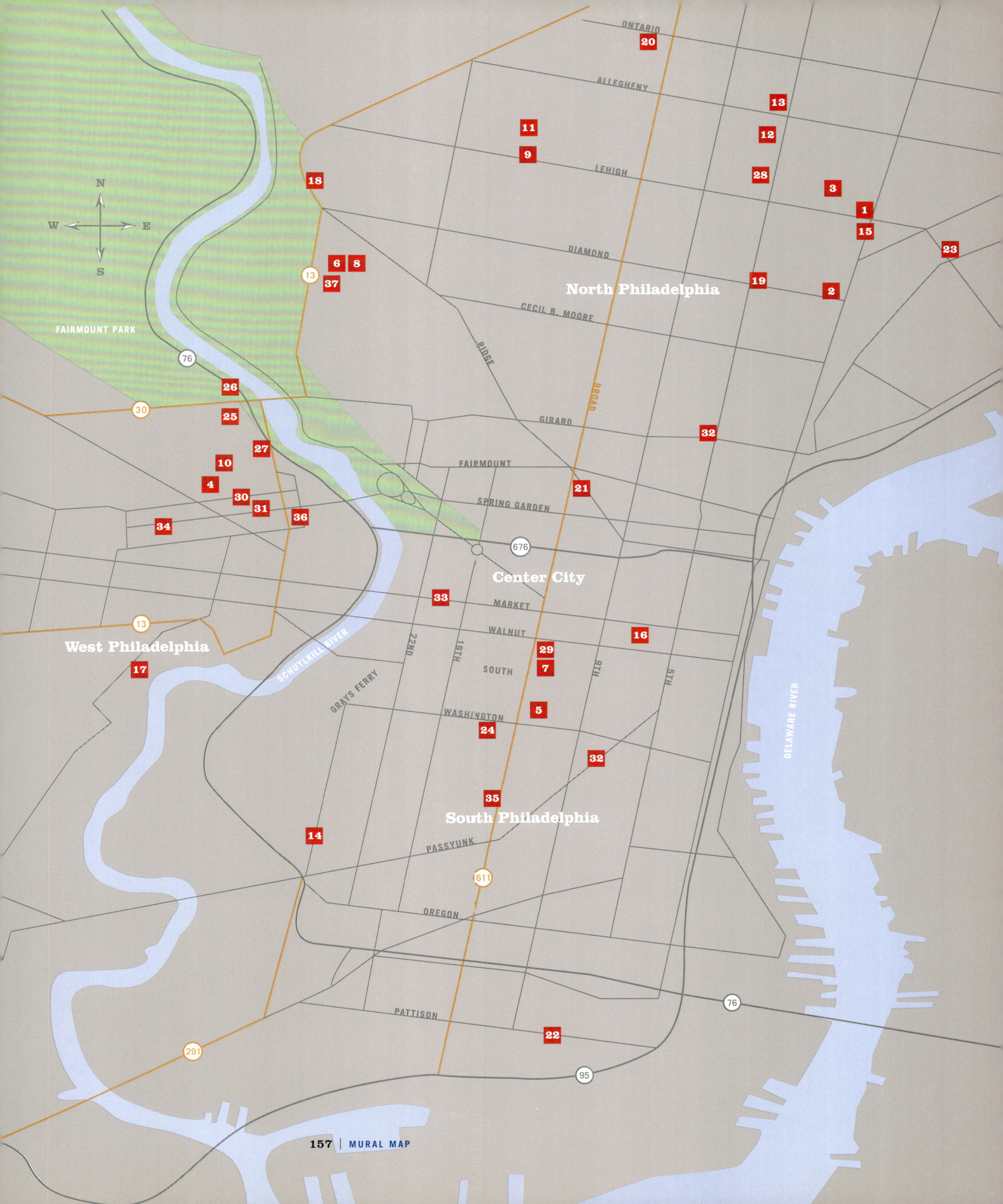
ONTARIO
ALLEGHENY
LEHIGH
DIAMOND
CECIL B. MOORE
RIDGE
BROAD
GIRARD
FAIRMOUNT
SPRING GARDEN
MARKET
WALNUT
SOUTH
WASHINGTON
PASSYUNK
OREGON
PATTISON
22ND
19TH
9TH
5TH
GRAYS FERRY
SCHUYLKILL RIVER
DELAWARE RIVER
FAIRMOUNT PARK
North Philadelphia
Center City
West Philadelphia
South Philadelphia
N
S
E
W
76
30
13
676
611
291
95
20
13
11
12
9
28
3
1
15
23
18
6
8
37
19
2
26
25
32
27
10
4
30
31
36
34
21
33
16
29
7
17
5
24
32
35
14
22

Index

Photography Credits

The sources for illustrations appearing in *More Philadelphia Murals and the Stories They Tell* are listed below.

David Graham pages 9, 24, 34, 46, 53, 58, 70, 75, 80, 81, 92, 96, 104, 112, 130, 131, 139, and 146.

Jack Ramsdale pages 2–3, 14–15, 22, 25, 26, 31, 32, 33, 35, 36–37, 39, 40, 41, 43, 44, 45, 47, 48-49, 51, 52–53, 54, 55, 56, 59, 60-61, 63, 64–65, 66, 69, 71, 72–73, 76, 77, 79, 82–83, 85, 86, 87, 88–89, 90-91, 93, 94–95, 97, 98, 100, 103, 105, 106-107, 109, 110, 111, 112-113, 114, 116-117, 118, 121, 122-123, 125, 126, 127, 135, 136, 139, 140–141, 147, 151, and 155.

Also

Josette Bonafino page 149.

Betsy Casañas page 145.

Rachael Clark pages 133, 134.

City College of San Francisco page 19.

Heather Fenton page 42.

First Presbyterian Church in Germantown, Philadelphia page 21.

D. S. Gordon page 144.

Chuck Isaacs page 150.

Library of Congress, Prints & Photographs Division page 20.

David McShane page 152.

James Prigoff pages 143 and 148.

Paul Santoleri page 154.

Temple University Libraries, Urban Archives, Philadelphia, Pennsylvania page 150.

Authors
Jane Golden
Robin Rice
Natalie Pompilio

Photographers
David Graham
Jack Ramsdale

MAP Researchers and Editorial Assistants
Brian Campbell and Amy Johnston

MAP Coordinator
Kevin Gardner

Design
Phillip Unetic/3r1 Group.com

Manuscript Editor
Laura Lawrie

Production Director
Charles H. E. Ault

Acquiring Editor
Micah Kleit